THE TRUTH ABOUT
BLACK PEOPLE

THE TRUTH ABOUT BLACK PEOPLE

How Determined People Can

Rise to Greatness

Shelton Vaughn

To order additional copies of this book, contact:
Xlibris Corporation
1-888-795-4274
www.Xlibris.com
Orders@Xlibris.com
69939

CONTENT

This book is dedicated to all generations:
To those gone before, to those here now,
And to all of those who are yet to come.

THE NEED

THE NEED IS this. We, the black race, must if they are qualities we have, use our intelligence, imagination, and initiative, combined with discipline, coherence and determination to develop a public policy that lifts us from the bottom rung of human society to the status of a first-class, first-world, world-class people second to none in building social systems that meet human needs in politics, religion, economics, and civic affairs. This we must do before we can ever be equal, thus before we can ever be accepted as equals. Forty-nine is not fifty, and ninety-nine and a half is not a hundred. You must be equal to be accepted as equal. This is an immutable law, fixed and eternal; and no man nor people, no matter the race or color, can alter or abolish it. If we do not do it, it will not get done by us. Since it is us, therefore, who must do it, if we don't do it, it shall not get done.

As individual functionaries under the tutelage and dictate of whites, we have written great books, have made great speeches, have earned hundreds of billions of dollars on jobs, in business and other endeavors, have earned every degree level offered at the university including bachelor's, master's and PhD's, have earned the Congressional Medal of Honor for bravery in America's wars, have won the Nobel Prize in various categories, have held the highest office in practically every stratum in American society, the lone exception being, the presidency of the United States (and some day one of us will achieve that also, whether we blacks are ready for it or not), and have been the world's greatest athlete, the world's greatest entertainer, and the world's most famous personality; and yet our status as an inferior, lazy and stupid people minus the manifested intelligence, imagination and initiative necessary to conceptualize, cohere, and carryout a public policy that builds the black community into a tower of social strength and regard is always a constant presence.

This book, to the question, can this condition in us be cured?, says, "Yes," if we as people choose to do so. It is, therefore, a hopeful prospectus about black people, about the composite of black humanity, not about black individuals as such. When a black individual is called by name it is in the context of black society and his or her role in it—either negative or positive. It is about what black leaders must do to lead us forward to the goal we must reach to be equal in every manly way. All the help in the world from others cannot do this for us; this is something only we can do, perhaps with the help of others, for ourselves. This book is a lesson for us now and for future generations, because it addresses a need human beings have whatever the time or place.

The prophecy above that a black would be elected president was written long before President Barack Obama ever came onto the political scene. It was due to my serious study of black people begun in 1981 that I knew America was willing to elect a black president. What brought me to do the study and to that knowledge is made clear elsewhere in the book. This insertion is to recognize Obama and the nation's victory and to give the reason my research saw the likelihood of the occurrence. America has had three immanent transformative black leaders: Booker T. Washington who saw in blacks a yearning to learn and the veil blocking their progress being ignorance and lifted the veil of ignorance from his people, unlike W. E. B. Du Bois who saw blacks as the sons of night and saw the veil not as ignorance but skin color and race; Dr. Martin Luther King, Jr. who went to those great wells of democracy, said that we as a people will get to the promised land of civility;

SHELTON VAUGHN

he saw in us the ability to build the beloved community; and, now, Barack Obama. The first two are highlighted elsewhere in the book; therefore, what I will do here is make clear what makes a black leader transformative.

There are three groups of black people: transformative, Talented Tenth, and the broad mass of black humanity. The black transformers acknowledge America's lights and her blind allies. The lights in brief are these: All men are created equal, form a more perfect union, and secure the blessings of liberty. The Talented Tenth lingers mainly in her blind allies; and the mass go where their leaders take them in self-imaging and in governance. The Talented Tenth teaches that blacks do not need leaders. I was in a literary conference recently, in the breakout was eight, six whites, two blacks—a male and a female—plus the facilitator, a black. Of the nine people in the room, three were black and six white. We discussed lack of social responsibility by black people, how their negative behavior fractures communal society making civility, a preferred social value, virtually impossible. I said this problem exist because black people refuse to teach the view that we need leaders. The black female, highly educated, a teacher, nearly bust a gasket, screaming with much repetition, "We don't need leaders! We don't need leaders!" She on the instant turn to the female blond at her side and asked, "Do you need leaders?" The blond's demur came with a downcast countenance. She no doubt would have had no problem agreeing with the questioner, if the questioner had asked, "Do you believe black folk need leaders?" She might have been happy to say, "I agree with you." So the inquisitor screwed up twice; being so viciously anxious to drive her point, she leaped beyond a bound for any sensible white person to agree to such twaddle about themselves, but would likely have been glad to agree with a black dumb enough to utter such crackpot tripe about the needs of black people.

Transformers see the veil holding blacks back to be ignorance; the Talented Tenth or TT sees it being skin color and race; and the mass of blacks follow TT's lead most of the time. TT, as in the case of the teacher, practices laziness and teaches indifference to group betterment. Their basic position is take responsibility for nothing; never blame black failure on laziness and indifference to their own wellbeing but blame it, instead, on racism and white prejudice. If some one says blacks should seek to be civil toward each other, charge him aggressively with the assault of blame the victim, while taking no measure to improve communal living.

Obama locked in the lights, and they led him to lead the nation. Cynics say they thought they would never see a black elected president. They have not seen the lights. They are blinded by the veil of ignorance, locked in darkness by a malevolent refusal to take in the lights, accept them and allow them to illume their minds, thus making themselves lights in the world. With out a doubt, the lights are the greatest practical gift men have ever given to the human race.

Resentful of Obama for digging into those great wells of democracy Dr. King went to, some wish like his father he had been born in Africa, and not like his mother born in America, the land of lights. But no man yet has ability to make what is not be. True, any man can say what is not is, but that exposes a darkness in him needing exposure to the lights. Resisting the lights delayed by many years a black getting to the White House. When Dr. King was asked if he had thought a black would be elected president in forty years, having himself made use of the lights, he said he thought a black could be elected in twenty-five years. However, he likely knew no black would ever get there without first going to the wells.

The lights of mind are given by the founding fathers of the United States of America to all mankind in recognition of man's imperfections, while willing yet to strive for perfection. Any man can use these lights individually, and any people can use them collectively in state craft and in communal life in general. They cannot open man's mind; but oh what, as shown in the case of Obama, they can do for him once let in.

POINTS TO PONDER

HAVE YOU EVER wondered why black leaders in Africa sold blacks to whites and why blacks let whites enslave, segregate, and in other ways abuse them?

Have you ever wondered why blacks would rather live in a community whites build than to use their intelligence, imagination and initiative necessary to cohere and build their own to be as good or better?

Do you believe that what makes people rich is their own initiative, imagination, productivity, and cooperative spirit which allow them to do together and with, perhaps, the cooperation of others the best they can with the bounty of natural resources that are theirs?

Observe two races, one white and one black. Observe the behavior of each. One by his behavior builds a complex, sophisticated, industrious and highly advanced technological society, while the other's leads to enslavement, segregation, despair, and so—called poverty. This shows that this disparity is not due to skin color or race, but behavior.

Some blacks will say that blacks had full employment during slavery, but in truth, they did not. A job is had when the worker knows the value of work, of having a job for pay or for other gratification sort by the worker: a volunteer, for instance, may not be paid but is gratified to render valuable service. Mules were worked but had no job, and nor did blacks during slavery. That is one of the things that made slavery in America a peculiar institution, under that regime blacks not only had no rights as citizens, but also they had no rights as human beings. They were not according to its form and practice human beings. It was that practice that made America's peculiar institution the most evil system ever practice by man.

It is a most puzzling occurrence that blacks submitted to whites' dominance, and worked on their orders with due diligence for hundreds of years, yet they will not cohere and work together for themselves hardly at all even today. (Look how quickly the Southern Christian Leadership Conference fell apart after Dr. King was assassinated, because Jesse Jackson, Andrew Young, Ralph Abernathy, and others could not or would not talk to each other, cohere and make the accommodations and compromises necessary to lead it strong). Why should it be whites decision to determine whether blacks act sensibly toward each other, or be productive? Why do they not make that decision for themselves? Is it that they are flawed by nature, as white theorists say, and cannot on their own do so, or is it that they refuse to do so by the will of their own choice? That situation puzzles mostly every body including whites and some blacks. It is a mystery this discourse seeks to unravel.

Do you believe that the black community today, a blight of crime filled with hellish rage, neglect, indifference, incoherence and stifling laziness by its best educated and positioned, can one day rise from its ashes of despair and so-called poverty to be a beacon light of hope for all mankind?

If you answered, "Yes" or "No" to either query, it would matter not whether you are black or white, Jew or gentile, Protestant or Catholic, or other enter this book now at the beginning and do not exit till you have read and studied every word through to the end and know its essence from cover to cover. It will benefit you immensely.

SHELTON VAUGHN

PROFILE OF AUTHOR

I WAS BORN to write this book. From my youth up, I have always wanted to make sense to people with words. I came out of my mother's womb, it is believed, wanting to do so. It was December 20, 1935, to Willie and L. C. Vaughn, in Parkdale, Arkansas, County of Ashley, that I was delivered. I am the fifth of seven children, the youngest of four sons. I was not a whiz kid in school. My grades lacked luster. (I was not to get "A"s consistently in school till I became an upperclassman in college). Some community people and my mother, however, thought there was something special in me. About the age of seven or eight, I was put in a youth program at church to preach. The church that night was packed to hear the boy preacher. And I preached. I did so well that the program producer, by popular demand, put me on again the same year or the next. That time more people came to hear me than perhaps for any other event ever in the history of my hometown; there were more people outside the church than inside; the buzz was that a great preacher was about to be born, but I did not preach that night and I have never preached again. When my name was called, I stepped to the podium but said nothing. (That statement was true till 2006. That year I was called to preach the Gospel of our Lord and savior Jesus Christ).

People thought the little fellow suffered stage fright, and that he would be a great preacher some day. I had no idea what was to be the purpose for my life till, several years later, on my twenty-first birthday, in Ramstein, Germany. There was a clarity in my head and before me saying study black folk. At that time, the idea of studying black folk seriously was, as a practical matter, more of an example of one's insanity than of one's good sense. To call black folk black back then was risky business. However, I accepted the assignment and went about my task with sustained alacrity. From that instance I began to read, listen to and observe blacks intensely every day. I was not long into my study before I learned this lesson: black leaders as a class did not have a clue what their duty is, which is to formulate a public policy that makes the black community a safe, clean and prosperous place in which to live, raise a family and do business. That reality pounded away at me for many years. But from the start I have had moments of intense joy but for more moments of intense sadness. I savor the joys when they come. No amount of sadness will steal my joy nor overwhelm me with its volume nor its crass and savage barbarity. No human being, not even white, can answer ultimate questions. So what I may propose on these pages as the answer to what Du Bois mistakenly called a race and color problem is strictly from a practical perspective.

In some sections, I focus intensely on Detroit, not to promote it so much; but that is where I have lived since 1960. So I know other places may be similar, but what I know about it should lead us to action wherever we are on the planet with sober determination.

Some say, when Detroit's need to develop a public policy that makes her safe, clean and prosperous is pointed out, she is being not promoted but picked on. But that is not so. History shows when America had a need for rail transportation from the East to the West Coast, when this fact was pointed out, she did not claim she was being picked on; she instead responded to the need by building a cross-continental railroad. Likewise when a need to connect the boroughs of Manhattan and Brooklyn brought a maze of complaint, under innovated leaders they built the Brooklyn Bridge. In neither of these cases of pointing to the need was it seen as bashing America

SHELTON VAUGHN

or New York City. To the contrary they were used as opportunities to display good old-fashioned American ingenuity. So instead of us meeting the need for safety, cleanliness and prosperity in Detroit, lazy-headed leaders say to point to the need is bashing the city. Doing nothing to meet the need we have is un-American. And there is no greater a way to promote the city than to develop a public policy that makes it a safe, clean and prosperous place in which to live, raise a family and do business.

ACKNOWLEDGMENTS

IN A BOOK of this magnitude, there are more people to thank than space could ever allow. But it is incumbent to list some. First, my mother and father, Willie and L. C. Vaughn; they did not have university degrees, but each of them taught the two types of lessons that have made this work possible. If asked, my father would say he went to the third grade, yet with that small amount of formal training, he learned to read and write; and he held significant positions in his church at the local, state and national levels. My mother finished the eighth. Mother taught by words and father by example, not by giving an example as in a seminar, not even by demonstrations with pictures and props. His example that informed me about him was in the life he led. He would help people; sometime they would call him at midnight or 4 o'clock in the morning. Would he take a spouse or a child to the doctor or come and pray with and for the family or come and help them bear some other horror that weighs heavy on the human condition? Sometimes he would make a judgment whether the person was in his predicament because of bad luck or because he was a bad person. He would always give advice to the latter and sympathy to the former. Mother wanted every child of hers to get as much education as possible. It was these two characteristics one in each of these two people that complemented each other and have guided my life to this hour and shall continue in that vein for the rest of my days.

Two siblings, my sisters, Sadie and Cora—they would always let me know whether in my correspondence with them I made sense. There was a woman, we called Baby, who could not read nor write; not knowing this, I sort her to be one of my first customers on my paper route. She accepted with great enthusiasm and always paid promptly. She died young at the age of forty-two. When I learned later she could not read nor write and that she did it for a boy she thought would make something of himself, I was inspired in my spirit and touched to the very core of my being.

It was from these people at home including my teachers in school who instilled in me a desire to learn, but it was not until I went to school in Switzerland that I learned how to learn, in two significant ways: one was how to learn to get good grades; and the other was how to apply that learning to life. That experience helped me to know that there is more to learning than grades one gets in school. I was able to discuss and argue points without ranker. That learning has proven to be invaluable to me. I am constantly learning how invaluable that kind of learning is. In a conversation recently with a boy of seventeen who has superior grades in Trig, chemistry, and in all core subjects including English and has scholarship offers from several major universities. Yet when he said he and the young people of today would not take what members of our race took in the old days, upon being asked what the people of old times took that his generation would not, he stood silent. When one learns more than how to get good grades, standing mute on one's own raised point will never happen.

To all of these wonderful people, I give my most hearty thanks.

And I owe a special thanks to William Kloefkorn, PhD, the university professor of English for many years and author of more than seventeen books; he read the manuscript, and called it "impressive, emphatic with clarity of purpose, a major piece of work, passionate, focused and relentless, eloquent, well written, powerful."

Any fault found herein is to be laid to me. And those black leaders, herein called out, should be proud to be called out, because African leaders, instead

SHELTON VAUGHN

of defending the continent, chose to round up their people, bring them to the shores of Africa and sell them to foreign buyers. And the international slave trade did not end because Africans chose to stop selling; it ended because foreign buyers became industrialized and chose to stop buying. The traits of those African leaders are still reflected in African descended people in leadership positions today in Africa, in Islands of the sea and in America.

THE PURPOSE

T HE MAIN PURPOSE of this book is not to explore the brutality of whites against blacks. What whites have done against blacks has been, as it should, explored in other venues, including books. This book, after the writer's more than fifty years of study, explores why blacks by the choices they themselves have made let whites enslave, segregate, and in other ways abuse them, and what they must do to attain greatness. It reinforces King's view that others cannot ride your back if your back is not bent and the insight of Booker T. Washington's admonition: "No race that has anything to contribute to the markets of the world is long in any degree ostracized."

PREFACE

THIS IS NOT a complete synopsis, but is a partial list of some of the broad themes herein discussed.

It explores the phenomenon that seems most strange even to a great number of blacks, that is, why such a large number of blacks of means, such as politicians, pastors, teachers, business owners, civic leaders, the wealthy, the famous, those in prestigious positions of authority, etc., move or wish to move out of the black community into the white, and think that is a move up and a sign of "having made it." Ignorant it seems of the degree to which such actions demean them and affirm the charges that they are lazy and stupid, and lack the intelligence, imagination and initiative necessary to cohere with one another and with others in ways that cause them to formulate a public policy that makes the black community a preferred place in which to live, raise a family and do business.

To bring this discussion to the reader with as much clarity as possible, from time to time the voice of the Street Philosopher may be heard. This is a voice heard sporadically in every stratum of black society. It is the voice that says to keep it real; as opposed to the tendency in his view of blacks, especially the black elitist, to be pretentious, fallacious, pompous, phony and shallow headed.

I will discuss the exact and precise charges whites made against us of being a lazy and stupid, subhuman, impulsive savage people, lacking a high degree of human intelligence, imagination, initiative, and coherence in a cooperative spirit necessary for formulating and carrying out a public policy that would lift us to greatness. It has a glossary and a sampling of letters written mainly to blacks with a public voice.

CHAPTER 1

The Big Mistake

I T IS FACTORS like behavior, attitude and choice not color nor race that are the root of what is called the race and color problem. If what is not the problem is blamed for the problem, it is very unlikely that the problem will ever be solved.

Using the scientific method of inquiry, over many years of researching and studying what is called the race problem between black and white folk, I have learned one thing for certain, and it perhaps more than any other, whites have never enslaved, segregated nor in other ways abused blacks, as W. E. B. Du Bois thought, and as blacks loudly proclaim erroneously, because of their race and skin color.

William Edward Burghardt Du Bois opened the twentieth century with the troubling, pessimisitic and false view that: "the problem of the twentieth century is the problem of the color line." In contrast to that gloomy, false and blind-headed proclamation, we shall open the twenty-first century with the truthful optimistic affirmation that the problem of the Blackman has not been, is not, and shall never be his color nor his race. That is good to know, after being beaten over the head for decades with such a crass, inane, and idiotic fallacy. But if this lie is not truth, a reasonable interrogative has to be, what then is truth in the matter, what is the cause of the Blackman's problem vis-à-vis white folk? High in the ranks of causes of the Blackman's problem has to be behavior, his and others, for if he is ever to improve himself and his position in the world his condition has to be caused by something that can be changed, not by something that cannot. It is just that simple. Du Bois' concept of the color line may be a cute turn of a rhetorical tag line. But the idea that color and race are ultimate barriers to black's progress or that they are the causes of white discrimination and abuse of him is a concept not sustainable by fact, logic nor reason. For how can his color or race be a problem, when he has no control over whether he is either? And likewise with white, for it is not white's race nor color that has positioned him where he is. After more than twenty-five years of research and study of black folk by listening to their voices and reading their commentary, as well as living the black experience, I, beginning in 1981, using the scientific method of inquiry and through thoughtful contemplation, have made the profound breakthrough to the practical solution to this enigma—that is at the core of every evil act ever committed against blacks by whites is a psychosocial dynamic that caused it, that is, an attitude formed in the mind and manifested in a public policy, not his color nor his race. Furthermore, no advance or setback ever experienced by black was caused because he changed his color or his race. It occurred because somebody changed behavior, not race nor color. The quote that follows is a writ that has doomed blacks (not intentionally I hope) by one of their own now for more than a hundred years to seeing their problem being caused by their race and color.

"Color and race are not crimes, and yet it is they which in this land receive most unceasing condemnation, North, East, South, and West," W. E. B. Du Bois in his book, *The Souls of Black Folk*, 1903. To declaim the essential and unalterable aspects of people's very being to be the cause of their problem is to affix them in a cask out of which they cannot come nor be delivered. This is a heavy burden to be placed unnecessarily, and erroneously, on an already beleaguered and downtrodden people by one of their own brilliant academicians. And make no mistake about that; Du Bois, for mere mental acuity or academic absorption ranks, perhaps, among some of the greatest minds who ever lived. He was the first black accepted into America's College of Letters. But it is a grave mistake, albeit unwittingly, for this falsehood to be laid on people who are formally labeled by whites as a lazy and stupid people with loose bonds one to the other and loose morals, people in the aggregate with the mental strength at best of a retarded child (as depicted by Jim in *The Adventures of Huckleberry Finn* and as Tom is treated by the prosecutor in *To Kill a Mockingbird*, 1960), deserving at most the insulting title of boy, never the courtesy title man or Mr.; and in their all around are seen more as animals in human form who, hardly with an effective, coordinated act of sustained resistance, submitted to the most horrific, barbaric, savage and tyrannical system of chattel slavery ever practiced against mankind, a slavery that in its complete severity rises no doubt to be the most monstrous crime ever committed in human history. If racist slavery is the biggest and the most evilest crime ever, the Du Boisian falsehood, adhered to by an elite element of lazy blacks as if it is a divine law, has to rank as one of the biggest and most towering and destructive lies ever told. To counter this falsehood with truth, there has to be a structural change in what the Blackman sees as the cause of his problem, if he is ever to master the process of the abstract thought in the social context necessary for any people to rise to a high level of abstract social growth in politics, business, religion and civic affairs.

The thesis here is that black humanity himself must develop a new consciousness, which, in spite of his current apparent, spiritual and moral deficiency, can eventually with innate industry lift the race above and beyond the fear, ignorance, social and intellectual laziness and indifference which beset him today; and allow himself to be a full and equal player on the world stage, in the global theater. This advance will replace the insulting label of boy now so firmly affixed on the marquee of his collective persona with the prideful and grown-up label of man. The growing possibilities of our time must begin to point to this new reality that the individual person and the collective person must supplement and integrate each other. The presence of this fact is obvious in dominate groups or races, and its lack is obvious in groups and races dominated.

The composite or collective individual that all members of the race make up determines whether whatever we achieve individually is seen as exceptions to the rule of blacks as stupid, or as an example of an individual excellence in a together people with enough intelligence to cohere in developing abstract social frameworks that allow them to exercise the level of self-control that results in them building those political, religious, economic and civic institutions in their community that transform it from a pit of despair into a haven that is as safe, as clean and as prosperous as any other people's.

Understanding this concept is necessary before the race can effectively counter the double attack against the composite by two very destructive internal factions. The war in the black community is not between blacks and whites, but blacks and blacks. This schizoid condition has the black criminal attacking blacks in the community while the so-called elite blacks, instead of providing the insight and actions that transform it to a safe haven, try to flee from it. A black today, for instance, is likely to move or want to move into the white community not for variety nor for social integration but because he thinks it is better. He is likely to think it is safer, cleaner, and more prosperous and prestigious than the black. He thinks this, it seems, ignorant of the fact that he cannot divorce himself from the composite. Cannot divorce himself from himself or said another way, one cannot run from one's shadow. The black criminal, on the other hand, is ignorant of the fact that by murdering a black individual, the composite bleeds, but the composite will never die completely till every black individual person is dead. His attack on the composite has the same effect as the slave holders had on the black individual. They could not destroy all black peoples' hope unless they destroyed every black person, and the black race will never rise to greatness till those of her children who try to run away from her stop trying to do so and the black criminal stops his murdering habit, thus stopping the bleeding. White cannot make the image of the black persona better or worst, only blacks themselves can do either.

While the Du Boisian pronouncement is false, for neither race nor color is treated as crimes in this country, it may perhaps at a certain level be understandable as mindless ignominious drivel, because it was written when the boot hill of whites was still ensconced firmly on the neck of blacks: he wrote it at a time when lynching cases like Roosevelt Townes (twenty-six) and Bootjack McDaniels (twenty-six) were almost daily occurrences. These two black men pleaded not guilty to a charge of murder in court. When they stepped outside the courthouse in 1937, an angry white mob came forward, took them from the custody of the guards without a struggle, chained them fast to trees, and asked one to confess to the murder. When he said he was innocent, a mobster stepped forward with a plumber's blowtorch and lit it; and, when the accused refused again to confess, the mobster trained the blue-white flame on their bodies and seared into their chests. They are listed in history as the blowtorch lynching in Winona, Mississippi.

Clearly, this was a miscarriage of justice, yet neither this page in history, nor any of the others including segregation, not even slavery itself, was written because whites hate black or even see black as a problem.

What is Not the Cause of the Race Problem

These atrocities were committed. But not as Du Bois concludes because the casualties were black and the predators were white. His conclusion is wrong because his premises are false, which are that whites abuse blacks because of their color and race. He supposed that such crimes were committed because the prey was black and the predators were white. But I say do not suppose the case as you want it to be; but take it as it is. And everyone knows whites affinity for black.

And say what you may, the evidence shows that whites like black. One day I opened my mail and in it was an invitation from a white man for me to attend his wedding. The bridegroom wore black and the bride wore white; they were a perfect match. White and black wore well together.

During the days of Jim Crow when a black person down south had to enter a white's house in the rear, I went by a white man's house down there on an errand. He was sitting on the front porch, a black cat in his lap, and, as I gave my purpose for coming, he stroked the cat with a soft and tender touch. After hearing my reason, he placed the cat on the floor and went inside. While inside, he called the cat by name, "darling," he said, and the cat with a trained paw opened the front door and went inside. That the black cat entered in the front door did not bother the caller in the least.

I attended a formal state dinner. White men there were dressed in black. I was in a formal state procession, and the cars of state loaded with whites were black. I went to a funeral; the body was white, and white men in mourning wore black. On their most regal and solemn occasions, whites use black vehicles and dress in black to dignify themselves and the occasion. They would not do this if they hated black or felt any enmity at all toward it.

And in the arena of sex, evidence is, that the white man did not rape the black woman—246 years as chattel—because she was unattractive or bad looking; he raped her because he had low morals and bad manners.

As if these reasons are not sufficient to dispel the claim or suspicion that whites hate black, let us go to what was behind the use of blacks as slaves, which was the bottom line. Whites would rather see black on it than any other color. And the more the better.

The claim that whites hate race strains credulity, because they are a race. We have been taught in school that there are five races of mankind (black, brown, red, white and yellow), and white certainly is one of them. (And as all the others, black is a color that comes from God). To say, therefore, that whites hate race is to say whites hate themselves. Whites claim the white race is superior to the black, but they do not base that view on color but intellect. When the intellectual achievements (a safe, clean, and industriously prosperous society) of the white race are placed beside the intellectual achievements (an unsafe, unclean, un-prosperous and un-industrious society) of the black race, the white race indicates that it wonders if the black race has a real human mind, but mind like life has no known color; thus as nobody knows the color of life, nobody knows the color of mind.

What Is The Cause of the Race Problem

Color in this matter is similar in kind to the bell in Pavlov's experiment with his dog. The Blackman's mind is wrapped in black skin; and he thinks, therefore, albeit fallaciously, that his problem is his color and his race; but it is not his color nor his race. It is how he processes and makes use of information in his mind. Because it is wrapped in black skin, when he is seen, one reacts negatively to him not because his skin is black but because of the poor, incoherent way he uses his mind. His situation is demonstrative of the experiment Pavlov did with his dog. After ringing the bell, he would give the dog food; and the dog, after a time, began to salivate whenever he heard the bell only. But his nature still required food to live. Though the bell caused him to salivate, it would be unable ultimately to pacify his hunger. To conclude, therefore, that the sound of the bell would really be food for the dog would be to miss read the effect of the bell. And likewise to conclude black skin causes racism is a fallacy; because as the sound of the bell cannot feed the dog, neither blacks' nor whites' color can be changed. And the cause of racism can be changed. At the core, therefore, of every discriminatory act committed against blacks by whites is, instead of race or color, a psychosocial dynamic that caused it.

Color nor race then is the cause of racism, because neither race nor color is changeable. To charge either one of them would be to charge God with causing it. And He is too good for that. Color and race are realities that people cannot change; whereas the cause of racism is something they can readily change. Therefore, on the face of it, neither race nor color is the culprit.

The cause of racism is an evil in whites who choose to take advantage of blacks' laxity of mind. There is a mind in the body of blacks (and there is a body of black humanity) as it is in the body of whites. The problem blacks have with whites would dissipate like air from a leaky tire, if blacks would do two things: one, make their community as safe and clean and industriously prosperous as any other people's; and two, respect themselves, respect others, and earn respect of others. That is what white people do, and they say they do it because they are mentally superior, and blacks do not do it because they are mentally inferior. And blaming their problem on skin color and race, and not on the miss use of their mind, is defeatist and is a surefire way for them to keep a firm and unholy grip on the bottom rung of humanity or, as the Street Philosopher put it, stay at the dunghill of mankind in general and whites in particular; because if what is not the problem is blamed for the problem, it is very unlikely that the problem will ever be solved, because you cannot hit the bull's eye, if you are not aiming at the target.

God has been good to blacks, but they have not yet been good to themselves. They have not been good stewards of God's gift of mind to them. Today in for too many instances, a black with money, fame, education or position would rather live in the white community than in the black, would rather present himself before the people of the earth as a lapdog than a human being—a lapdog being a famous, educated, wealthy or positioned black whose choice it is to move into the white community before, with his help, the black community is comparable to the white in safety, cleanliness and prosperity. Some would want to call such a move integration, but it is not. I will discuss integration elsewhere. But let me say here that Martin Luther King Jr. was probably the greatest advocate for integration in American history; but he never moved into the white community, because he was too busy working to improve conditions in his own, and because he knew exactly and precisely what integration is.

The black—white conversation in polite society today, unspoken of course, goes something like the following:

"I accept black inferiority and white superiority."

"Boy, do you want to move into my neighborhood?"

"Yessuh."

"Why?"

"Because it's better."

"Who made it better, boy?"

"You did sir."

"Why don't you make your community a preferred place in which to live?"

"Sir!"

"You heard me boy."

"I lack that amount of intelligence, sir."

"If you are ever to be taken seriously, that's what you must do, boy."

"Yessuh."

Such words would never be exchanged openly today between the white agent and the newly assigned black professor at Harvard (Harvard used here generically) as he is shown some of the nice, spacious, exclusive properties in the white section of town. This is a situation, therefore, that says for more than what is ever actually uttered. And it matters not whether he gives the big toothy grin; or is sully, truculent and reserved, or is bodacious; or has the, "I am as good as any white" attitude, or is very bold and crass; or is pithily stupid to the degree that he would say within himself that he does not give a damn about Haiti, the black ghettoes of America, or the starving, stupid, lazy-ass Africans in Africa: I know I am not accepted by this white man and never will be; but he has let me move in and I am the happiest black person on the planet; and, being so possessed, and with an internal hope, that his house will not be bombed and that, when he drives through the neighborhood, he will not hear some white yell, "Go back to Africa Nigger," he, whatever his personality type, settles in with conscious or unconscious trepidation.

It is this unspoken conversation, this interaction carried on daily, however, between the upper echelon of the races that keeps afresh blacks misuse of mind relevant to whites. A black individual, for instance, can become the richest person in the world, the black athlete the greatest Olympian, the black entertainer the most famous personality in history; the black academician a most distinguished scholar; but until blacks build a first-class, first-world, world-class community, where the streets are safe, the homes are secure, and the gaiety in the voices of their children is heard around the world, they will never break loose and be free of the snares of what Du Bois calls "white condemnation and contempt."

In the main, the black elite acts as though there is no black public domain, as if there is no body of black humanity, and as though this body, which they ignore at their own peril, I might add, has no head to think, to plan and to carry it forward in an honorable and dignified manner. No other race including the white can ever treat blacks any worse than that. Thus the black is his own worst enemy. This helps to explain why so many blacks with money, education, fame or position opt to live in the white though treacherous community and enjoy their culture; ignorant, it seems, of the fact that this action is a powerful argument that blacks as people are too lazy and too stupid to cohere one to the other to plan and build together, perhaps with the help of others, their own community to be as good as or better than any other.

As long as the black community in America is seen as a black ghetto, filled mostly with hellish rage, a black's individual achievements in wealth, education, fame or in other ways are effectively truncated. Our new reality must be to integrate the individual person and the collective person in ways that supplement each other.

If we blacks have a good mind, and there is no evidence that we do not, though there is plenty of evidence that we have not to date used it wisely, and the future of course is yet to unfold, how long shall we as a race blame whites for our depravity, when it is us who must use our minds to transform our community from the baneful stench of crime, careless neglect, elitist clicks and recklessness that it is today to an oasis of hope, peace and good will, from a blighted scene of murderous destruction of human life to the beloved community of optimism that reigns as the hallowed sanctuary of safety, cleanliness and prosperity?

Some Examples of The Cause of the Race Problem

If we blacks say that whites discriminate against us because of our race and color, and if we say that we cannot change our color nor race, and that whites, therefore, should not discriminate against us on the basis of something we cannot change, this is a fallacious, and is essentially a convoluted and specious argument, because just as we cannot change our race nor color, neither can whites change theirs. So if we think whites can do better by us, it is because, evidently, we think there is something in or about them they can change. And if there is something in or about them they can change, there is something in or about us that we can change. This tells us then that we are not discriminated against by whites because we are black and they are white. So, therefore, race and color are neutral entities in the conflict between the races. But, though this neutrality has now been shown not to be the cause of what is called the race problem, there still is a problem between the races; and it is caused by something in each race that it can change. And it is incumbent upon blacks to change that, which they can change in themselves; and then whites will inevitably have to change that in themselves that blacks have tried so hard to get them to change without making first the necessary change in themselves, which is to change from the stupid to the intelligent use of mind. And whites would then of necessity have to change from the arrogant and contemptible to the respectful use of mind.

If we the blacks can understand that no white has ever raised a hand against us because we are black and he is white, we will then be on the road to solving the race problem, because that understanding will free us to look for and find the real cause for whites' discrimination against us. The real reason is we let them. And the question then becomes why do we let them? They have told us not only by their actions but also in words. They have said that they have, and will continue, to discriminate against us in their own words because they see us by our behavior to be a lazy and stupid, impulsive, subhuman, savage people, closer in intelligence to apes than to the white man.

There is a cause and effect for the race problem, whereas we have tried to make it be an effect only—white discrimination; but there is a *cause* for whites' discrimination against us, and the cause for it is in us not on us, for whites, like any other people, will do to us only that that we permit. After observing us very carefully, whites found that the lag headed way we as a people navigate our way through life makes us a fit specimen for subjugation. We are the victim of that principle in nature that says, if this is done it will have this effect. If you give over how you are to be treated into the hands of others, the consequence could very well be extremely harsh and brutal. You could be enslaved, raped with impunity—no recognition nor acceptance of paternity resulting from such unions—worked without pay, segregated as a matter of course, have done to you whatever they choose and, after a time, that that they have chosen becomes their right. And they then convert that right into a doctrine that says "blacks have no right a white is bound to respect."

A Simple Truth for the Black Individual

You must realize that graduating from Harvard with a 4.0 grade point average does not prove you are as smart as the white who wrote the books you studied, built Harvard, taught the classes you attended, and granted the degree you received.

To prove your smarts, to shine the light of your humanity, and in short to show that you have initiative and imagination, you must go out among the members of your race cohere with them, build a Harvard, develop a curriculum, write the books, teach the courses, and grant the degree.

If you don't do that, you effectively become the classic definition of an animal; for an animal can be trained to perform some astounding feats, a lion to jump through rings of fire, an elephant to spin round on a spindle, and a horse to walk up on two legs; but you will never see the trained animals out training other lions, elephants or horses to perform these feats. So the sign of black superior human intelligence is not that a member of the race can be trained by whites to receive a degree from Harvard as Du Bois thought, but can and will he use that learning to train or so direct his race that his like the white builds a safe, clean and industriously, prosperous community, where the atmosphere is friendly, sociable, and likable; where the ambiance is soft, dignified, splendid and learned; and where every child, boy or girl, enters the world into the bosom of outstretched arms that renders unto the new born babe a joyous, warm, and healthy embrace, which says in a loud, distinctive voice we are glad you came.

After whites labeled blacks lazy, stupid, impulsive, and savage, there came a time when white described black as an ugly, savage brute. Yet when black was called ugly, he did not manifest his beauty; when he was called a brute, he did not assert his civility; and when he was called a savage, he did not manifest his humanity.

Black's silence in these matters affirmed in white's mind that he was correct in his assessment of the black condition. And white proceeded to act in concert with his now—stated view of the black race. But none of this was done because black is black or because white is white: it was done because white chose to use his mind to execute his will over black, whereupon black chose not to use his mind to block whites' rule over him, and build for himself a superior, innovative and prosperous, world-class society, working perhaps jointly with his white brother.

When called impulsive, he did not show a thoughtful manifestation of his superior humanity over the impulsive animalistic side of himself, which landed him under the control of others in the first place. He acted more from external stimulus than from his own mental reasoning and thoughtful contemplation. Being impulsive at this time does not correct this error in black judgment; it only affirms it. All impulsion does today, other than the mayhem it creates in the community, is get black locked up in prison, where he is told what to do and is made to do what he is told. Thus today he is in the same essential position there his forebears were during slavery when they were told what to do and were made to do what they were told. Most blacks in prison today, however, are there for either stealing from a black, raping or murdering a black, or for the commission of some other heinous and vicious crime against another black.

How to Solve the Race Problem

There is no other human being, who has ever loved a city more than Coleman Alexander Young loved his, the city of Detroit. So his failure to build a public policy that would have stopped its decline and transformed it into a city of safety, cleanliness, and prosperity was not due to his lack of love for it. He had love for it, but he did not know how to deliver it. He did not know how to effectuate a public policy that would have made his city a first-class, first-world, world-class city. His lack of this knowledge was due to the fact that he had not made a careful study and proper analysis of the black condition. If he had done so, he would have found that white prejudice did not cause the black condition but it was the black condition that was the fodder that continuously fed the craw of white prejudice. With that level of ignorance in full possession of him, though he thought he should do the best he could to make the city the best it could be, he had no knowledge of how to do it, and so while he held to his limited view, he watched in harried sorrow as his beloved city kept drifting and spiraling downward into the abyss of the bottomless pit.

While some of his fellow residents ran about the streets stealing, burning, raping and murdering with almost total abandon, he stood by with prestige and authority of high political office in his possession and watched as killers made his city a murderous crime scene. While these two crown jewels of prestige and authority were his, he had not one, single, solitary clue how to use them to make his city what he wanted it to be, which was a safe, clean, and prosperous place in which to live, raise a family, and do business. He did not know how to use these honors, these great assets, bestowed upon him to formulate a public policy that would make his city the most prestigious and preferred destination point on earth for civilized people from around the world to come and see and bask in the ambiance of its excellence. Instead of this, many came to be an eye witness to raging flames leaping from house to house as the city he loved burned in the night, a direct result of action taken by some of his fellow residents, and perhaps others, who willfully and deliberately set fires with tragic effect in the neighborhoods.

The main tragedy here, though, is not the willful burning and the deliberate acts of savagery committed by the arsonists. It is that those blacks with education, wealth, prestige and authority who included Mayor Young were impotent, as those who would, at Halloween year after year, burned their city to the ground. And, while his mobilization of thousands of residents did quell the massive burning at Halloween, the impulse to burn was never replaced with reasons manifested in a public policy that transformed the community into a safe, clean and prosperous place. It is said that youth is too precious to be wasted on the young. Whites did say some time ago that education, money, prestige and authority were assets too valuable to be put into the hands of blacks; for if they were given possession of them, they would not know how to make proper use of them.

The Proper Role of the Black Politician

When the honor and prestige of being one of the elect, who has a seat in Congress bestowed upon him, a black politician, when he stands in the well of that hallowed place, or any where else, and says that his jurisdiction is riddled with crime and festers in despair and lack of hope, and not that he has built a consensus in and out of it that has now transformed it from an index of misery into a jewel of social progress and congenial accord, he is seen by civilized men more as an animal baying like a dog than an intelligent man who is fit to have the honor and privilege of bearing the title of Congressman or any other high office. And likewise with any other black politician at the local, state, or federal level whether elected or appointed. Holders of positions of political power and prestige are there to serve as a catalyst to bring together disparate elements to solve problems, not merely to list them as though the mere listing of them or that show of concern is a solution. Concern is for the ordinary citizen to have for the politician to tap into. The politician's duty is to use the prestige and authority of his high office to tap into citizens' concerns to build a consensus that resolves problems in his jurisdiction. That is what white men do. Are we blacks men or children? Jefferson's pithy revelation that "all men are created equal," his hypocrisy notwithstanding, was not merely brilliant; it was inspired. Flesh and blood did not reveal that to him but directly from the mouth of God.

Because Jefferson and his countrymen veered from that truth, the nation paid a heavy price in blood and treasure with the guts and bones and the flesh of men strewn about the field. And there have been many a crass and evil despot who have tried over the years to steer America away from the path of her promise, but so far not one has succeeded. Her stride to form a more perfect union is, I believe, still on course.

Some blacks, and some whites, have said Jefferson was speaking only for whites, but certainly not for blacks. But that is not true. The only people who think his statement does not mean what it says have to be those who do not see themselves as men, because it is a straightforward, unequivocal and universal declaration; for there is no exception in "all." So if blacks think they are not included, it must be because they think they are not men. But the words are clear, and they are written; if blacks do not see themselves as men, that is not the fault of Jefferson nor the revelation; for it does not say that all people are created equal, nor that all people are created men. It says what it says, and what it says is true. I think it is correct to say that if the black elite, which, in this instance, are the educated, the wealthy, the prestigious, and the ones with authority, do not know how to sit down at the table with members of their own race in peace and calm tranquility and map a strategy that effectively lifts their jurisdictions and their race to the heights of greatness, it is doubtful that they will ever know how to sit properly at the table of any other. If they are allowed at the table of others before they have built a table of their own, it is because they are being seen as lapdogs, not equals, and are being tolerated, not welcomed nor respected. Others do not want them there because they do not yet know how to behave.

The least productive human resource in the world today is the black politician. Every profession pursued by blacks can boast of some measure of success but the black politician. Some run for office but don't know how to win. Some run and get elected but don't know how to formulate a public policy to effectively cut off the spigot that feeds so many youthful blacks to the prison system. It is said by some that the feast sharks had of those of us thrown overboard as we met death in the belly of slave ships at sea in route to the New World was not so good as the bloated walls of prisons are today as they greedily stuff their jaws with young blacks jumping and leaping from their mother's belly in a mad dash to enter in behind the doors of prison.

Our two most noted and worthy leaders were Booker T. Washington and Dr. Martin Luther King Jr. Washington opened his school, Tuskegee Institute, July 4, 1881; and Dr. King began his leadership seventy-four years later, December 1, 1955. Washington was an educator who lifted the veil of ignorance from his people in what is still the greatest institution ever built in American by black intelligence, and Dr. King was a preacher and a pastor who developed a public policy that transformed America from a Jim Crow nation to an open society. Most intelligent people know it was not the arrest of Rosa Parks (many blacks of all stripes had been arrested and otherwise abused by Jim Crow tyranny) that made the difference but it was what members of her race and millions of others did about it. This response was carried out under the leadership of Dr. King. He saw blacks' backs were bent. He taught white he should not ride the bent man's back but should, instead, assist him to straighten up and walk upright. He knew, however, that white could not give black dignity, for dignity like life itself comes only from God: and that only black himself can live his life and build his dignity. Dr. King was a preacher and pastor, and Washington was a teacher and educator. I will expand elsewhere on the true significance of the roles these two men exercised in blacks' struggle to rise to the level of their potential.

There is no comparison between the effectiveness of these two men in their leadership roles to bring black up to par and the black politicians. They, so far in actuality have been a negative energy. It is not just a problem Coleman Young had: but of black politicians throughout America and worldwide. Black politicians in black jurisdictions in America, whether mayors, legislators, judges or school boards as well as worldwide, whether on an island in the sea such as Haiti or on the continent of Africa, most suffer mainly from the same syndrome, the inability to formulate a public policy that builds their black jurisdictions into a first-class, first-world, world-class community in which the streets are safe, the homes are secure, and the gaiety in the voices of the children is heard around the world.

Instead of this effect, the destructive force of the black politician has now negatively impacted the black church. The most noted example of this is the Rev. Dr. Henry J. Lyons who, instead of being an honest pastor and president of the National Baptist Convention, USA, Inc., became a thief who stole money entrusted to his care to rebuild churches torched by arsonists.

Called upon to guide the flock aright
The malignant lying skirt chasing thief
Fleeced the sheepish flock both day and night
And spent the loot on hunks of human beef.
He stole from his church, from both man and God
In amounts that would make angels angry.
The vile action of this malignant clod
Caused the needy children to go hungry.
His actions caused real preachers to turn gray
For this malignant one could hurt the church
And cause members to curse and walk away
And cause parents not to give quite as much
 A thief is a disgrace in all nations
 A lying preacher an abomination.

And now a great many black churches today at election time look and smell like a cesspool of whores with politicians of practically every stripe and kind parading before the congregation, and sometimes they are actually allowed to speak to the people from the pulpit on Sunday. So now the honesty of the black pastor is compromised, and what was once a potential moral force in the community has become a painfully lying force. Thus there is no potential protective shield any more between the mass of blacks and the corrosive effect of the black politician.

Those pastors who care about morality and the righteous call of the church should never let a politician speak again to the congregation from the pulpit or anywhere else in church on Sunday. And they should let no other politicking go on at church on Sunday, including introducing the politicians.

Every congregation and pastor who care about such matters should instead form a political committee and, anytime but especially during election season, politicians could be given the opportunity of coming before the committee and the public at the church on a designated week day set aside for that purpose. The committee could serve two purposes: one, hear the promises the politicians make; and two follow up and see how many promises the politicians who came before it had kept. This it seems would be far more preferable and beneficial than making the church a sluttish, whorish, cesspool for politicians.

Somebody said the Constitution of the United States was a living, breathing document. When asked what that meant, a black politician said that it lent itself to interpretations in keeping with the times and cited *Roe v. Wade* as a case in point. As I watched this person, I waited for him to go on from there and state what the true essence of the said statement is: what is it that makes the U.S. Constitution a living, breathing, ever-alive document? When I finally saw that his beginning, though good, was also his end, I realized all over again why certain people call black folk shallow headed. For though this black politician was a Harvard graduate, he did not take a moment to think about the question and the answer; for if he had, he would have found that the answer to the query was basically in the question. For the answer is simple: the U.S. Constitution is a living and breathing document because members of each generation absorb and internalize its precepts and seek to make them the guiding principles of their political lives.

As I hear words and read books by and about (I don't think it's necessary to specify names here) some of the most noted former leaders in the Civil Rights Movement, what shows up most on these pages are swelled heads with the main purpose being, it seems, to express pride in achieving a political office and/or to bask in their fame. So there are many famous names, but there is no black community or black jurisdiction that has, under its political leadership transformed itself from the misery index to the index of plenty. To the contrary, usually, under its leadership as local, state, and federal elected and appointed officials, as executive, legislative, judicial, and administrative persons, the misery index in the black community has risen exponentially. After what is called now a lost generation, the black population in America is beginning to see a strong similarity between black politicians here to those in Haiti and Africa. In Africa and Haiti, blacks are trying to get from under the leadership of their black leaders there by coming to America or by going to Europe run by whites; and in America, blacks in black jurisdictions run by blacks are trying to get out of them and into jurisdictions run by whites.

The black politician should know that the high honor and awesome responsibility placed in his hands should add up to something more than a pack of lies made in promises not kept. He should know that the end is not to be called mayor, congressman, councilman, judge, school board member, and the like but to be effective at solving problems located in his jurisdiction, and to do it so well that those outside of it would find his example something they would be proud to emulate.

The black politician must not act as though he is a disinterested sideshow put out to make noise, and not as the holder of a high office of prestige and authority who must serve as the catalyst to solve the problems of crime, out-of-wedlock births, economic devastation, poor schools and low academic achievements, and debris and blight and filth in the streets. His vision should be so bright and so clear that all by it should strive to follow his lead with zeal, commitment, joy and constancy; the light of his vision should cover, penetrate, and inspire every person; and it should clean out every nook and cranny in his jurisdiction. The mediums and earthen areas along the sidewalks throughout the community should be aglow with green well-groomed grass and bright, beautiful, cultivated flowers. The black politician should not stain and demean the prestige of his high office with childish, irresponsible talking and speech making but, instead, he should enhance its statue by effective leadership, which means only one thing, solving—without excuses—the problems within the confines of his jurisdiction.

CHAPTER 2

The Journey to Excellence

The Intent

THE EXPRESSION, REACH for excellence is easily said. However I am going to draw a blueprint here that if studied carefully will be helpful to us as we struggle together as a people to reach for and attain excellence; as we struggle to make our community rise in rank from its third-world rating (and to say that sounds almost hyperbolic) at the bottom heap of mankind to rank among the most prestigious in the world.

Definition of Excellence

We have shown convincingly that under the dictate of whites there is hardly anything, we cannot achieve individually. We have not, however, shown the world yet that we have the initiative and intelligence to build, as Dr. King challenged us to do and sort to lead us to do while he lived, the beloved community, a community that is safe, clean and prosperous, a community where the streets are safe, the homes are secure, and the gaiety in the voices of our children is heard around the world. My question is not, did a black get elected mayor, speak to a national political convention, get elected president, make a great movie, win an Oscar, earn huge sums of money, become famous, or any other individual achievement that whites allowed him to do? It is, is the black community civilized? Is it prestigious, clean and industriously, prosperous? Is it a preferred place in which to live, raise a family, and do business? Are the streets safe, the homes secure, and gaiety in the voices of the children heard around the world? Is it indeed a first-world, first-class, world-class community that is second to none, reflecting without a doubt the intelligence, imagination, initiative, coherence, genius and unity of black people? This is something the white man cannot do for us with programs and money. This is something either we blacks have the intelligence to do or we do not.

The Need

The black community needs to reach for excellence; to do this, its leadership has to establish by its own initiative and intelligence unity and coherence in a public policy that achieves the desired goals. Its function therefore is to determine need or issues and set and achieve goals.

Du Bois said that the greatest deterrent to crime is the public opinion of one's community. He got that right. But in typical Du Boisian fashion, he then muddled that truth by saying in effect blacks are exempt from adhering to it because they are discriminated against by whites. We must generate in our community a public opinion that stifles high crime, while generating oxygen aplenty for decency, cleanliness, safety and prosperity.

In every community there are general issues on which most everyone will agree; saving the lives of children is an example. Determining key issues then is relatively easy; the difficulty is in building a public policy that molds agreement into an indelible plank in the standards of the people, making it so strong that an individual predator or hostile gangs inside the community, no matter how contrary, can never uproot and destroy that effective consensus of the people. Effective here is key. Because today to the survey question, "Would you rather black people live than be killed in high numbers by blacks in the black community?" blacks answer verbally, "Yes" but then go about saying and doing nothing to stop the killing. Doing nothing means not developing a public policy that stops it but instead continuing to say and do those things that allow the slaughter of our sons and daughters mostly by black males in the black community to go on unabated.

That an individual or gangs in the community would find it impossible to destroy the plank is easily understood, because they essentially would have no place to take root and grow. But the effectiveness of the plank against an outside force, such as racism, is more of a challenge. This is so because the outside force may be large, powerful and unrelentingly evil and vicious and, therefore, it may seem overwhelming. Even if it is large and an unyieldingly evil, the indelible quality of the plank will still hold; it is therefore indestructible, because it is an intricate part of the character and the fabric of the people. And as long as the community itself lasts, the safety and the well-being of its children and its people at large to the extent that it is humanly possible is assured.

Determining the issue and learning what to do, which in this example is to develop a public policy for the safety of children, lead to the most daunting task of all: who should head the effort and why? What should the goal be relevant to the issue (if for instance homicides are sustained at a rate of over five hundred per year, should the goal be to reduce it to less than fifty or twenty and should the goal be reached in one, two or three years, etc.?)? How to develop the public policy? How, in other words, to cohere, to reach and to maintain a set goal?

Exactly How to Formulate the Policy.

First, key people of the community must come together: business, religious, political, civic and any other class of people out of which leaders are formed. They should establish a general board, an operative board, and an executive board. The general board should meet once a year, the operative once a month and the executive board once a week. Each board should be allowed to meet more often if needed but never less. Committees should be formed to do the work of the organization; and times should be established for their reports and recommendations. No murder or killing should go without notice.

To talk outside of such a public policy would be like trying to go to the moon without a rocket—you would go nowhere fast. With the policy, every citizen's voice reinforces the social contract and the mayhem practiced in the streets of black America since 1968 would become unthinkable. To accomplish this our leaders have got to stop tap-dancing and showing their teeth in front of the television camera and roll up their sleeves and go to work in the community building the public policy needed to move us forward, to save the lives of our sons and daughters, especially our children.

Education Alone is not Sufficient

There is a pyramid of demonstratively appalling active contempt and abysmal ignorance and lazy or stupid indifference to the absolute needs of the black persona by the academically achieving blacks as well as most other achieving blacks in business, politics, religion, civic affairs and academia.

The black economic and business minds have not transformed the black community into a coherent economic giant; the black preacher and pastor have not transformed it into a bastion of morality; the black civic leaders have not transformed it into a scene of civility; the black politician has not transformed it into a safe, clean and friendly harbor; and the academician has not transformed his hall into a reservoir of academic excellence. Yet the black business person, the black politician, the black civic leader, the black preacher and the academician, each is an educated class in America today. So though these classes are educated, they have not led the race to build a safe, clean and prosperous, first-class, first-world, world-class community.

Failure of the educated class

Once educated, Dr. Martin Luther King Jr., returned to the black community and found opportunity to render useful service. From there, he spearheaded a movement to benefit the community, the nation and all mankind. Members of the black educated class today, unlike King or even sympathetic whites after slavery, missed the aim of the struggle. They do not make their expert knowledge responsive to the social or communal needs of black society. Instead, they use it to the detriment of black people.

To say to the contrary would be to ignore a bloody reality or to argue as some do that blacks are genetically flawed and, therefore, are incapable of developing a society whose image is not of criminality but of civility who point to black degeneracy worldwide, including the mess in Haiti and on the continent of Africa and the tons of murdered blood spilled by black criminals in the homes and in the streets of black society in America, as proof.

Let us examine briefly what the response of the best-educated black Americans has been to the desperate howl of their people for leadership during the years since 1968.

A black Harvard man, an MBA, who has worked more than twenty years in a Fortune 500 company says that it is unfair for blacks to expect their best educated to give something back. He states that he does not know the answer to the economic deterioration of black society. If that is true, to whom is the black mass to turn? He further says that nobody asks his white Harvard classmates to give anything back.

Is he saying that the great advances made in white society are made by the best-educated whites not giving anything back, or that it is unfair for the white masses to expect them to do so? Or is he, in effect, saying that white intelligence is superior to his black intelligence and, because that is the case, white intelligence can build desirable communities without the white mass demanding it?

With his black intelligence being inferior, at best he can only beg and request of whites their permission to move into their neighborhood. Even an inferior, if permitted, can move into a desirable neighborhood erected using the initiative, imagination and coherence of others but it takes a man and people of superior intelligence to build one.

A black male product of Princeton sees the situation of blacks murdering blacks in high numbers in the black community as a condition that is a greater shame on white America than on black America. In effect, he is saying whites have enough intelligence to be ashamed of black criminality against blacks but blacks do not. He expects white humanity to be more genteel toward blacks than black humanity is toward himself.

These people do not realize that when they say and do these things they are affirming the mental inferiority that others claim about them. They do not understand that when a problem with the magnitude of the barbaric, no not barbaric, impulsive savagery that fills black society today occurs, it is precisely what the best-educated people of the race are saying and doing that is causing the problem.

The black educated class missed the whole point of the Civil Rights Movement. Because of their negligence, the young and the ignorant do not know that this struggle ever existed. It was not about how physically close a black could get to a white; it has always been about whether the black's ability for thought and action was inferior to the white's.

A highly perfumed, dressed-to-the-nines, black female, PhD, sat in the waiting room at a radio station waiting to go on air to ask white males in the boardroom to stop promoting the black woman's black son's lyrics that call her bitch, whore and slut. Listening to her made it obvious it had not dawned on her the fool she really appeared to the world to be. Though highly educated, her low level of basic human intelligence, clearly at that moment, was not enough to inform her that it was not the duty of the white man to teach the black boy to respect the black woman. Respecting her is something the black woman's culture should be teaching him from the time he is conceived in his mother's womb. Do not raise him to see you as a b-w-s; and, when he begins to play back what his mama and black society have taught him, go running to the white man as if he is his son.

These examples show two things. One, the Blackman thinks his ability is inferior to whites, though he may verbally say to the contrary, but even blacks know actions speak louder than words; two, he uses whatever thinking ability he has against himself. The line between sense and thought is a thin one. He raps aloud, but his intelligent thought lies dormant on the other side of the line. When his thinking skills match his rapping skills, he will then be able to move himself and his people from the ghetto, because the black ghetto is not based solely in geography but in black degeneracy. This thought process will not get him a residence in the suburbs of his people, but a home in their midst and a place of abiding love in their hearts. It will astonish him to see that his children will then follow his constructive and thoughtful course with as much devotion and zeal as they now follow his thoughtless and destructive course.

The actions and assertions of the people I have described and the bloody reality of black society appear to argue vigorously in support of the racist theory that blacks are incapable of productive, abstract, coherent social thought and action. But the evil committed against black society by this black educated class and the black criminal is not the last word. It is not the ultimate and final expression of black people.

From the belly, bowels and womb of this race, now trodden down and bludgeoned by these vicious elements, shall spring forth a fruit rich in substance, unbounded by ignorance, unchained to defeat and not prone to self-slaughter. This fruit will know, that when whites say they are better than blacks that is a white problem. When whites manifest this faulty thinking with acts against blacks, this fruit will seek to improve race relations. This fruit will also know that when whites say blacks are incapable of thinking of ways that will lead them to building safe, clean and prosperous communities and blacks, as they have done since 1968, prove them right, that is a black problem.

It is my hope that one day black PhDs, MBAs and other black graduates from colleges and universities will come out of these institutions and not try to run from their people, but will plant themselves, as King did, firmly in the midst of the black community and cultivate it until its roses bloom and its diverse crops yield an abundant harvest.

That was the dream of Dr. Martin Luther King Jr. I believe that this community and its people can be so transformed that the black male will no longer be seen as a predatory scavenger weaving a web of theft and murder, but as a son, a husband, and a father. The black female will no longer be seen as loose, with low morals and standards, but as a daughter, a wife and a mother.

CHAPTER 3

The Destructive Legacy of the Niagara Movement

The Call

IN WHAT, AT the time no doubt seemed a sensible and doable undertaking, W. E. B. Du Bois, Harvard graduate, and first black PhD, class of 1896, made his call to form the Niagara Movement. It was on July 9, 1905, that twenty-nine of America's best-educated and wealthiest black men from fourteen states answered the call and, after being rebuffed in New York, came to a hotel in Niagara Falls, Canada, across the river from Buffalo and with what seemed a possibility for hope, and some contention, formed the Niagara Movement. It was incorporated in Washington, DC, January 31, 1906. Some of those who came were Du Bois's fellow Harvard men, Clement Morgan, a lawyer and class mate and William Monroe Trotter, a publisher; present from Georgia was the wealthy Alonzo F. Herndon, businessman from Atlanta.

The Fatal Flaw

But success for the Niagara Movement was not to be; it did not fail because white men set up on them with guns and clubs and whips and chased them down like animals, beat the squat out of them, bust some kneecaps, shot some in the back and murdered two or three in cold blood yet it still would become the most destructive and humiliating failure in all the annuals of black humanity because its best-educated and wealthiest men failed in a very doable effort to form a successful organization up North to help move the race forward.

So, instead of the new organization providing real hope, it highlighted among other things a fatal flaw in the so called Talented Tenth, the crux of the black elite, especially so in Du Bois's ability to be a leader: "I was no natural leader of men," he said. "I could not slap people on the back and make friends of strangers. I could not easily break down an inherited reserve; or at all times curb a biting, critical tongue. Nevertheless, having put my hand to the plow, I had to go on. The Niagara Movement with less momentum met in Boston in 1907 and in Oberlin in 1908. It began to suffer internal strain from the dynamic personality of Trotter and my own inexperience with organizations." There is no evidence that the men he invited to Niagara were strangers to him. What is strange about that statement is, he made it. Nay, the real tragedy of the Niagara Movement was not the scholar's inability to slap backs or check a biting and critical tongue. It was that America's best-educated and wealthiest black men could not or, at least, would not check their bloated egos and cohere for the purpose of building a strong institution up North of which blacks could use and be proud of for all generations to come.

The need to backslap to lead men was contradicted in his own report of an interview he had with Booker T. Washington, a great leader of men and the builder of Tuskegee Institute, the greatest institution ever built in America by a black person. "Booker T. Washington," he said, "was not an easy person to know. He was wary and silent. He never expressed himself frankly or clearly until he knew exactly to whom he was talking and just what their wishes and desires were. He did not know me, and I think he was suspicious. On the other hand, I was quick, fast-speaking and voluble."

Those are not traits of one reserved. "I had nothing to conceal. I found at the end of the interview that I had done practically all the talking . . . . In fact, Mr. Washington had said about as near nothing as was possible." So while it was true that he was no natural leader; it was not an inability to slap backs that caused the failure of the Niagarites. Let us now examine these self-serving comments. He said he had nothing to hide, but he did. This will come out later. It is self-evident based on this report that being quick, fast-speaking and voluble is not a recipe nor a qualification for leadership, nor is backslapping.

The Reasons for the Niagara Movement

The Niagarites were not men enough to understand what was stopping their social progress, and were not wise enough therefore to devise and execute a coherent plan for improving their role in the unfolding drama of race in the nation. They complained bitterly of discrimination, but never advanced and executed an effective idea to end it. They said it was wrong, that they would submit if forced; that is the most lame-headed statement. That is like saying they would die if murdered, for any idiot knows it goes without saying that if forced, one would submit; but they thought that was one of their brightest assertions. So they said much, but provided no evidence of their manhood. They never executed a coherent plan to end discrimination. They seemed unaware that they held sway over the locks that could unleash a torrent of freedom and fair play in America for every body including blacks. It is in this area of the Niagarites views that such paucity of understanding of how childish, pathetic and sick their intra-group situation was. They were perfectly willing to demand of the white man their manhood rights, but were not willing to demand of themselves coherence, discipline and manly action to achieve them. If they were not acceptable to each other, why think they would be acceptable to other men?

They did not want the white man to treat them like niggers, yet it seems their every move in terms of being destructive for the race was niggerish. They wanted to be treated like men, but their every act was childish. In their circumstance, you do not just say you are going to protest. A dog will bark when hit. Men of superior intelligence to get what they want devise a plan of action and then execute it with discipline and esprit de corps.

As strange as it may seem, the basic problem the Niagarites had was that they did not accept the American ideal of fair play. That is why they could not cohere in a plan to have America live up to her promise. They wanted her to accept them because of their book learning, not for anything they had done to advance the possibility of fair play for all. Therefore, they wanted to be accepted as men while they acted as boys.

Du Bois thought he was more than he was and wanted to be something he was not. He thought he was too important and too learned to be black; that is why he called blacks serfs, peasants, hordes and a headless host; and he wanted most desperately to be white; that is why he lied on his application to Harvard, calling himself mulatto when he was not. He seemed totally ignorant of the need of people to have institutions of their own. He jumped, therefore, at the chance to be an employee and board member of an organization founded by whites; and when they rapped his knuckles he took it like a sheepish animal. This says he had little or no ability to control himself socially; and by not being willing to work with BTW, he demonstrated that he would rather not work in a black institution striving mightily to improve the race. In falsely proclaiming himself a mulatto, he effectively declared that he thought mulatto was better than those he called full blooded, and having failed at trying to run an organization of his own, the next best role he could possibly play in human society was that of a lapdog.

The Reason for the Failure: Bloated Egos

When Du Bois made the call, chances are, he thought he was exhibiting high black intelligence; but in actuality he was revealing the most universally identifiable trait ever found in the black elite; and, therefore, in black society. He would not join BTW at Tuskegee to build a strong and powerful synergy for the race. He made the call and thus exposed and, thereby, raised high the partition of divisive tyranny, a destructive sentiment, and behavioral pattern that separates the black elite from the mass of blacks and characterizes the separation of the black elite from that small group of transformative black leaders who are truly dedicated to working to improve the condition of the race as exemplified in BTW; and it demonstrates the muddleheadedness they had among themselves. Divisive tyranny destroys any possibility for blacks to cohere and build social institutions to meet their daily needs for food, clothes, shelter, athletics, entertainment and safety in their communities where they live, draw their breath and have their being. Unlike BTW who saw blacks as people yearning to learn, Du Bois saw them as serfs, peasants, hordes and headless hosts. He earnestly saw blacks as headless people. You cannot have it both ways; you cannot claim credibly people to be headless while at the same time claiming yourself to be their leader. Unless of course your claim of leader is false, is purely empty rhetoric.

Du Bois was a brilliant scholar, but as evidence shows he was highly deficient in good social judgment. And in addition to that, the record makes clear that he was evil incarnate. He was evil for the following reasons. He attacked BTW most viciously for not fighting strongly enough for the following three social items: "the right to vote, civic equality, and the education of youth according to ability." Now let us see what he did while a professor at Atlanta University. Being without doubt the best educated black in American, did he ever present himself to the election commission in that state and demand that he be permitted to vote? No. Did he go to the head of civil government in that state and demand that he be treated on a par equal to white men there? No. Did he go to the leading white university in that state and request that it open its doors to blacks? No. Why then would he demand that BTW, working his fingers to the bone in the neighboring state of Alabama, building an educational institution that was training blacks on how to provide food, clothes, shelter, athletics, entertainment, as well as arts and science, and safety in their community for themselves, speak out on these matters when his actions were speaking out so brilliantly for himself, his people and the nation? If you have tears, prepare to shed them now for the reason is simple. His Talented Tenth made a high and haughty, self assured boast that Tuskegee Institute would not survive. That white folk would take it out. That is what they wanted. They thought by goading BTW, he would say something stupid and whites would go in, burn the institute to the ground, and murder in cold blood tons of blacks as they would do later in the Greenwood section of Tulsa, OK, June 1, 1921.

He said he had nothing to hide, but he did have something to hide. He did not like it when BTW sort to enhance the quality of life for all blacks, but was not honest enough to say so in those specific terms. So he claimed he was for blacks, and that BTW was an accommodationist for whites; he gave the word "accommodationist" a negative tone. But he never defined what an accommodationist is, because he could not be honest about his desire for the black race, because his intent was evil and meant the race no good. An accommodationist is someone who would rather compromise than be confrontational, would rather win than fail, would rather be victorious than be defeated, would rather be respected than held in contempt. This lack of candor in Du Bois made him a hypocrite. He reported that a lynching was prevented but did not identify Ida B. Wells-Barnett as the preventer. That in effect put him in bed with those racist publications that would report an incident involving whites without identifying the race, but would if it was a black. So if racism was evil, he was evil.

We know what racism is, but what was evil in Du Bois? Let us define racism exactly. Racism is an evil in whites directed against blacks. But Du Bois was not white. True. The evil in him is called niggerism. Niggerism is an evil in blacks directed against themselves. This is the great tragedy of black people; they have been under continuous attack from this twin headed monster of racism and niggerism now for hundreds of years.

When returning to the United States, after white philanthropy had paid for him to be educated at the prestigious University of Berlin, Du Bois said he came back to "nigger-hating America." Of all his much writing about America being a nigger hating nation, he never was inquisitive enough about the matter to ask why whites hate niggers. He thought, no doubt, that he knew the reason why but no evidence is given in his writings that he did. Chances are he thought their being racist was the cause. While racism is incontrovertibly the most monstrously evil ever to infect human personality, it is not the only evil to do so, because the reservoir where racism gets it sustenance is in the field of niggerism.

Racism here means that evil in whites directed against blacks, and niggerism means that evil in blacks directed against themselves. Racism and niggerism both are lethal, but racism is worse because it comes against the race from outside. They in a way are like homicide and suicide. In either case, the corpse is dead but in society murder is a heinous crime, whereas suicide is a horrible tragedy. The former requires justice; the latter requires sympathy and pity, which is what the whites showed by forming the National Association for the Advancement of Colored People.

Du Bois's enmity for BTW and his program for "lifting the veil of ignorance from his people" was so intense that even though the founders of the NAACP told him it was not to be used as an attack base against BTW, after they brought him in, one of the first things he did was to use NAACP stationery illegally to tell a lie on BTW in a broadside attack. He did this because he figured he could get away with it because weighing his leverage, the likelihood of them kicking him out so quickly for this dastardly deed was highly unlikely. They checked him but did not kick him out then, so he was right on that point; but the deed showed him to be very calculating when it came to acting against the best interest of blacks. Nonetheless, his devotees would rather lie about what he did not do, than tell the truth about what he did. They claim for instance that his Niagara Movement was the forerunner of the NAACP and that he was the inspiration for the Civil Rights Movement. Both of these claims of course are unmitigated, boldface lies that insult the honored memory of those heroes who served the race and all mankind so honorably. The truth is the NAACP was founded by whites and not forerun by Du Bois and the Niagarites; and the Civil Rights Movement was lead by Dr. Martin Luther King Jr., who rejected the elitist point of view of the Talented Tenth. He got his inspiration from the longing of his people to end Jim Crow and got his philosophy of nonviolent direct action, from Mohandas Gandhi and Henry David Thoreau. What Du Bois did was to show inability in the black elite to cohere and build social institutions to meet the needs of black people in every manly way. This truth is too painful to tell, so they choose to lie instead. Dr. King did say, however, that a lie shall not live forever, and the truth though trounced to the ground shall rise again.

Forerunner means that something occurred or went before for the purpose of what was to follow. That here is not the case. The Niagarites earnestly thought they were men. And building institutions for social advancement is something men had been doing for many years, including BTW who had been doing it since July 4, 1881. To say the NM was a forerunner of the NAACP is like saying Great Britain is the forerunner of the United States. This Talented Tenth's lie is a smoke screen to hide a miserable and humiliating failure. The reason the elitist use it is it suits their purpose of subterfuge, and not because there is one iota of truth in it. Make no mistake about it; the NAACP was founded by whites to help advance, as they said, coloreds; it is not an organization founded by the black elite to help the race.

The white man was convinced that blacks did not have the executive grit needed to build social institutions to meet their daily needs in every manly way. Rather than uttering purely and unadulterated scholastic gibberish and prancing around in a self made fog of pompous, ignominious pretense, BTW actively contradicted that conviction by building an institution in the heart of Dixie, in the cradle of the Confederacy, so strong that the evil, vicious, envious and industriously lazy and socially deficient black elitist, led by Du Bois could not destroy it. And today it still stands and serves every race and gender who enters within its hallowed walls yearning to learn. It is an example of black industry when it dares to get off its lazy bottom and stir about and do good for himself and for all mankind.

Washington showed success at institution building, and Du Bois showed failure. The black elite is still failing. Black heads of black churches, of civil rights organizations, of high academic degrees, of educational institutions, of high political office, and of business acumen, all of these in the tradition of the Niagarites are failing to organize and formulate a public policy that meets the daily needs of blacks in every manly way for food, clothes, shelter and safety in their community. They, it seems, would rather be lapdogs in white society than men in their own. They talk about poor whites and poor blacks getting together to make a difference. But poor whites already have leaders looking out for their best interest. Why should they hookup with a pack of what Du Bois called headless poor blacks? That is the same old scam he cooked up, claiming white gentry would think better of blacks if they had more contact with educated blacks rather than having almost all of their contact with black flunkies, not understanding that the similarity between the lapdog and the flunky was close in quality with a preference for the flunky because of his utility and against the lapdog because of his social crassness and inaptness in terms of building institutions and formulating a public policy that would transform black society into a preferred place in which to live, raise a family and do business. And in terms of work, the white has to provide both with a job, having to tell each one what to do and when to do it. Du Bois spoke much about the contempt whites had for him personally and the black elitist in general.

The Effect of the Failure

The effect of the failure of the Niagara Movement was monumental. The legacy of it regrettably is still the bane of the race today. Highlighting a deficiency in the Niagarites collective will, it has served to stunt the social growth and development of the race; and it has fueled a pattern of consistent neglect of the race by its best educated. No people deserved to have this example of failure cast in their midst by their best educated and wealthiest men to plague them as it seems without end as they try against the odds to move forward. The Niagarites said they wanted to provide "wise and courageous leadership." They did not define what they meant by wise and courageous. But BTW's leadership meant building an institution that would meet the needs of the people. Theirs obviously was a false estimation of their ability to be wise and courageous and to cohere and execute like rational and reasonable men a common will. Each of them, no doubt, went to the grave unaware of the harm that failure had done the race. Ignoring the enormity of it, they without guile glibly excused it by saying it was due to dynamic personality and inexperience; but those who fathered America had men among them with dynamic personalities, and they certainly had no experience in founding a nation; but being reasonable, rational and accommodating men, they, unlike the Niagarites, knew and understood that being superior men, failure for them was not an option. Pride in their manhood girded their resolve and would not let them, because of dynamic personality and inexperience, fail; unfortunately, irrationality, unreasonableness, incoherence, refusal to accommodate and a false pride in the Niagarites assured theirs.

It was because of their failure that the hope for the formulation of an organization up North to help "advance colored people" came not by the actions of intelligent, coherent, scholarly, and wealthy black men but by sympathetic, liberal whites. That call, paradoxically, was made by William English Walling, a white Southerner. The organization he founded along with a committee of whites who responded to his call is the National Association for the Advancement of Colored People (NAACP). They, after some discussion, invited Du Bois to join, and he accepted. And he had the unique distinction of serving it simultaneously as a board member and an employee as head editor of its publication, the Crisis until they kicked him out.

In his book *From Slavery to Freedom: A History of Negro Americans*, Vintage Books Edition, March 1969, John Hope Franklin gives the following account of events in Springfield, Illinois, that spurred liberal whites to act to help to advance colored people: "The town officials saw that the mob was becoming unruly and several unsuccessful efforts were made to disperse it. Finally the Governor called out the militia. The mob, oblivious to the appeals of high state officials to respect the law, raided secondhand stores, secured guns, axes, and other weapons, and began to destroy Negro businesses and to drive Negroes from their homes. They set fire to a building in which a Negro owned a barber shop. The barber was lynched in the yard behind his shop, and the mob, after dragging his body through the streets was preparing to burn it when the militia from Decatur dispersed the crowed." While this was occurring in August 1908, the Niagarites were being too boyish, too lacking in manly stamina and superior human intelligence to hunker down, cohere, compromise and accommodate to deliver success for their people and for the nation.

And one of the most demeaning comments ever made about a black public figure was said about Du Bois by one of his longest and strongest supporters, Mary White Ovington, chairwoman of the board. After he had run afoul of procedures and they were looking to rebuke him, she said,

"His career has been made by the whites." How did this titan of black elitist intelligence take that insult? He took it like a pathetic, whipped, sick puppy: no biting or critical tongue. Silence! Mary Ovington knew him when he was a professor at Atlanta University and argued for bringing him into the NAACP; she saw him as a brainy fellow, referring to him on occasion as the man with a "noble head." So her rebuke of him in those words comes from one who was sympathetic and had followed his career for many years. The comment also is evidence that she knew he was not what he thought he was and that she, and other whites, endured him by allowing him latitude to pretend he was a man of substance and not a surly malcontent voluble and full of pretense merely. It shows that she always saw him as nothing but a disgruntle sorehead who would rather hang around whites who would tolerate him mouthing insidious, ineffective verbal epithets at their social short comings toward blacks than to dig in with his fellow blacks and do the hard manly work absolutely necessary to form and build an organization that would add credit to his race and improve race relations overall. When the Niagarites proved to be incompetent in organizing themselves into a coherent rational and reasonable body of men, this confirmed for whites, her included, that their assessment in the main of the adult black male as a boy who had to be under the charge of white men was true and accurate. And out of pity for this pathetic man child (pointedly and ironically, in some moments of pompous exaggeration, Du Bois called his people a "child race"), they then formed an organization to advance himself and his race and allowed him a role in it.

When considering their Declaration of Principles, the men at Niagara quoted that part of the Declaration of Independence that says, "All men are created equal"; but at the end of that historic document, the founders of the nation closed with words of commitment to each other that they kept. The words are these: "and, for the support of this declaration, with a firm reliance on the protection of Divine Providence, we mutually pledge to each other our lives, our fortunes, and our sacred honor." Thus the Declaration of Independence became a monument to unity, power and influence; and their Declaration of Principles a diatribe to infamy, humiliation and failure. We can only wonder what the race situation would be like today if the Niagarites had made that same pledge also to themselves and kept it. Because without forming institutions of your own to reflect and store evidence of your intelligence, to abide in this world, you must of necessity accept the largesse of others to provide organization for you and then allow you a place in it. And in that subservient, insulting, demeaning, embarrassing and humiliating arrangement, you must conduct yourself within the limits allowed for you that they think fit for it is true man will be controlled. By whom? Himself or by others.

The Importance of Organization.

Organization is the key to exercising the common will of people for their betterment within their own society and in determining whether they will have inferior, equal, or superior relations with other men. Though educated to the highest degree, this point was missed by the Niagarites. They proved it was an inability to organize, unify and execute their will, and not a lack of education that was the example of their inferiority. Organization requires giving up a portion of ones individual autonomy for the strength and power found in group unity. For them as individuals, whites had done about all they could; they had educated them in the best schools here and, in the case of Du Bois, in Germany as well; but obviously this training was not enough for them to act manly and execute a common will in unity for the advancement of themselves, their race, and the nation. They proved to be unable to establish and execute a binding consensus among them. Their challenge was similar in terms of a need for unity and power to that band of men who founded the United States and established its form of governance. Had those men come back from Philadelphia and said they could not beat out a declaration nor establish a constitution, they would have appeared as inferior as that group history now records as the Niagarites.

Three Schisms

These three schisms have been referred to in other parts above, but because of their impediment to black social development, it is important to summarize them. There was a schism between the black elitist and the mass of blacks and between the black elitist and the black leader striving to advance the race and there was also a huge schism between the Jeffersonian ideal and the black elitist desire. As part of their hidden agenda, they wanted to be accepted by whites because they thought being educated made them better than the mass of blacks. They wanted to be accepted for their book learning not for their humanity. However, the social contract (which if the truth be told, the Niagarites being bane elitist did not accept) whites had was for self governance. It was that they, or any superior people, could govern themselves under constituted laws that made the governor or prince no more human than the ditch digger. Looking at one of the most destructive debacles in history, the impact on the black race is that it affirms its inferiority, and that simple fact only is devastating. The fact is: white men at Philadelphia proved that they could accommodate, compromise and unify for their common good, and the black men at Niagara given the same exact challenge proved that they would, or could, not. To call their debacle at Niagara anything else would be the same as calling dung a rose. It is not the name that is the fragrance of the rose; it is its essence. Booker T. Washington saw the black man capable of building strong institutions for the common good and built one; he saw the mass of blacks as people yearning to learn, and he taught them. Du Bois and his fellow elitist thought they could do it better than BTW but found in the end they could not only not do it better but they could not do it at all.

We must, therefore, rid ourselves of the notion that we are a headless people espoused by Du Bois and reflect the yearning to learn view saw in us by Washington. As Washington saw then, we must see us now people yearning to learn to feed, clothe and house us, as well as providing entertainment, athletics, cleanliness and safety in the hood. Despite the crass and ignoble catastrophe of Du Bois, we must reject that insulting slimy social disaster; choose the route of intelligent success; and labor honorably and coherently together for the mutual good of us all.

CHAPTER 4

The Cosby Call

L ISTENING TO THE debate whirling around Bill Cosby's call for poor blacks to improve themselves, you would think the lid had just jumped off the cuckoo's nest, or the debaters are cracked in the head really. A faction of the black elite claims his call was an attack on poor blacks, thus implying that some blacks are outside the stigma, "poor blacks," and that it was unfair of him to attack the ones who are not. But to think that the poor black stigma can be applied to certain blacks only is an example of self-delusion in the highest. The stigma is a destructive condition in the body of the black race, especially so in the black elite. There are blacks physically outside the black community, seen mainly as lapdogs but there is no black outside the race; thus, no black is outside the stigma, poor blacks. When a black gets a superior education, acquires great sums of money, or becomes well known, he does not as a rule invest those assets in the people of the community to stimulate them to build a field of hope, civility, goodwill and power, as whites do, so that the community is slowly and decidedly transformed from a den of despair and death to a place preferred, full of life and joyful living, made possible in a public policy that cleans up the neighborhood and opens stores that provide products and services in a safe, clean and profitable environment suitable for building a synergistic life style that is respectful of the decency that is in the very core of their own humanity.

Thus, what Cosby spoke to, though perhaps unknowingly, was the unique quality and universality of the poverty of black humanity to develop a public policy in the black community that makes it a first-class, first-world, world-class place in which to live, raise a family and do business. Good or bad, the leadership people get from their elite bespeaks the whole clan to be either inferior or superior

Clearly, there are blacks with and without money, educated and uneducated, famous and unknown. But that is so in other groups. Whites, for instance, some have large amounts of money and others very little; some are highly educated and others hardly at all; some are famous and others not so famous.

The call, however poorly articulated, Cosby made was for black people to address the issue of poor black public policy in the black community. Since it is the wealthiest, the best educated and the most noted of any people who set public policy among them, the inescapable fact is it was the black elite to whom the call was made and, by implication, against whom the charge of laziness was launched. However, being acutely lazy, and cleverly cunning, they deflected the charge. Then attacked Cosby. Now we have the nonsensical babble going in the ranks of the black elite, with one faction claiming to be a shield for poor blacks against Cosby's attack against them. And another faction claiming Cosby has a right to say what he wants. But both factions are degrading their own humanity and the elegance of the race by craftily avoiding the issue.

Personal Attack

Attacking Cosby personally, a woman on *ABC's "Nightline,"* instead of focusing on the issue of poor black public policy in the black community, got personal and got into his sex life, a subject of which she seemed well versed, thus showing a streak of downright ignorance and laziness on the matter of poor black public policy in the black community. Her breadth and depth of knowledge on what questions to pose to develop a base of knowledge useful for advancing the quality of life in the black community were extremely deficient. But her discomfort was not for long. She began aggressively to squirm in the chair. Once comfortable, she began to pepper him with a series of "got you" questions about his sex life, completely oblivious it seemed of the fact that he was not there to discuss the sexual proclivities of black folk nor spousal infidelity.

As a researcher of black people since 1981, looking for the cause of blacks killing and murdering blacks in such high numbers in the black community, I have found the tactic of personal attack to be the main tool of the black elite whenever a black tries to help the race in general. They jump him like a pack of crazed, ferocious dogs to prevent any chance of advancement by what they call, the black underclass. Though the mess in the black community speaks to its veracity, that statement, would have seemed crazy even to me in 1981 when, using the scientific method of inquiry, I began researching black folk in a quest to learn the cause for us killing each other in such high numbers after the assassination of Dr. Martin Luther King Jr., April 4, 1968, through the decade of the 1970s and beyond. One thing you learn real fast is that every people have a head and that the body of people like an individual body goes wherever the head goes. So whatever state of degradation or greatness they are in, they are in it because those who head them took them there.

Historical Personal Attacks

The tactic of personal attack by the black elite on any black who tries to improve the common lot of black folk is historical. They used it against Booker T. Washington, Marcus Garvey and Dr. Martin Luther King Jr. Booker T. Washington performed one of the most remarkable miracles in history. He asked a former slave if he was ever sold; he said his master sold "five of us," himself, his brother and three mules. The fact that a human being in the most modern nation on earth would speak with conviction his equivalence to a mule spurred Washington, and in relentless toil, he "lifted the veil of ignorance from his people." The legacy of his labor still lives in them today. One would hardly find a black person in the United States today who would speak of his humanity in tones equivalent to a mule. Yet the black elite attacked him then and are mad with him now. They claimed then and now erroneously that he was against blacks getting the highest education possible and participating fully in the affairs of the nation. When the truth is he did more to get blacks into Harvard and other prestigious schools than other Americans. He did not just help to get them in those schools, being America's greatest black industrialist, he also hired many black graduates from those prestigious universities.

The Talented Tenth was mad with him for the same reason they are mad with Cosby; Washington made education available for all blacks, and demonstrated that a black man could build and run a great institution. He sort to have every hand of every person be useful in something. The Talented Tenth said the final thing a people should be remembered for is their poetry. Washington knew that poetic words were not the full measure nor the greatest expression of a people. He knew that a people should be known for how well they feed, clothe, and house themselves and how well they manage the affairs of their community. He knew you learn the efficiency of these qualities in school also. That he sort to address the complexity of black people and to place them on the plane with other men galled the Talented Tenth. They were mad with him for two reasons: he was seeking to educate the mass of blacks against their will, and they could not stop him.

The Talented Tenth will have us think that there was a debate between them and Washington. But there was no debate between them and Washington. The debate was then as it is now over the Cosby call; it was between two factions of the Talented Tenth over how vicious their attack against Washington would be. As they attacked him, he kept building Tuskegee Institute strong. They boasted that whites would destroy it and that it would not last. They wanted it destroyed because they would rather it be turned to ashes than be proud of what a black man had built to benefit the whole black race, and all mankind. But whites did not destroy it and they, the Talented Tenth, could not. So it stands today—a monument to black industrial potential—as the greatest institution ever built in America by a black person, and it is still taking potshots from the Talented Tenth. To get a reasonable mind-set of the Talented Tenth today, one should read the national bestseller, *Our Kind of People: Inside America's Black Upper Class* (2000) by Lawrence Otis Graham.

The attack against Garvey was at best grotesque. They talked about his shape, size, color and height. These things were of great concern to them because Garvey's full-frontal charge was for universal human rights. When studying the assaults on Garvey, I looked at a broader spectrum of African-descendent people. This pattern of the elite acting against the masses was a keen aspect of the Atlantic slave trade, when African kings, chiefs and potentates rounded up African people for hundreds of years and sold them to foreign buyers. That has to be the most monstrous and ghoulish crime in all humanity. No other people or race has ever done that to their own. So the attacks against him must have seemed almost natural for the Talented Tenth.

But the most fatuous attack of all was made against Dr. King. A faction of the black elite joined him to use him. Jim Crow put a huge crimp in how they could enjoy the American life style. They saw in him a means of ending it. The other faction was comfortable the way things were and did not want them shook-up and were, therefore, unrelenting in their attack. Those who joined him, once Jim Crow ended, began to destroy the Southern Christian Leadership Conference. Today, that great institution that broke the back of Jim Crow tyranny in the United States, which led the nation to the conclusion that no citizen has a birthright to lord it over another, is mostly a mere name on paper. And the two dominate civil rights organizations whites formed, built, and won't let blacks destroy are now mostly meeting and chitchat societies. If the whites who founded and built them could see what blacks have made of them, they would no doubt turn over in their graves. One of them is most noted for issuing an annual *State of Black America* paper. And the other caused this exchange in a baffle people in a baffle nation:

"Did the National Association for the Advancement of Colored People bury the "N" word?"

"No, I don't think it was the "N" word they buried."

"If not the "N" word, what was it?"

"It was its symbol."

"If that was its symbol, that means the "N" word is not dead. Why would they say they buried it, if all they did was bury the symbol? Isn't that like burying the flag, then saying you've buried the United States?"

"That is the way they chose to be irrelevant, while doing great harm to black people. Black people need to be encouraged and motivated to do right things, like make their community reflect their superior intelligence by manifesting their desire for safety, cleanliness and prosperity. Rather than do that, they chose to bury the symbol of a word not yet dead. May God help us all!"

"If I am understanding the point, they should have killed the "N" word first. How long would it take to do that?"

"It may take a thousand years, but they should cause its demise and then bury the rascal dead."

"Where does the "N" word live?"

"It resides in black people. They are full of it from the soles of their feet to the crowns of their heads. That's the reason they are sick of it. Not sick enough yet, however, to kill it."

"How would they kill it if it's in them?"

"Plant and cultivate in them its antidote, civility."

A Basic Tenet of Psychology

A basic tenet of psychology is that you teach people how to treat you. Because Washington taught that to blacks, the Talented Tenth asserted falsely that that made him the enemy of black people. Saying, the black man had a say in how the white man treated him meant that he was excusing the white man's wrong doing. However, more than forty years after Washington's death, Dr. King, standing on the shoulders of Washington, told black folk that the white man cannot ride the black man's back if the black man's back is not bent. Yet after a white man assassinated Dr. King, instead of the black man standing up and cleaning up, he, in a lapdog style, has been knuckle dragging in the filth and laziness of despair and pretense with a sway in his back making the white man's ride shamefully and embarrassingly pleasant.

The highest academically achieving blacks have a greater responsibility for advancing the race. But they use their training to slick talk themselves out of acting in the best interest of the community and take instead those actions that are extremely detrimental to the advancement of black people. Specifically, they will not cohere and formulate a public policy that builds the community to its best potential.

It is wished that the black elite would stop their sham debates and being lapdogs in the communities of others, return to the black community, present a plan for its development, and then work the plan and plan to work till the blight and horror of the community is cast aside and replaced with a brightness reflective of their best manhood intelligence. As segregation was no way for the white man to prove that he was civilized, being a lapdog is no way for the black man to prove that he is not lazy. The need is now for black humanity to stop playing the inferior game of pretense and get real, heed Cosby's call, and cultivate his community for a wonderful harvest of civility.

We must note the effect of what the Talented Tenth say and do, not merely what they say. They mainly like to issue useless position papers on the *State of Black America* and make symbolic acts, but they have not yet done their duty which is develop a public policy in the *State of Black America* that transforms it from a den of slaughter, mayhem and despair to a place preferred, where people, because of its cultural ambiance, scramble with joy to get in rather than try in desperation to get out.

CHAPTER 5

Blacks' Quest for Reparations

THE QUEST FOR reparations by blacks is fraught with doubt and challenge. The doubt is in the fact that many including some blacks think that any reparation is owed them for their ancestors many years of enforced servitude without pay and peonage with underpay in the United States of America. The challenge is to thrash through the pros and cons of this matter to the answer that will at last resolve the issue with complete and total finality.

The reasoning for the quest is that from 1619 to 1965, blacks in America were under one form or another of enforced servitude; from 1619 to 1776, it was slavery in what became thirteen Crown Colonies of England. In 1776, these colonies mounted a successful rebellion and became an independent nation state and named itself the United States of America. This independent nation retained blacks as chattel till 1865 and after it ended slavery, it practiced a form of enforced peonage called Jim Crow till 1965. From 1965 till now, blacks in America have been basically a free people.

Certain of this free people now request of America payment for work done by their ancestors as slaves from 1619 to 1865 when they worked allegedly for no pay and as peons from 1865 to 1965, when they were underpaid. Some from the peon period yet survive.

On its merit, this request in the claimants' view seems to be an open-and-shut case based on the essence of two credible principles: if one works for another, one should get paid and there is no free lunch. Once work is done, the principle holds; wages become a debt against the enterprise that caused the work to be done, and it remains so till it is paid. The enterprise in this instance is the United States of America, a nation that prides itself in the diligence with which it pays its debts. Some key questions in the view of claimants are will this debt ever be paid? If yes, when? If no, why not? Or is it a cloud hanging over the nation that will forever blight its name in shame?

There is no doubt that America enslaved blacks and abused them during Jim Crow; yet there is strong resistance to paying several trillion dollars, or any dollar, to them in reparations for their labors during those years. This is so for any number of reasons. Let us look at a few. Black is faced with the challenge of proving to white, and some blacks, that white enslavement of black was not a favor to him. White constantly points out to black that he is glad he is here under white rule and is not in Africa or Haiti under black rule. Some blacks think blacks don't know how to make proper use of economic resources. I have heard hundreds of blacks say that if white would put into the hands of black all the money in the world today, with in ten years or so, black would be in greater economic poverty than he is today. That certainly seems like a strong argument for not paying black one red cent in reparations. But this stance though it seems strong is not only odious, but also it's dangerous, because it says that what a person does with his pay should determine whether he gets paid and because to refuse to pay one for one's labor based on whether the enterprise or some other entity disagrees with how the recipient is going to dispose of his earnings is a concept that is illegitimate and is alien to the notion of one being paid for one's labor.

When I hear this kind of resistance from black or white, I listen intently beyond the key statement, however, for the supplemental reasons. They come most in examples of a black's poor stewardship of properties that he did get after slavery. I have listened literally to hundreds if not thousands of blacks who when coming North from the South left millions of acres of land there that went back to whites due to lack of payment of taxes or a family member left there gave it to white for a few gulps of liquor, or they mortgaged the land for a few pennies or didn't pay the debt, putting the land squarely back into the hands of white. I have personally attended meetings in the North where some black was trying to raise the consciousness of blacks to the huge loss of land resource. And while at each such meeting—there was some minimal interest shown in trying to save their property and protect their interest while thanking the conveners for their effort—more than ninety-five percent of the people present showed no keen interest in trying to protect their interest nor was there a fervent "thank-you" offered to the conveners for their effort. At one of these meetings, a man stood up and said, "What blacks want is a job that pays and somewhere to spend the money." Somewhere to spend the money. That is why some feel that, if given all the money on earth, black would in ten years be poor again. But we have shown that argument to be invalid.

Another way the resisters view the matter is that a person works to learn how to work and to learn the value of work, and while he is learning, he is not paid, because the lesson is as much or more of a benefit to him as it is to the enterprise engaging his services. This principle too is strong; it is established most readily in school where the student not only is not paid for his labor, but he actually pays the school for giving him the work. This relationship is effective because it is expected that when the student completes his course of study, he will be so proficient in the subject matter that people will then pay him handsomely for his services or he will produce products people will buy. So once one completes his schoolwork or studies, he then gets a job that pays him to do what he knows or he opens a business and provides products or services for which people will pay.

It is in this crucible that blacks' claim for reparations is stuck for white says that though he made blacks work for no pay for 246 years and for underpay another hundred, black today still works harder not to work than he does working. In other words, black today still does not know how to take initiative. Blacks suing for reparations say white worked black, but did not teach black the value of work. White says one learns the value of work by working: that principle is, one learns by doing, if one has the ability to learn. White says that, if after being made to work 346 years, black still does not know the value of work, that puts him intelligently speaking really in the category of animal, where he (white) had put him all along.

Blacks point out that reparations were paid to Jews by Germany and to Japanese by America, but these examples have hardly any resoluble effect on dislodging resistance for paying reparations to blacks. This resistance is found in a point of view that says there are two types of slaves, learned and unlearned or natural and unnatural. Nobody has to teach unnatural slaves the value of work. And each type is known by which takes initiative, which, in other words, take the initiative necessary to build his community into a first-class, first-world, world-class community.

Learned slaves are skilled and proficient, are knowledgeable, and know how to cohere as a group and how to take initiative. They are captured as part of the spoils of war or sold into slavery. Once in slavery the learned slave is made to work in services or produce products to benefit his master, sometimes performing skills he already knows.

The unlearned or natural slave is in a whole different category; he doesn't know how to work, and once he has been made to work, he never learns its value nor how to take initiative. He has to be told what, when, how and where to do anything. He lacks, it seems, the ability to comprehend the complexity present in community building. He will work himself to death for his master as long as he is told what to do in the case of the so-called successful black or is made by his master to do it if he is incarcerated. If given the opportunity to take initiative, the natural slave will reject that opportunity out of hand and act with due diligence to move or want to move in with his master if his master lets him or to become a criminal to get put in prison, so he can be told what to do and made to do what he is told.

Now you may say but every black does not either want to move into a white neighborhood or is in prison and is not, therefore, a natural slave; but that would be a misreading of the situation. Let us understand something. This discourse is about the composite body of black humanity. That one thing that leaps into one's mind when one sees a black, whether he is a billionaire or a pauper, lives in the plushest white suburb or in the nastiest, crime-ridden, so-called black ghetto, has a PhD from Harvard or a degree from hard knocks; it does not matter who he is or what his status is; it is that he is of that branch of humanity that lacks initiative that would rather in many instances live, if admitted, in some other group's community than to build his own. Because today in America, it matters not whether a black is the president of a highly prestigious Ivy League College or University or is an ignorant, illiterate criminal locked away in prison, it is the genius of the white that feeds, clothes and houses them both.

The black today that is called successful in the main is not called so because he has taken the initiative that has caused the black community to become a safe, clean and prosperous place in which to live, raise a family and do business. He is called such because white has told him what, when, where and how to do something, and has allowed him to hold positions he was once denied, and he has performed some of these tasks reasonably well for a black and has been paid well by white. But white cannot make black have initiative; that is an inner resource that only black himself can employ.

It has been said that in the real world, people tend to take care of their own first. I don't know about that for we blacks tend not to take care of our own. We as a people tend to do just the opposite. We in America, by world standards are educated and rich yet our community is in shambles. We don't provide the outlets in our community that provide our food, clothes nor shelter. Once a jurisdiction becomes all or mostly black, foreigners come in to provide us with these necessities of life. For their safety, they use guard dogs, bulletproof glass and bars of varying sort. And though so-called black leaders declare black to be poor, the deliverers of these necessities take many billions of dollars out of the black community each year to theirs. Now you may well say that black leaders are correct, for if the money is earned by others and taken out, that would leave the black community poor. They say this, however, before the money is taken out. They use the poverty excuse not to build businesses to provide these necessities and to meet other needs that a civilized people need to have the good life; they use it as an excuse not to. With all this wealth in black hands, it became necessary to look for the exact definition of poverty. The word "poverty" means "lack of" or "deficient in." Clearly, by world standards black is not deficient in wealth nor education. In his book, *The Debt*, Randall Robinson says we have had done to us an "enormous psychic wrong." His way of saying we are messed up in the head. But he goes on to say that this wrong that has caused this psychic problem has been committed against us by somebody other than ourselves. And that is where his and most of the main focus of black thought today is, in my view, in error. White did not mess up our psychic; we did. White took full advantage of our messed up psychic state. But he did not mess it up, nor can he fix it. And until we realize that it was us who messed us up and that it is us who must fix us, we are going to stay messed up a long time more. Because it is impossible to hit the bulls eye when you are pointing at the wrong target.

A black's biggest problem then is convincing somebody, including himself, that he would know what to do with reparations for he has not shown yet that he knows what to do with freedom. And it is written that because "you have been faithful over a few things, I will make you ruler over many things."

There is no real present sense (remember when I use this generalization, I am talking about the composite body of black humanity and not that there is no black individual anywhere who does not counter this profile) of black acceptance of black humanity. I was invited by a group of African American business students at Wayne State University to talk to them about black business development. After the program, some of the students gathered round me for further discussion, when an eighteen-year-old freshman said to me and to the others present that he had "developed a word game" that he was going to market to whites because "Niggers are not in the mind game." Since only people are in the mind game, he with that attitude had effectively concluded that blacks in his view are not full-fledged human beings and since he was black, he was saying in effect, albeit in ignorance, that he too was not a human being. This kind of rejection of black humanity by us is found among us far too frequently. This negativity in us about us is manifested in our refusal to provide for ourselves the business outlets of food, clothes and shelter in our community. And the better attitude in others toward us is manifested in their willingness to come into the black community with guard dogs, protective glass, and various types of bars for their protection to provide these basic necessities of life for a fractious people with a fractured psychic.

There is a great effort today to try to prove that blacks had great civilizations thousands of years ago. The problem with such efforts is not that there is no truth in the claim; the problem is that the effort makes the searchers look stupid in that if there was something back then, there should also be something today. In other words, it may be important to know that water was wet several thousands years ago but it is more important to know that it is wet today and will still quench thirst. So the argument goes that it is okay if blacks built great civilizations thousands of years ago, but it is more import that we actually build a safe, clean and prosperous jurisdiction today, where we take the initiative in our community and organize, operate and properly manage the businesses that provide our food, clothes and shelter, and recreational activities.

One of the greatest hoaxes ever pulled on us is the claim by us that whites abuse and discriminate against us not because of our lag headedness and lack of initiative in caring for our humanity but because of our color and race.

Historically blacks, using the Du Boisian model, have whined, chafed and complained to whites about wrongs whites commit against blacks, while ignoring wrongs blacks commit against blacks. When told he should show concern about black criminality against blacks, Du Bois in his own words said he called the idea, "silly." Black can never advance with this one-sided focus about his well-being. The time has come for this pattern of self-neglect to cease and for us to make our requirement be respect of black by both black and white and others.

Work done by black during slavery was done not because black took initiative, but because he took and obeyed the orders of his master. By looking at a slave, white knew of what he or she was capable. He would tell a medium-sized female to bring in two hundred pounds of cotton for the day. If she did, she was praised. If she brought 190, she was stripped and whipped. The next day, he would tell her to bring in two hundred and she would bring in 215, enough over to make up the short fall for the day before. This kind of response by black during slavery made it the most productive period blacks have ever had, and the Jim Crow period was next, and the free period is dead last. It is most amazing that black people would submit to beatings and all forms of brutality and would work themselves without end for their slave master, but will not get up and use their own initiative to work for themselves to make their community a safe, clean and prosperous place in which to live, raise a family and do business. And in the free period, that is, the period since 1965 when they became able to enjoy the blessings of liberty, almost all the work blacks have done has still been work white told them what, when, where, and how to do. The amount of initiative blacks have shown since they have been free could be sold for a penny with some change due the buyer. And as long as there is high sentiment in the black elite with preference for living as lapdogs in the white community rather than taking initiative to build the black community to be as good as any other, the question of their full fledged-humanity will hound them all their days.

Since black has been free, there have been practically all failures in the body of black humanity; but there are three that give cause for great anguish: the failure of black educators to use the Booker T. Washington model to properly teach and train the youth; the failure of black politicians, especially mayors, to formulate a public policy that makes their black jurisdictions safe, clean and prosperous; and, perhaps because of the history, the greatest of the three is the failure of the black church in its preacher/pastor to create a moral climate in the black community in which the sanctity of human life and the family is inviolable.

So the quest for reparations by blacks has a question staring it in the face: is what is owed to us by white greater than the debt owed to us by us? If we truly are a people too fractured to pay ourselves first, it is not likely that any other people are going to pay us any reparations at all. White has shown himself to be good at organizing the social energies of men to work together for the common good. When black make that reality operative in his community, America may rise to a level of desiring to clean her plate of the sweat of men's unrequited toil and pay up.

CHAPTER 6

Commentaries for Improving the Black Persona

Why the Blackman Should Respect Himself

THE BLACKMAN SHOULD first respect himself because embodied in one's self-respect is the obligation of others to do the same. The Blackman, therefore, ought to bring himself under the law of self-respect and make it an integral part of his very being. This principle teaches him several things but let us here consider two. One big lesson is when he refuses to enforce the law of self-respect, that puts the Whiteman in the superior position and conversely that puts him in the inferior position. When he does that and the Whiteman then acts superior in his dealings with him, the Whiteman is acting on the grant given to him not by nature but by the Blackman himself. When the Blackman acts as if he is ignorant of his enabling role in his inferior relationship regarding the Whiteman, he does not help the matter but exacerbates the situation. If the Blackman opts to adhere to the principle of self-respect, now universal among civilized men, he will come to know something that at the moment he cannot imagine, that the Whiteman hurts too when he sees so much social laziness, indifference, mental lag headedness and calculated incompetence in whom is obviously his black brother, though he has his PhD from Harvard, a billion dollars in the bank, or an MD degree from a top medical school, and permission to practice at John Hopkins.

The second lesson is that the ritual dance of condescension by the Whiteman and the whining complaint of the Blackman will lose their eminence of place in their conduct toward each other, if the Blackman would bring himself under the law of self-respect in every manly way. His sense of his self-respect must engulf him. It should echo in his talk, his walk, his gate, his every posture of standing, sitting, reclining, as well as in his role in the black community as leader or helper.

For instance, the white men, who abused Rosa Parks on the bus in Montgomery, did so out of the view that the Blackman did not respect himself; this assumption allowed them to order her out of her seat for a white man. When she refused to submit to their will but chose instead to assert her self-respect, white men arrested her. But because the Blackman chose on that occasion under the leadership of Dr. Martin Luther King Jr. to demonstrate his superior intelligence, his next trip on that bus was in dignity with no limits on where to sit from the back of it to the front. But today, because of the Blackman's truculent laziness, rife indifference and calculated incompetence, the white men's abuse of Parks now seem kind and tame when compared to how she was treated by a young black male who intruded her home in her senior years and robbed and slapped her around. Yet on her passing, the black gatekeepers of the Blackman contacted rejected all the self-respect taught by Dr. King and stood mute when it was suggested that if the bus she sat on deserved a place in history as a reminder of how whites treated blacks, her home, which the black male invaded, should be made a shrine to remind us of how much we need to do now to develop and sustain a synergy of self-respect in the black race today that would end such savagery, making that pattern of behavior not only undoable but unthinkable.

Why Me-ism Failed Black Folk

Me-ism is a destructive philosophy opposed to what is in the best interest of all. Its adherent sees no idea or purpose more important than himself. There is nothing he would assertively commit to that would benefit the common good. The only commitment he makes is to himself. If he dies pursuing that commitment, well, so be it. But that attitude is exactly polar opposite to the meaning of the statement by Dr. Martin Luther King Jr. that if one does not find something so precious he would die for, he is not fit to live. The King statement is to the "Me" person, a none register. There is a call upon every leader to do his duty and to understand that his call to lead is not the same as his personal agenda and generally it is the pursuit of ones personal agenda that interferes with ones call to lead.

The philosophy of me-ism has proved itself to be not a friend to us but has instead shown itself to be an enemy unparalleled in the measure of its destruction committed in our homes, streets, neighborhoods, and the greater community. This philosophy, it seems, showed up the instant Dr. King was assassinated. The men heading the Southern Christian Leadership Conference—Jesse Jackson, Andrew Young, Ralph Abernathy and others—after Dr. King was assassinated, chose, without any obvious forethought as to what the consequences would be for the people, to leave SCLC, an organization with a track record of working for the common good, to pursue personal agendas. That behavior is the very definition of me-ism.

Their acts of me-ism reverberated from the top down with a crushing and devastating effect that blew our can-do spirit from us and brought in its stead a legacy of despair fraught with a pattern of killing, slaughter and murder that continues today. Because they refused to get along and do what was needed to make SCLC continue to be a reliable resource in service to our community, our community became a death trap, where our own black sons roam around in the community, killing their own people, sometimes in cold blood.

When listening to or reading what each of these men say about their cause for leaving SCLC, it is always a personal reason. But the question is what is in their psychic that fits them in such away that they would walk away from a cherished and honorable organization that had just successfully ended Jim Crow in America and was primed to take us from the back ally of American society into the realm of full and respectable citizenship?

SHELTON VAUGHN

Well, for some odd reason, Young thought winning a seat in Congress, being mayor of Atlanta, and being America's ambassador to the United Nations were more deserving than the advancement of black people and evidently, Jackson thought making a symbolic run for the presidency of the United States was something he would rather do than disciplining himself for the awesome task of continuing in the leadership at SCLC. There is hardly anybody now except the very naïve who thinks his runs were for something he could do, when the biggest item in his resume was his participation in the destruction of SCLC. And Abernathy, it seems, thought becoming a Republican suited him better than hunkering down and making SCLC continue to be an institution reflective of their best intelligence. Not that being republican is bad in and of itself. What made his move sinister was why he went republican, which was to spite his cohorts. Each of these men turned against working for the common good and became me-ism personified. And all the social capital built up in SCLC during the Civil Rights Movement got washed down the drain with the murdered blood of black people, whose sons in the main began to kill and to slaughter black people with little or no regard for the sanctity of their lives the year Dr. King died. It is their example that led to the "Me" generation, whose tagline became the lost generation.

I have been puzzled that Jackson did not realize that his action would have this destructive effect and would go and talk to the leaders in the Middle East, but not to those at SCLC. Why would he urge the United States to talk to leaders of the Middle East, rather than talking himself to the leaders at SCLC and effectively transitioning its focus from acquiring our rights and opportunities to disciplining us on how to make proper use of them by cultivating a fine sense of social intercourse and civil coherence?

That he would go to the Middle East without portfolio to negotiate release of Lt. Robert Goodman but would not stay at SCLC and negotiate to stay the release of tons of murdered blacks and flowing rivers of their murdered blood marks him as well as the others to be men of very poor social judgment. That he would run for the office of the presidency of the United States with the most outstanding thing in his resume being his participation in the destruction of SCLC compounds this idea further.

Black Folk do not Know How to Argue

It is not a small wonder why we blacks are making such a mess of things in our attempt at self-governance in America, Haiti and Africa. We try hard to be good functionaries, but hardly any at all to build organizations to reflect our superior human intelligence; we do fairly well when we are told to do or allowed to do something by others in charge of us. We can entertain and function in the trades and the professions but we have not yet demonstrated our prowess in the art and science of self-governance. I will sketch here briefly what research shows to be the cause of this blot in our record as people and how we can best correct it. That is the good news: it can be corrected by us and if we put forth that effort, it has been shown that others will be more than willing to help. Black America's two greatest leaders, Booker T. Washington and Dr. Martin Luther King Jr., found that to be the case. Washington got white philanthropy to assist in funding the building of Tuskegee Institute, where he lifted the veil of ignorance from his people and King got whites to assist in helping to end Jim Crow.

One of the great dramas in American history was played out at the Edmond Pettis Bridge in Selma, when the Alabama State Policy chose to beat and club people seeking to exercise their citizenship rights to march for justice, Dr. King asked for people of goodwill to come join them in their march to gain their citizenship rights; his call brought some of the wealthiest and most influential people in the country from all over America to Selma, and a judge in a court of law said people had a right to protest for right. And Washington with his industrious spirit tapped wealthy industrialists like W. K. Kellogg, Andrew Carnegie and others to finance the building of a library and other buildings and to supply resources to help meet other needs on the campus of Tuskegee Institute.

But I digress. Let us look briefly at what is a glaring deficiency in the social fabric of us as people. After more than twenty-five years of researching us, using the scientific method of inquiry, looking for the answer to two questions: what was causing black people to murder black people in such high numbers in the black community? and how could the killing best be stopped? After finding the answer to these questions, I found something else was necessary before these two questions could be properly and effectively answered.

I found that we do not know how to argue as a people, among ourselves, in our community to make our society first-class, first-world, and world-class. We know how to argue academically. In debates, we do very well. But when engaged in a debate for the development of the race and thus of our human society, we always reduce ourselves and the argument down to a rant and then we breakup with no lofty objective accomplished. The inability to argue is what caused failure in the Niagara Movement, founded by W. E. B. Du Bois and his Talented Tenth, and likewise with Jesse Jackson, Andrew Young, Ralph Abernathy and others in their failure, after Dr. King was assassinated, to sustain the Southern Christian Leadership Conference as a prime and stellar organization reflective of their best intelligence.

Two essential elements in argument are logic and persuasion, and the main thing we blacks should have in our community is organization. To build organizations that meet the needs of the community, people have to be able to persuade each other with logic. However, in our community among our best educated, when it comes to building organizations to meet our daily needs, the one thing rarely found is logic.

The Rhythm of Culture

My reason for writing this book is to share with the reader what I found to be, if there is one, the answer to the problem of blacks and all, or at least most of it tenants. Hoping that if we get to know the joy and the sadness in common, we can and will regenerate the joy and reduce the sadness.

In *The Souls of Black Folk*, 1903, W. E. B. Du Bois, PhD, said the double aim of the black artisan was to "escape white contempt" and "to plough and nail and dig for a poverty-stricken horde." Claud Anderson, EdD, in his book *Dirty Little Secrets*, 1997, says, "While black labor was the engine that drove civilizations around the world, black people were never allowed to develop their material and human capital nor control their own destiny." Are these two men saying essentially the same thing or are they saying something essentially different? One sets out what he feels is the duty of the black artisan to blacks; the other by saying what blacks were never "allowed" to do sets out the duty of others to blacks. I am going to argue that the black problem is not that others have not allowed blacks to develop; I am going to argue that blacks have not allowed themselves to develop and that, furthermore, it is not within the power of any other people to stop blacks developing themselves if they choose to do so. At first, this may seem an agreement with Du Bois and a disagreement with Anderson, but I don't think so. Stay with me. Both recognize a hostile adversary, but neither makes clear what we must do about it.

Anderson wants others to allow blacks to do what blacks themselves must decide for themselves; and Du Bois wants a few blacks to do for all blacks what all blacks must do for themselves.

The essential weaknesses in Du Bois' position are two: one is that while it states the duty of the artisan to the masses, it does not state the duty of the masses to themselves; and this leads to the second, which is an impression of an aloft or unconnected elite trying to argue for the poverty-stricken blacks in the halls of hostile whites. The very fact that one is chosen or chooses to speak on behalf of the masses makes one an elite. But you do not go into the halls of the adversary as an aloft elite, as though you are above those you are supposed to be speaking for; you go in instead as one of them, not as a big shot above them.

The weakness in Anderson's position is that it seems almost to deny the very humanity of blacks. Who are any other people that they can, or not, allow blacks to develop their material and human capital or control their own destiny? If blacks are human beings, it is they and they alone who must determine to develop their resources both human and natural.

The Du Boisian position is a big contrast to today when the black artisan laps up white contempt like it is sugarcoated candy. Whether it is Rev. Jesse Jackson playing to white liberals or Warren Connolly showing teeth for white conservatives, it is a certainty that the black artisan today is not ploughing and nailing and digging for the black masses.

Du Bois wrote his argument of black double-ness or its "two-ness" when the end of slavery was less than fifty years old, when the stench of former owners was still odious in the nostrils of former slaves. The major two sides to the black problem of that day, as best he could see, was the avoidance of whites' contempt and to labor for or pretend to labor for the masses.

Enough time has passed now both since the end of slavery and the Du Bois' concept of the double-ness for blacks to modify not the concept of double-ness but its focus. We are still faced with a double-ness. However, the double-ness today is not so much about the problem blacks have with whites as it is about the problem blacks have with blacks. For the facts known today, perhaps unknown to Du Bois, argue that it is the problem blacks have with blacks that is the cause of the problem blacks have or have had with whites.

What is white contempt or racism? White contempt is a belief by whites after observing closely black behavior that blacks are a lazy and stupid, impulsive, savage people vastly inferior to whites. It is a belief that because of these, in their view, natural attributes in blacks, they are incapable of the initiative and imagination that will allow them to build a world-class community, where their streets are safe, their homes are secure, and the gaiety in the voices of their children is heard around the world. These conclusions

SHELTON VAUGHN

did not come about by whites from observing the black individual; they came about from observing the black race, which is made up of millions of individuals. White contempt is another way of saying racism.

The word "racism" was not in use when Du Bois wrote his monograph on the matter; racism is a word that came out of World War II. To know what white contempt is helps facilitate understanding why the problem blacks have with themselves is for more significant than white contempt. There is a causal relationship between what Du Bois calls white contempt and what is understood today as blacks problem with themselves. Because of the closeness of Du Bois to the brutal period of slavery, he, perhaps, could not see then what we can now in the light of passing time. The two-part problem of white contempt, or racism, and the problem blacks have with themselves is not a mystery but it is difficult to understand.

The Problem of Criminality, Black and White

1. He knows it is wrong to steal, but not why. He does not know why, because his race has not raised the objection sufficiently in black society for him to gain the amount of understanding necessary for him to restrain himself. A question is advanced of how he knows it is wrong. He knows it is, because he does not want his property stolen and the reason he does not want his stolen is he wants to keep it. He knows the injured party wants to keep his but his impulse to steal overrides any understanding he might have of why the injured party would want to keep his thus, he steals. When they come for him, his defense yells poverty, despair and racism. The prosecutor simply brings the charge. If the thief is convicted, he is jailed for a spell. But not having been taught sufficiently why stealing is wrong and being too demented to figure it out on his own to a level of understanding that would cause him to slam the governors on, while sitting in jail, he plans ways to steal more skillfully when released that will cause him not to be caught again. But he is, and thus there is a high rate of recidivism.

2. When whites see us defend rowdiness, stealing, hooliganism, and utter almost total disrespect for law, they fear that if they give up their hold of fear over us, general society here would degenerate to what it is in Africa and Haiti. And they would rather fight till the last man is dead than for that to happen. Therefore, the two races, albeit for different reasons, are scared of each other. White is scared of us because of our propensity for criminality at street level and lack of industry, and we

are scared of white because of his superior intelligence and power in building complex social systems that work well for them but all too often criminally against us. If we cannot live but as a den of thieves and whites only by laws made by them for their advantage, this dichotomy of wills makes for a peace that can never come between the races. There is a corroding and deleterious effect in whites in the boardroom that must be cleaned up, for though they switch around in the pristine suburb, saying to themselves, "We can't be all that bad; the blacks are still begging to move into our neighborhoods," not understanding that we are begging not because they are well, but because we too are sick. The criminality committed in the boardroom is in its way just as antisocial as the thuggery is in the streets.

3. God made man, one man of many colors, called by men the races of man. All colors are beautiful. America split man, segregated man, separated him from himself; thus, she created a breach in nature, which is a crime against humanity. And there are only two other events relevant to man to surpass it in effect; both are divine—the fall of man and his redemption. This split in nature, this core evil, this division of man can have unintended consequences; it has already caused a civil war.

4. Unintended consequences can humble the most brilliant strategist, the most powerful nation, and can blunt and break the teeth of the sharpest minds. To wish you had not bought us from us in Africa and brought us here to labor for free to build the nation while your great minds planned its growth and development is too late, is now beyond your ability to counterman, beyond your ability to cause it not to be. There has to be a day of reckoning, when the price must be paid, for there is no free lunch. Nothing is free; there is a price for everything. The price you must pay is to express constitutional sorrow for the horror.

5. When talking law, especially the Constitution, we talk about it in terms of it being a document whites have formulated, promulgated and ratified; therefore, they must obey its precepts. We see us in America, but not really a part of America, because so far it has not been up to us to say. We would rather be in America now than in Africa but that is irrelevant and is beside the point, which is that we did not choose to come here but were instead brought here in chains and held in chattel bondage for 246 years by a nation and people claiming themselves to be civilized. It is that crime that cries out into the ears of mankind and must be heard and reconciled. Without reconciliation, there is a doubtful chance whether America can ever be at peace; for the stench of the carcass of

SHELTON VAUGHN

slavery, of her Peculiar Institution, will continue to fester and poison all within. Reconciliation can heal that open-sore festering in the pores of the nation, can put it behind her but it is not behind her yet.

6. There are three men (and two others, Abraham Lincoln and W. E. B. Du Bois, deserving a mention) who have seen the core evil of America: one white and two black—Thomas Jefferson, Booker T. Washington and Dr. Martin Luther King Jr. Abraham Lincoln knew slavery was evil, but was blinded against the core evil of the nation; he thought ending slavery would cure the nation, would in his words "bind up the nations wounds." But it did not; it saved the union. He never came to know America created a breach in nature, separated man from man, a division that must be repaired if America is ever to be at peace. Du Bois could not see it; his anger over the issue of slavery and the aftermath blinded his vision. Jefferson's vision, however, caused him to shudder when he dared to think God is just. Washington, in the midst of extreme barbaric savagery in the form of lynching and other forms of brutality being committed in the system against us by certain whites, lifted the veil of ignorance from his people. Dr. King promulgated three truths: "A lie will not live forever; truth trounced to the ground will rise again; and the arch of the universe, though long, bends toward justice." These three men could see there is no defense against truth nor for a lie. Jefferson saw his country on the back of the tiger; Washington knew for the good health of the nation his people would have to learn that "no race that has anything to contribute to the markets of the world is long in any degree ostracized;" and King declared what the remedy must be, justice. In their scope, it is clear might does not make right: right makes right; and right is right, win or lose. Right is right when right, and wrong is wrong when wrong. Might does not always win. There is wisdom in the words "When you don't have what you don't have, use what you got." If David had had an atom bomb for Goliath, his Hiroshima, he might have used it. But since all he had was a slingshot and a rock, that's what Goliath got. And David the victory.

7. In addition, King recognized love. Love is not merely a four-letter word, it is directional. It is the forward emotion. Love and hate are to life what gears are to automobiles. Those who say hate is never useful and is always wrong are incorrect; it is on rare occasions not only useful but also necessary, but it is always a backward motion; you can only go forward on love. And in the end, Jefferson evidently concluded God is not just or there is no God, because the optimism shown during the

revolution soon vanished, and unlike George Washington who at death freed his slaves, Jefferson dying twenty-six years later did not.

The False Solution: Reparations

8. Arguing for or explaining why reparations are owed us in monetary terms for enslaving our forefathers here for 246 years without pay and another hundred years of underpayment under the segregated and separate but equal laws of Jim Crow is to argue for the wrong type of reparations. (In the *Merriam Webster's Collegiate Dictionary*, tenth edition, is this series of definitions for reparations: 1a: a repairing or keeping in repair b pl: repairs 2 a: the act of making amends, offering expiation, or giving satisfaction for a wrong or injury b: something done or given as amends or satisfaction 3: the payment of damages: indemnification: specifically: compensation in money or materials payable by a defeated nation for damages to or expenditures sustained by another nation as a result of hostilities with the defeated nation) The damage done to us was not monetary; it is not an uncommon belief that if white would in our present state give all the money on earth to us, we, in a year or two, would have returned practically all of it back to him and would be begging once again for jobs, food, clothes and shelter. "Unless some critical number of renaissance blacks can wrench us away from the minced-step rusted strategic template to which our noses have been welded . . . no Marshall Plan for our material renovation can work." This is in *The Debt*, 2001, from Randall Robinson, the foremost proponent of reparations in the country. Clearly, white knows how to build and manage a complex social system that works, and it is obvious to anyone with eyes to see that we do not have a clue how to do such a thing and where things stand now, we have no reason to believe that, without an effective leap of faith, we ever will.

9. No intelligent black can defend the mess in Haiti or Africa or in the black enclaves in America. Africa and Haiti, however, are Old World. Haiti is in this Hemisphere of course but practices Old World savagery. If America is truly a New World nation and not merely an Old World nation in a new suit, it will integrate itself. And integration is not having a bootlicking, lapdogging black next door to an arrogant condescending white. Integration is incorporating for the first time in history black into the American mix, being truthful about her history, seeing herself

as one nation under God indivisible with liberty and justice for all. Not liberty and justice for all but blacks.

10. It is the mess in Haiti and Africa and the black enclaves in America that shows we do not know how to handled wealth, because by the book the riches of Africa in diamonds and gold and other innumerable items of value are immeasurable, yet it is called poor, and its people starve, die of HIV/AIDS without hardly any help from their governments, and take constant actions to destroy life and property on a par with their brothers and sisters in America.

11. But if monetary reparations are not proper compensation for the crime committed against us, what is? Let us take 1a and 2a from the dictionary definition. One "a" says repair and 2a, amends. These are two kinds of reparations that can reconcile America and heal her festering sore.

The Real Solution—Amend the Constitution

12. There are many issues of race in America, but there is a fundamental issue of consent America has never addressed but must regarding the American of African descent. Anger is not the tool to use to right this massive public wrong. Anger is felt by a wife toward her husband, when the objective is release of anger. What is sought in this public arena is not release of anger but the security of justice. The propellant for justice is determination. Anger blinds the vision, is an enemy, not a friend. It is all right to use anger when release of it is the purpose but when the goal is justice, the use of anger is dangerous, is as dangerous as using water on an electrical fire.

13. Using John Locke, the English philosopher's definition of tyranny, America is today and has always been relevant to us a tyranny, because it is the will of whites being exercised over us without our consent. This is the classical definition of tyranny, the use of authority arbitrarily and unfairly against people. There is a need for capable men, black and white, with calm minds to go into conference and thrash out and promulgate a formula for working cooperatively to create one America, for now there are two, one white and one black created by the founders of the nation. Today, America is a house divided against itself. Evil is wrong in whatever form or guise it selects to adorn itself: in a three-piece suit, in the garb of a swell, the rags of tramps, with billions of dollars or no money, with recommendations of millions of his kind or dupes, or with armed force unparalleled, its nature is still the same; camouflage cannot

alter it. A slave is bound to obey his master. Du Bois said we were made to bend our bodies till the master stamped the red stain of bastard on the foreheads of our sons and daughters. Though the issue was as much his as hers, it mattered not for he had another property to work without pay or to sell on the hoof at auction for quick cash.

A free man is obliged to obey the law of which he has consented to be bound. Tyranny makes people give way to its arbitrary, capricious will and appetite but it is not lawful to be a tyrant. The best way to get a fix on whether white thinks America is a tyranny is to see if he would want done to him what America has done and is doing to blacks.

14. To give constitutional standing to us, there should be a constitutional convention called by us and supported by the nation for us to ratify, or not, the U.S. Constitution. Americans will say that America sinned against God and man in founding herself on the enslaving of us, and that wrong, they, her current citizens, deeply regret and apologize for, and are privileged to join in partnership with the injured party to eliminate every vestige of that evil from the essence of American society. We, descendants of slaves and members of the black race residing in the United States accept and agree to obey and abide by the U.S. Constitution as thus amended and with the following Bill of Challenges: We will resist the urge to steal, lie, vandalize, rob, rape or murder. Keep our community pristine clean. And work individually, and cooperatively to invest time and capital in it to make and keep it prosperous. That way, from a black stealing a chicken, to murdering in cold blood, to lying under oath will be seen by us as that black having violated our constitution, our agreed-on social code, and the social contract we agreed to uphold and that every one of us, each black person, is duty bound to uphold, honor and obey.

15. This could be the first time in history that blacks anywhere have been asked to give their consent to be governed and obeyed the agreement, and upheld the precepts, which are their own.

The Role of the Black Citizen

1. Looking where we are now, I have concluded that we must learn how to be citizens or suffer the consequence. Like a woman who has given birth but does not know how to be a mother, we have come through the blood of the slaughtered, gained freedom from the bondage of chattel slavery and, under the leadership of Dr. Martin Luther King

Jr., have ascended into the realm of the citizen; but we do not know yet how to exercise our rights nor how to enjoy the blessings of liberty. Nothing comes easy to us. Our freedom, nor did our civil rights come easy. So neither will be the proper wearing of our citizenship. We have now the rights and privileges that the nation can bestow upon the citizen, but his practice is as illusive to us as is the pot of gold at the end of the rainbow. We must learn, however, that his primary trait is duty, and his primary duty is respect for self, for family and for fellow citizens. We must learn that being a citizen is no sham role; that to walk among men and know that you have the high honor and distinct privilege of wearing the grandest title that can ever be worn by any man is to know that no other honor bestowed upon you can ever top the simple role and title of citizen. We must learn that the hallmark of the citizen is self-discipline, not impulsiveness; simplicity, not bombast; dependability, not indifference. These traits manifested bring the citizen from an outcast state into the inner circle and from the station of downtrodden to the position and status of equal player. Though we now have the freedom and rights of the citizen, until we learn and perform the duties of the citizen, though we individually are billionaires or have PhDs from Harvard or are famous personalities, we will continue to be the skunk at the party.

2. When you have attained the freedom of a man and the rights and privileges of the citizen, your challenge shifts then from how to get them to what to do with them. When a white treats a rich or famous or educated black like a maid or butler at a swank hotel, that is his genteel way of calling him lazy or stupid or both: lazy, if black understands what's being said; stupid, if not. It is the white's way of saying to that well-to-do black, "Your stake is in the black community now go you lazy, trifling, lag-headed bum and help to improve it." It should be the ambition of every black male to be the best citizen in his community. His hunt should be to make it better, to build it up, to improve it inside and out, and to identify needs and make the improvements by developing coalitions that bring them to fruition. Thus, convert naysayers' quivers to green pastures of goodwill. To leave your community by choice, when it needs you, makes you a stench on the thread of time, not a beam of light in the path of men. Thoughtful men build for all; everyone turns a stone. Mary makes the mortar John makes the bricks Bill lays them the house is built Sam and Sue make it a home baby Jessica makes it a family and the neighbors love the whole scene. Now the community is assured a

good future. It is this discussion that has not taken place among us. And it must if others are to know our thoughts on these matters, are to see us performing them. Since possessing the privileges, our behavior, in terms of their use in our community, has not, with one glaring exception, been pleasing even to us. Except the vote, we have fallen for short of the mark in the performance of the duties of the citizen. It is the purpose of this discourse to generate discussion and productive action in our community and elsewhere about the proper role of us as a free people: what should our goals be and how should we go about achieving them in the community?

3. We have seen a black perhaps, who, because of a display of personal prowess, has received a Nobel Prize or a PhD degree from Harvard or an appointment as head of an Ivy League College or University or an elevation to a top spot in a Fortune 500 company or proclaimed the athlete or entertainer of the year, etc., etc., ad infinitum. All of these achievements were wrought, however, on the basis of whites performing their role of the citizen; whites provided most if not all the props for the success of most of these individuals' personal recognition and basically, all the individual had to do was show up. These are not achievements of the black race, but of a few black individuals due to the largesse of white citizens. These achievements cannot be accredited to the black race anymore than the fame, and achievements of Lassie, the dog, can be accredited to dogs.

4. So far when ever black genius surfaces, it is in a specific gift like a genius for music or law or mathematics or science or as an administrator and so forth, and all of this mostly is in the context of whites performing the role of the citizen. These individual black achievements are wrought after whites form a corporate nation state or a corporate company, and upon performing the role of the citizen by providing opportunity for all, which means training blacks to develop their genius, black genius blossoms individually. But rarely does it bloom in a corporate cooperative task among blacks themselves to build the black community to be the safest, cleanest and among the most productive and prosperous and dependable in the world, becoming thus by us performing the duties of the citizen within it. Rarely do we make it the center of opportunity. Booker T. Washington did but was and still is hated by the Talented Tenth. The darker side of us, it seems, is not our color but our lack of dependability and cooperation one with the other for the betterment of the community and all within it.

5. This lack of dependability is usually reflected in the tone of the successful black individual that says that he is better than his community, which is a way of trying to say that he is better than his race. This attitude is prevalent in such comments as these: I bettered myself; I got out of the ghetto, or I want to better myself; I want to get out of the ghetto or I was lucky I got out of the ghetto; or I was never in the ghetto. To which I say, if you think you are out of the ghetto, you are brain-dead, a walking carcass; for wherever you go, you are you, and you are black. You cannot run from it nor out of it; only within it can you run. John Donne confirmed this sentiment in words unalterable and immutable more than four hundred years ago, when he said, "Never send to know for whom the bell tolls: it tolls for thee." No black is from, or out of, the ghetto; every black is the ghetto and that is so as long as black is ghetto, and you are black. The only way for you not to be a ghetto black is for there to be no black ghetto.

6. Here are two examples that illustrate this point. When a very successful, high-profile black woman went into a store in rural Michigan, one white female clerk said to another sneeringly, "A Detroiter." The black woman, overhearing this snide remark, did not say anything; but was deeply hurt, because she did not live in Detroit. She lived in one of its plushest white suburbs. When I heard her complaint, I wondered if she would have been offended by the same comment if blacks in Detroit with her participation had, by performing the duties of the citizen, built its educational system to be second to none and had made it the safest and cleanest city in the state, and that it was recognized nationally and internationally for such, and its reputation for its ambiance ranked among the best among all the cities of the earth? I doubt that she would have felt hurt—proud maybe! No doubt the same kind of pride a black Nobel laureate would feel if he walked into the same setting and a white had said there was a Nobel laureate. Even in a case of mistaken identity, the person's chest would still stick out. A black multimillionaire heard a white with far less money refer to him as boy, and he was unglued for a whole day. These kinds of peptic remarks and condescending treatment can effectively crush a black's ego, because against them he has no defense, because he feels guilty about the mess his community is in and feels helpless because of his laziness to do anything about it. He can try to cover them with banter and bluster and pretense, but his psychic can no more ignore them than the body can ignore the heat of a fiery furnace. And he is further frustrated because he knows that yelling racism does

not help his case one bit, because the effectiveness of the epithet is in the pathological condition in himself and his community.

7. And the Blackman knows for more than he will ever admit to in public. He knows, for instance, that the only way to rid black of ghetto is for us to perform the duties of the citizen in our community. He knows that white has accepted two premises about himself: one, he is a human being; two, a man is not a boy. But he knows also that a black as of this hour has not accepted fully either of these premises, in terms of his behavior, about himself. And he knows that when he accepts the former, he will use his mind to think, to get in the mood of the citizen and when he accepts the latter, he will realize that white as black is formed too in his mother's womb and, therefore, has no natural authority over another man; but a man not only has natural authority over a boy, but also has both a natural and legal duty to control a boy till he is mature enough in both mind and body to control himself, and to understand the ramifications if he does not. Where things stand now, this could very well be a thousand years, if ever, because the element for our progress in the practice of the citizen is now, where it has been for many years, in our hands.

8. The sad part about these situations is that we know how to feel very keenly the insults, but we do not know how, it seems, to build dignity in our community, because we do not know how to perform the duties of the citizen. I hear us all the time say "they" watch us; they grab their purses when we show up; or they assume we are the maid or the butler in a swank hotel. But I never hear us follow such grievances by asserting that our community is just as safe and clean and swank as theirs. And it is this dichotomy in the races that white thinks gives him license to tweak our noses, and he is shrewd enough to know that the yell of racism is an ill-fed disguise of a cover-up for gross negligence, indifference, and just plain old-fashioned down-home laziness on our part, even though we are rich and famous and educated by him. And he knows that the only way for us to improve our situation is to practice the duties of the citizen. To practice them is something the woman felt impotent to perform relevant to ever-building dignity in herself and in her community. And she felt the absolute absurdity of calling the white woman a racist while proclaiming a separation from her own race and her entrance into the community of the very race the woman being called a racist belonged and she felt that, while calling the white racist, she was saying something

worse about herself and her race from which she cannot separate, nor run from, no matter how hard she tries.

There is a descriptive difference between what is the black persona and the black individual that such situations speak to. The individual is one person, but the black persona is the composite of black humanity in the aggregate. When it is said as a general commentary that the black person is lazy and stupid or some other negative, the reference is to the composite person. But no black can extricate himself from the charge till the composite is free of it. And this is so whether he is rich or poor, famous or infamous, educated or not or lives in a plush white suburb or in the midst of black squalor and depravity heaped to the neck.

9.   The woman should know it ennobles the spirit to perform the duties of the citizen and demeans it when you do not. Importance to her was in her renown and ability to reside outside of the black community in a plush white suburb not built by black genius performing the duties of the citizen; this misplaced emphasis caused her to miss altogether the point of nobility found in performing the duties of the citizen, whether rich, famous or educated; and the countervailing demeaning effect when you do not perform them, whether you are rich, famous or educated. Her move to the white suburb was not to integrate it but to be in a safer, cleaner and more-prestigious community than she and her race had built in Detroit.

Here are two ways we can use as a starting point to help improve the image of our community, a.k.a., the black race.

10. **Religion**: Using the Bible as the supreme guide on marriage, pastors must raise the consciousness of the people to a level that stirs in them the absolute need to join in the bond of holy matrimony and abide there by the principles of fidelity with the strength that causes them not to swerve from the course that builds the family and fortifies it against the hounds of hell that would seek to prevail against it. Expressed cleavage, back ends in motion, pretty legs and wild imaginings made real are a few of the hounds that can gnaw at and tear down the walls of a weak heart, thus causing fathers and mothers to lose focus on the family and the best interest of the children, causing them to lose the sight that having both parents in the home reduces the need so many youth have to try to find the missing one in prison.

11. **Business**: Many voices in the black community call for jobs, jobs, jobs. To call for jobs, however, is easy, but a community must do more than call for jobs; it must also do more than provide a pool of willing, able, and capable workers. It must perform the duties of the citizen by providing a milieu of safety. This is necessary because the employer has to invest capital to provide jobs. And if it is placed in danger due to excessive crime, the employer could very well choose to invest in a location less threatened by it. So calling for jobs is well and good, but providing a safe, hospitable community is a prerequisite for job growth.

12. Professing ignorance of this principle, some black leaders, rather than acting to reduce crime, stress that jobs are needed to bring it down.

    But this position is not backed by use of their own financial resources to provide the capital necessary to produce many of the jobs they insist the community needs. In our community today in America, if people other than blacks did not come into it and for their safety use guard dogs and get behind iron bars and thick glass in many instances to open up grocery stores to provide us with food, clothing stores to provide us with clothes, and construction companies to repair and to build our homes, we would literally starve and would be in the condition so many Africans find themselves today; we would be without garments to cover our nakedness and without shelter to protect us from the ravages of the weather. Some of our leaders' refusal to do their part for job development take the strength out of their professed desire for jobs as well as their view that safety concerns should not be held by others providing jobs for workers in our community. A community of citizens should build institutions that meet their needs for food, clothes and shelter—and for those extras also that make for the good life. No black person should ever move into the white community because the black community is less safe, clean or prestigious as the white.

13. Finally, there has to well up in the body of black humanity a demand for greatness. When that happens, we will pull up our pants, roll up our sleeves, put on our thinking cap and, compelled by our own initiative, join the other people of the earth in constructive labor, laboring in our community to make it the best and the most preferred haven known to man. The very idea at that time of presenting ourselves in public as a lazy, stupid and foolish people, whether rich, famous, educated or other will seem oxymoronic. I heard a black man say that he can do

anything a white man can do. To that sentiment, I say, black man, we do not have anything to prove; but we do have something to do, and we should get about doing it with all deliberate speed. For to say that we can do anything whites can, but offer no evidence that we know how to build a coherent social system of opportunity that supports and sustains the individual, the family and the total community in a first-class, first-world, world-class fashion makes us appear impulsive, bombastic and ludicrous.

A Call to Service

Were the head men at the Southern Christ Leadership Conference really evil, lazy and ignorant? These are the traits manifested by them when they refused to make SCLC a resource for developing and shaping the better character of the black community by transforming it into a place of pride and graphic civility rather than going off on personal individual agendas after Dr. Martin Luther King Jr. was assassinated. If they did not know that was their duty, that lack of understanding made them ignorant; if they were intelligent enough to do it but did not, that made them lazy; if they knew their duty and deliberately chose to ignore it the only reasonable conclusion is they are evil men. And because of their negligence, many thousands of blacks were murdered in their homes and in the streets of the black community. The breadth of murder and slaughter was so broad and deep that the generation following Dr. King's assassination is called the lost generation.

Rev. Jesse Jackson, Rev. Andrew Young, Rev. Ralph D. Abernathy and the others in leadership positions at SCLC had a chance rarely given. They had opportunity given to them by one of the truly great men of history and like loose-headed animals with no brain smarts they walked away from it, and the black press, black preacher, black civic leader, black educator, the entrepreneur, and the black politician, in the main, treated these men's behavior with approval by joining them in shirking their responsibilities to lead the race to greatness as well.

While Jackson sashayed in the Middle East interfering in the foreign policy of the United States which was paying trained diplomats to do the job, SCLC by his and the others neglect was, as a national resource for black social development, effectively destroyed. They jump to do something they did not know how to do, while leaving undone that they promised Dr. King they would. They promised they would keep SCLC going forward, but by the turn of the century, just thirty-two years after Dr. King was assassinated, it was mostly merely a name on paper and the major civil rights organizations (CROs) were the two (National Association for the Advancement of Colored People (NAACP) and the National Urban League (NUL) founded by whites who will not let lazy, trifling blacks, though they try, destroy them.

The problem most people have with Jackson, and the others as well, is how he could be over in the Middle East saying talk not fight, when he, Young and Abernathy could not sit down and beat out a strategy for advancing the race and the country. He brought home Lt. Robert Goodman, who the United States was going to bring home anyway, while the earth was drinking the murdered blood of tens of thousands of blacks slaughtered in neighborhoods in America.

The black media (black publications and blacks in media, blacks working in white media) are letting blacks down big time. *Ebony* magazine came out in 1945, when blacks were portrayed in white media as lag-headed idiotic buffoons. But John Johnson, its founder, saw blacks as teachers who cared about their students, preachers who set moral examples, not ashamed to preach the value of family life, where the mother and father were in the home. He saw whole communities struggling to be decent and carrying people.

He sort to capture that beautiful scene in words and pictures in a feature collage that excited black people and got them reading wonderful things about themselves.

But this is a new day now, and it is still stuck where it started. We do not need to know that Detroit has a black mayor merely; we need to know if he has put in place a public policy that has blacks respecting human life as much as or more than they did during the fifties. The list of one hundred influential blacks is an anachronism. It merely tells the office held. With the level of murder and mayhem going on in black society, we need to know what these people are doing in office and why they are not developing a public policy that makes the black community a safe, clean and prosperous place in which to live, raise a family and do business. In the fifties, whites treated us like animals; now we treat each other like animals. It acts as though we are still trying to open the system up so we can be elected mayor. Hello out there black media and blacks in media, we have been electing mayors across America since the 1970s.

CHAPTER 7

The Duty of the Black Leader

**(And Other Comments Helpful to Any
People Needing to Move Forward)**

The three greatest statements ever made

THE THREE GREATEST statements ever made are: (1) the truth will make you free by Jesus Christ (2) all men are created equal by Thomas Jefferson and (3) no race that has anything to contribute to the markets of the world is long in any degree ostracized by Booker T. Washington.

Booker T. Washington and Martin Luther King Jr. adhered to the principles of truth, equality and markets. And the white race with an obviously gross exception tries to adhere to these principles. If the Blackman would try to adhere to them with as much diligence as the Whiteman, he would find himself no longer ostracized. King also chimed men cannot ride your back if your back is not bent.

Jesus speaks of truth, Jefferson speaks of equality, and Washington speaks of markets. If we blacks use that line up, it would serve us as well as it serves whites. The Jeffersonian declaration is a denunciation of the claimed divine rights of kings. It well says all men are created human, and no man is divine. It ushered in the ascendancy of who under England's rule was called the common man. It said the division among men as divine and common was phony and should, therefore, no longer be honored. It was a bold commentary that sent packing the long-held idea that the common man needed a king in a pretense of divination to rule over him, and it was an excellent assessment of the view that the common man had intelligence enough to control himself and thus, a man capable of self-governance, who could, from time to time, pick among his fellows men able to hold those necessary offices affecting the lives of all the people. The concept recognized and made policy the idea that the office affecting the people belonged to the people not to the holder of it. And the people, based on established law, through elections or martial strokes—the thirteen colonies used both—would fill them with whom they thought would best serve the common good.

There is a significant lesson in the Jeffersonian precept for blacks: that men can change society and lift it up with truth. When the idea of the divine right of kings was brought before the court of public opinion in the thirteen colonies, the main friend it had was tradition, a tenacious foe, but in the end that proved to be far too deficient, when faced with the awesome might of truth, backed with the will of men to respect it. The flag is a pure symbol; it cannot order anything. If anything is ordered, written or uttered, the people know it was not the symbol of the nation that rendered it, be it good or ill. And they have honored the orderly removal of office holders from the beginning of the republic to the present. The precept, "To thine own self be true," will always inevitably and eventually corral men into the path of truth out of the haze of lies and the fog of pretense.

The policy of black and white men that have crushed to earth the hopes of blacks, the black man himself with the help of other men of goodwill must overthrow. Booker T. Washington understood this; W. E. B. Du Bois never did. He never had a clue. Being most pretentious himself, he thought the black man's color was the black man's problem, not pretense. When the black man understands what his problem is, he will then stand aright in the pantheon of men with his shoulders back, not slumped; his head up, not bowed, except in prayer; and his back erect, not bent. When blacks develop the level of self-control that will allow us the option of self-governance, there is no force nor power known to man that can stay our rule nor hold us back. Till then, we, like the common man was by the king, will be ruled by whites with the precept of haughty arrogance and the weapon of constant and unrelenting fear.

Lead people to be self-respecting. If people respect themselves, they will derive several benefits. They will thereby gain the same from others. Some of the big complaints one hears from blacks are that whites discriminate against them, whites disrespect them, and whites hold them in contempt. Now we know that one way to reduce this way of thought and behavior is to increase our respect for each other and our property. I can assure black leaders that if they conceptualize and carry out a public policy that increases blacks' respect for themselves and for property by 90 to 95 percent, whites' respect for blacks will also go up to nearly that same degree; that would be a good-good or a win-win situation. White folk do not discriminate against black folk because black folk are black, nor do white folk discriminate against black folk because white folk are white. Whites discriminate against blacks because they have conceptualized and carried out a public policy to do so, and blacks have not conceptualized and carried out a public policy to effectively prevent it. There are two black men who have tried valiantly, and for their efforts, their names have been lifted to the top of the page of honor in the annals of history. Booker T. Washington built Tuskegee Institute (now Tuskegee University), the greatest institution ever built by a black person in American History. This great man for this great feat, however, is thoroughly vilified by Du Bois, his Talented Tenth, and his other adherers in the class of the pretentious black elite.

They harp on the claim that it is race and color prejudice that is the problem. But the Whiteman has far more sense than that. He knows that to claim such nonsense would bespeak himself a fool. Being a brilliant social strategist and tactician, he knows dominance is caused by discipline bound in an effectively administered public policy. He has never yet fallen under the illusion that his dominance is caused because of his race or skin color. He may use that as a point because he finds blacks are gullible enough to buy such idiocy, but he has never once relinquished discipline and effectively administered public policy to the faulty illusion that his race and color are bulwarks against tyranny or any other human ill. If people can be convinced that their race and color, two things over which they have no control, are reasons they are discriminated against, that is like convincing them that to ingest, digest and excrete are problems. So to proclaim race and skin color to be problems is to any reasonable thought process illogical. That the so-called most brilliant black scholar of his day would propagate this claim wholeheartedly is evidence that the black race has to dress himself in a mindset that is logical.

What Makes a Good or Bad Leader

(Of the bad are W. E. B. Du Bois and Jesse Jackson
Of the good are Booker T. Washington and Martin Luther King Jr.)

The duty of the black leader is to effectuate a public policy that lifts black people from the bottom rung of human society to their rightful place of dignity among the peoples of earth, to lead them in from the outhouse of mankind to their proper position as an equal player in the affairs of men.

In this context, there are two types of men, leaders and led and two types of leaders, bad and good. And two types of results, success and failure. A good leader upholds the principles and standards of his charge and knows what to do but, because the strength of opposition, may not always be quite able at times to get it done; however, if he fails, he admits it but in general a good leader effectuates the policy that succeeds in accomplishing the mission. A bad leader does not uphold the principles nor the standards of a leader, and failure beckons him like carrion draws flies. He may or not know what to do; however, he may know but, because of a personal agenda strays from the task. A bad leader therefore rarely, if ever, succeeds and a good leader may not always in every instance be successful, but his record over all makes him a successful leader. Thus a good leader by the odds stacked against him may fail some time, but a bad leader by his very nature is a failure.

Being a leader of men is an awesome responsibility. He coordinates the brain power and the actions of the people within his jurisdiction and so directs them that they work coherently for the common good. He works for the best interest of every person within his jurisdiction and knows everyone has an important role to carryout. His duty is to build consensus around those issues he and the people think will raise the level of dignity, civility and productivity in the community.

Instead of organizing blacks as Dr. King did and leading us to desired goals, we point to disparity in arrest and incarceration records of blacks to whites to defend the fallacy that we are discriminated against because of our race and color and attack whites both liberals and conservatives: conservatives for wanting tougher laws and liberals for weak social programs. By doing it this way, we effectively take ourselves out of the picture and thus set us up as helpless animals with no human intelligence at all. We know what liberals and conservatives want, but we will not establish a public policy that lifts us to greatness. We have not developed a language to meet our needs, to speak to our aspirations as people of intelligence, as King and Washington did so brilliantly. I heard a black judge say a black would likely be better off in prison; I have not heard a judge or any black leader since King say they are effectively transforming black society from what it is to being its best.

Since no black leader since King has done this, every black leader, therefore, since King has failed black people; has stood on the sideline, not addressing the basic needs of black society, and watched disinterestedly, it seems, as blacks mostly males roamed the streets of the black community murdering thousands of their own people annually, many times in cold blood, including children as young as six months old. If black leaders cannot conceptualize and carry out a public policy in black society that so direct the actions of black people to save and protect their children, their sons and daughters, from willful, open, deliberate, and systematic slaughter by their own black sons, there has to be an error somewhere. And the error here is in the fact that the black leader may not know his duty and certainly does not do his duty. Even if he knows it, he may not have the intelligence to perform it but it is essential that he know it, and he should also know when he succeeds or fails. And if he fails, he should admit it and then, if at all possible, correct it.

Some think high-tone speeches are the duty of a leader, but all that reflects are strong lungs and a gift for rhetoric. The difference between the electrifying, high-tone, inspirational speaker and a good, effective leader is that the speaker spouts words and the leader pronounces policy. The speaker, before he goes on, looks up words to entertain and to be cleverly amusing; the leader consults with the various elements of the community to make certain that he properly proclaims effective public policy. While it is true both the speaker and the leader use words to convey their messages, the difference between the messages is as big as the difference is between firing a loaded or an empty gun. The speaker's words are empty rhetoric; the leader's are loaded with policy.

Some think getting high university degrees is the duty of a leader; this at most is mere preparation for the task. High university degrees can certainly be of help to a leader because they give him a broader perspective, but they cannot make him be a leader. There is so much evidence now that makes clear high university degrees do not necessarily make one a leader. It is said above that where leadership is concerned, there are only two types of leaders, good and bad. Du Bois, in his autobiography, written in the tenth and last decade of his life, admits, "I am no natural leader of men." If Washington is without doubt the greatest human leader in history, Du Bois, though a great academic, is without doubt an absolute fog of pretense. So when viewed with clarity, there was no competition between these two men. Du Bois certainly wanted it to be so badly he took to carping and whining like a little sorehead boy. Then one day, after a period of complaining about the one person doing what he could, while he did nothing to advance the race, he decided to try his hand as a leader of men and founded the Niagara Movement. This is a movement that went nowhere; it is the movement that did not move but it is loved no doubt by every member of the lazy, trifling black elite, especially his Talented Tenth, committed to doing nothing to advance the race. They will trot it out every chance they get as proof of the greatness of his leadership, but point to not one thing it did to improve the condition of the mass of black people.

After he saw he could not lead men, he, like a little child, a boy, put himself under the rule of whites in the new organization they founded called the National Association for the Advancement of Colored People. They made it clear to him they would not allow him to use the position granted him there to lash out at Washington. The NAACP is what the Niagara Movement should have been. Its founders, all white, conceptualized and began to develop and carry out a public policy to help America live up to her promise by seeking to persuade whites to stop lynching their fellow black citizens, many times without provocation and sometimes in cold blood. This organization complemented Washington's efforts, for he was busy as he could possibly be "lifting the veil of ignorance from his people," the first time this had ever been tried in history, a job he was doing ever so valuably and brilliantly at Tuskegee. Unlike Morehouse, Howard, Fisk, Hamilton and other black schools founded and headed by whites after slavery, Tuskegee Institute was founded and headed by Washington who built it into an institution of national renown that trained blacks how to meet all the needs of man, including food, clothes and shelter.

Some think being famous is the duty of a leader but fame means a great many people know you; being a leader means getting a great many people to do what needs doing to make the community a safe and friendly place in which to live, raise a family and do business. The black leader must get down in the community, use the Washington and King examples, roll up his sleeves on an issue, especially an issue as devastating as open murder of our sons and daughters by our own black sons, and stay there till black males are primed for excellence, till the chill of the bullet from the gun gives way to hugs, slaughter to laughter, ignorance to learning, and devastation to economic growth and prosperity. If we want to end the slaughter of us by us in high numbers, we must take specific and deliberate action to stop it. We cannot set around, hold irrelevant seminars, issue stupid reports and pass inane and silly resolutions on the status of black America, yell racism, and get this job done.

When the blacks of Montgomery wanted to end abuse of themselves by ill-mannered whites, they got in the trenches and stayed there united under the good leadership of Martin Luther King Jr. till the change came, which was 381 days. They did this with committed, unified black leaders and the support of whites of goodwill. When the leaders united, the people united. When the leaders acted with good sense, the people followed suit. Black folk, like all other human beings, follow the direction of their leaders too. We achieved Montgomery because of black leaders, and our black sons are murdering blacks in high numbers throughout the United States today because our black leaders have not conceptualized and carried out a public policy that makes such savagery by black males against their people unthinkable, thus uncommittable. There was a senior black woman so proud in that day in Montgomery to see the dignity rise in the step of her people that when offered a ride by young people, including black males, willing to walk in her stead, refused and walked on. When asked if she was tired, she said, "My feet is tired but my soul is rested." This experience, unlike today when young black males like predatory animals break in on old black women in their homes, rob, beat and murder them in cold blood, shows that black males are not genetically programmed to act like impulsive savages: that they can under the guidance of good black leaders act another way.

For as long as anybody could remember, they had been abused on the buses by the drivers, among whom were no blacks. They suffered abuse daily in many forms. Sometimes, it started before they got on the bus, for the bus would pass and not pick them up. But being a for-profit business, most of the abuse occurred after they were picked up. One practice was to have them enter at the front, pay the fare, get off and walk alongside the bus to reenter it at the rear door, if the driver didn't pull off with their money while they were in route to the rear door.

Once seated, they were made to jump up and give their seats to whites if none were vacant. If there were vacancies behind them, they were ordered to move back so that no white would be seated behind a black. And there was the rule that vacant seats in the forward-most section were reserved for whites, though blacks were stuffed in their area like sardines, no standing room, they were not allowed to sit in those.

In addition to these demeaning enforced physical performances, they endured a continuous barrage of verbal abuse. Calling heavy-set black women fat cows and all black people apes, Niggers and coons or any other assaulting term they chose to let fly from their filthy lips, bus drivers heaped on blacks daily. And as if these insults were not enough, quite often they would call the police to arrest a black if he did not jump as quickly as the driver thought he should have.

These were specific crimes being committed against black people riding the municipal buses in the city of Montgomery in 1955. These crimes were being committed daily against black people, though the NAACP (The National Association for the Advancement of Colored People) and other civil rights organizations were in the city and had been there for many years. The local heads, who were black, of these organizations had no clue of the duty of the black leader. Most of these people no doubt meant well and some may have in their way loved black people, but there is no evidence that any of them had a clue of how to formulate a public policy for leading black people and whites to end this abuse and make the bus ride safe for blacks. A new organization was formed and selected a leader, a rarity, who happened to know and was willing to perform the duty of the black leader.

Policy

Sample 1

Policy is all: without the right policy people will likely be trounced in the dust like the dung of dogs.

Knowing what they wanted, blacks of Montgomery went straight to work to build the policy needed to attain their goal. Policy is a plan of action or inaction that will be done or not to achieve a certain aim. In Montgomery the aim was to end abuse of blacks on the buses by whites. Whites had a policy of abusing blacks on the buses, and blacks had a policy of accepting the abuse. Blacks under King changed their policy from acceptance to nonacceptance. This new policy of blacks' none acceptance caused whites to assess their policy of abuse. After some jostling in the trenches and an affirming decision from the Supreme Court upholding the Constitution of the United States, whites changed their policy of abuse to non-abuse. So the problem was not, as Du Bois claimed, their colors; it was their policies. Neither group changed its color nor its race; each group, however, changed its policy and that made all the difference. What is most significant here is, it was blacks who changed their policy first.

They jettisoned a policy they did not know they had and exercised a unity they thought would never be and changed a city they thought perhaps would never change to the degree that a bus ride in dignity in Montgomery for blacks would become a nonevent, with less notice given to it than one gives to breathing. This result was not wrought with flatulent seminars, degreed pretension, nor theoretical concoctions, but by harnessing the energy of the people to work together for the common good, they developed an effective public policy that attained the desired goal.

Sample 2

A black man went to the home of a white family in a ritzy suburb to pickup a black female servant. She was not ready when he arrived; she did not invite him in; he said she did not because he is black. He said the whites told her she should have invited him in. When asked if he thought she would, if a similar circumstance would occur again, he said it had and that she did invite him in, and that was when he learned about the exchange between the servant and her employer about his first visit.

I said to him that should tell him that it was not his race nor color that caused the maid not to invite him in. He asked if it was not his race, what was it. I asked him if he had changed his race or color. He said he had not. I told him that what kept her from inviting him in was something that could, and obviously did change. Then after much fumbling and bumbling, he blurted obviously it was her attitude. It was not till the next day that he got my point. He said he had heard me say before that our race and color were not our problem but had ignored it as pap. He said he understood the point now, that if you want something to change, do not charge its cause to something that cannot. If you want a dog, do not order a chicken; likewise, if you want something that walks on two legs, do not order a dog. When you blame negatives on your race or color, you put yourself and the race in the pit. In human affairs, always place blame on what is changeable, sentiment, attitude or policy, etc. It is policy that forms and gives collective strength to attitude. Policy is all. Without the right policy, people can, and most likely will, be trounced in the dust like the dung of dogs.

Sample 3

Whites' ignorance of how to raise blacks to greatness and black's ignorance of how to raise himself expose a breach in nature not amenable to nor amendable by man. White knows the vehicle that got him there is civilization and that it is the only thing that will get black there. But having civilization yourself does not mean you can give it to some-one else. You can teach a man what you know, but you cannot learn for a man what he should know. This is one of the many limitations in the nature of man.

The black leader should accomplish three things within his jurisdiction: safety, cleanliness, and prosperity. These three things should be the first focus of every black leader. The focus being in the order listed, for though they go hand in hand, it is impossible to have a clean and prosperous community that is riddled with crime, because the investment in capital and human know how will go elsewhere or it will just never develop or spring up from within the people of the community. There should be a thousand well-attended classes each week in a city like Detroit, teaching blacks the value of civility and how to practice it and receiving reports on how it makes each feel as a person, as a member of his community, on his job, and in the greater society. Whites have had hundreds of years of conducting town meetings, accommodating, compromising, coming to consensus and developing their social skills.

With this as a backdrop, we can readily see that we as a people have had two categories of leaders: negative and positive. Under negative are bad and failed, and positive are good and successful.

For our discourse here, there are two areas of leaders, political and other: political has to do with official governmental entities; other has to do with the religious, economic/business, and civic elements of society. In each of these areas black leaders have failed to lead black people to be their best.

We talk about what we want and need; whites talk too, but they do more than talk; they *do* what they need to do to meet their needs. And they form coalitions necessary to meet the task. In this process, they build effective political, religious, business and civic institutions that not only meet the basic needs of food, clothes and shelter of their community but also provide for themselves those amenities that make for the good life. And all the while, we have done nothing basically but talk. When we were slaves, we wanted

SHELTON VAUGHN

freedom; we got it; we said we needed education and good paying jobs, we got them; the vote, we got it; the opportunity to run for and be elected to political office sweepstakes, bingo we got that too. Now with all these wants and needs fulfilled, we are still talking. When the whole list of wants and needs is reviewed, one big thing is missing, which is, what can we do with them? We said what we wanted, but we have never said what we will do with them once having them. And with the exceptions of Booker T. Washington and Martin Luther King Jr., no other black national leader has ever committed to the kind of discipline with planning and foresight that shows a real understanding of what we as people must do with freedom, education, the vote, ascension to high office, or the possession of much money.

The Discussion

"Well, I understand the policy bit, and it has merit without a doubt," he said. "It adds to the dialogue. But the whole point of policy, as you so ably presented it, is that it can be made and changed. So our concern is that whites have made policy that discriminates against black folks because black folks are black, and we want them to change that policy to one of nondiscrimination based on race or color. My mother's sister at one year of age died in her mother's arms because a white ambulance driver would not take the sick child to the hospital because she was black."

"If that was the policy of whites, what was the policy of blacks about medical care for members of the black race and for others? Reread the policy until you understand its meaning," I said. At his idiocy, I became almost totally disgusted with this Harvard graduate with a PhD. But I did not because in the throes of his depravity of understanding, he was showing promise, though very little very slowly, as a man. At this point, however, I became very fascinated with how intensely the bulk of the educated class of black humanity waste so much time selling themselves the fallacy that whites discriminate against blacks because blacks are black and whites are white. It is as though that if they were forced to give up that lie, they would be forced to think.

But I continued with this example, which is a no-brainer: If there are one thousand black bags and one thousand white bags and, in the white bags are ten dollars each and in the black bags are one thousand dollars each, which race, oops, bag would you choose, black or white? He said black. Neither the Blackman's color nor his race is a problem; his problem is the content of his character. Dr. King truly was a great leader; before assassinated, he was already coming to understand the significance of the content of character.

The Myth of the Black Middle Class

Education, money, fame nor position makes a black person be middle-class. Dogs have education and other things: Lassie is trained to act, is paid a lot of money, is famous, and has a solid, prestigious position in the hearts of people, but is hardly middle class. These are the amenities of the middle-class, but it takes for more than the mere possession of these things for a black to be middle class; otherwise, there would be such a thing as middle class dogs.

Middle class has specific social attributes that refer to the race as a whole. The key attribute of the middle class is coherence in the race. When it is said a white is middle class, it refers to coherence in the white race. When it is said a black is middle class, the question arises, middle of the class of what? When a black is referred to as middle class, the logic of the reference is blurred with facts contrary to coherence in the black race. Thus referencing a black as middle class is a fiction, is a lie that insults intelligent human sensibilities.

Middle class in a people is like a house, it has to be built. As shown above, amenities alone do not make a middle class. It is a combination of amenities and values that makes a people have a middle class. Just as one cannot be in one's house, if one has no house, a black cannot be in a black middle class, if there is no black middle class. If there is no black middle class, no black then can be in something that does not exist.

To say a black is middle class, and then refer to the black race as a poor, powerless, poverty-stricken people is an oxymoron, because other significant attributes of the middle class are wealth and power. Wealth means they have the material resources to pay for what is needed; and power means they have the intelligence, coherence, discipline and influence to get it done.

There are black professors of economics and there are blacks of position on the Federal Reserve Board; but none of these folk got these positions after first developing an economic plan that made the black community in Washington, DC or Detroit, etc., a booming, bustling center of black-economic activity. Their positions were given them, because they got degrees from some prestigious colleges or universities and because white is still willing to tell them what to do when. By giving them these positions with such sparse qualifications, the white man gets a win-win: one, he gets to tell them what to do and two, gets credit for being a nice guy to coloreds, while some other loudmouth black idiot runs around blaming him for the savagery being perpetrated by blacks against blacks in the black community.

And sometime, these positioned blacks refer to the mass of blacks as the black underclass. When all they are, are people in need of their black leaders to come in among them and lead them to greatness. To call, therefore, such positioned blacks middle class would be to purport oneself a fool or at least to have a high level of disregard for the truth.

Phenotype

There is a mindset in some light-skin and dark-skin blacks as well that only light-skin blacks should advance to certain high positions in America, because light-skin blacks are closer in skin color to whites than dark-skin blacks. Many black people think it was Clarence Thomas's phenotype not his politics or his social habits that was troubling Anita Hill and her disingenuous, hypocritical black supporters. This would explain why she pursued him with a keen interest but resisted with equal tenacity his advancement to the high court. This attitude in certain blacks being not highly publicized, but very prevalent and malevolent, made Hill's behavior seem bizarre, puzzling and loose headed; but more puzzling than that is why such an attitude exists in any blacks at all. It exists because of a historical policy in the social order in America of putting whites first and blacks last or whites on top and blacks on the bottom. That has been the whites' policy and the blacks' policy has been to accept the whites' policy, and some take that acceptance to extreme.

That attitude in blacks is manifested daily throughout American society, but not exercised in the extreme notoriety given to it by Hill in her resistance to the elevation of Thomas to the high court. Yet some people see it as natural as drinking water or breathing or using the bathroom. Here are two examples: there was the case when a dark-skin black citizen's experience with a high-profile dark-skin black political appointee. The citizen went to this appointee's office on business. He was greeted graciously, given a seat at the desk, and, for a moment, had the undivided attention of this official, until the official caught sight of a white woman outside his office. After the appointee caught sight of the white woman, the citizen could no longer gain any traction in the field of this official's attention, and without performing the courtesy of excusing himself, the official moved away from his desk and chased with quickness the white woman and rendered what service she was seeking. The black citizen did not wait around. He saw who came first in the service of that official. Another example of this was in line at the post office, a dark skin black fellow was next in line with a white woman behind him, the black PO clerk took the white woman first against her protest. In neither of these cases did the dark-skin person say any thing there then. And by the way black leadership has treated the mass of black people since Dr. King was assassinated, it is obvious that their anger at Clarence Thomas is not because of any right-wing political views he may have that would lead him to make decisions on the court that would be adverse to blacks. The reason they did not want him on the court is he was too dark, and the reason for their anger is he did not lay down and take what he obviously felt were unfounded attacks; but instead, he fought back and won. And that galled them all the way to the bone.

Hill's politics was right of Thomas; she campaigned vigorously for Judge Robert Bork, and his politics was right of Thomas. The black elite joined her against Thomas for reasons they dare not say in public. But once we see how quickly they dispatched the Southern Christian Leadership Conference after Dr. King was assassinated and how they stood by and watched blacks turn their neighborhood into a scene of slaughter, the once proud black family into a campus of destruction, and the black community into a wasteland of murderous rage and laziness it is not difficult to realize that no decision made by Thomas on the supreme court could ever match that, if he were to vote to re-enslave us all. That history reveals, therefore, that it is not Thomas's decisions on the court, but the policies of the black elite in the public square that is the bane of black people.

Not wanting to be what you are is not unique to blacks. I have seen Germans not wanting to be Germans, whites not wanting to be white, blonds not wanting to be blonds. And Dale Carnegie tells in his book, *How to Win Friends and Influence People*, of a Chinese child lifted into the lap of a carrier of blue eyes, upon seeing the blues, the child leaped from the person's lap and took his fright in extreme hysteria into the arms of a parent. So there are times when blue eyes are not looked upon as the epitome of what is beautiful. To the contrary, as in the eyes of the child, they are seen as evil incarnate. Man's mind is facile; he can place any idea in it he chooses. The fact that something is in one's head does not make it be true. Reality is true whether it is in a particular man's head or not. Man being fragile can succumb to any view of himself or of others.

Regarding the not-want-to-be list, when I was in Europe, I met Germans not wanting to answer questions about their Nazi past who said they were ashamed of what the Nazis did and wish they were not Germans; I have seen whites rub tar or soot on themselves to simulate blackness, and I have seen blonds dye their hair to fit in where they would otherwise draw unwanted attention. In Carnegie's case, it was not that he did not want blue eyes; he learned that they were not universally seen as beautiful.

The time has come for the Blackman to stop blaming racial discrimination on his race and color, for there is nothing wrong with his race nor his color. The problem is how he processes information in his head, what he does with it, and how he makes or refuse to make public policy.

CHAPTER 8

An Analytical Look at Black Society

Who's Murdering Black People in America

A S A RESEARCHER, I have thought for some time now of what to do about the issue of blacks killing blacks in such high numbers in America. The high rate is appalling. As late as 2003, the FBI reports black males' rate of homicides per hundred thousand nationwide was 38.9 to white males 5.4. This comparative fact is rarely pointed to when Talented Tenth talks about the high ratio of blacks in prison relevant to whites.

It is an issue that defies imagination. It clips along at an insane pace that nobody, it seems, can or will halt. It either rises year by year or it stays high; it certainly never makes a precipitous, deep and sustained drop down to where it equals or betters whites. It seems to be a problem that has taken on a life of its own, a hideous monster, a pit, without a bottom. At certain moments, it seems the only thing one can do is think about it.

Thought, however, is an important process. It aids in helping to discover what is not causing the problem as well as helping to determine what is.

To that perennial question, what is it that causes blacks to push against themselves this pattern of self-slaughter, some say it is due to drugs, guns, racism, lack of educational opportunity, lack of parental guidance, and economic deprivation, which means too few jobs and too much poverty. However, when drugs and guns are looked at as causes for this behavior, it is found that whites, at least in the view of more than 90 percent blacks, have more guns than blacks. And not only is it felt that whites deal more drugs than blacks, but also these same blacks state right out that blacks don't own the ships and planes that bring the drugs into the country.

That statement is interesting because it is an admission by blacks that at the point of importation, whites handle all the drugs. And according to the U.S. Department of Justice, Bureau of Justice Statistics, whites constitutes 72 percent of all drug users and blacks, 15 percent. Yet the FBI reports the homicide rate among white males is 5.4 per hundred thousand to 38.9 for blacks as late as 2003. That drugs cause blacks to murder blacks in high numbers is a lie that lazy, trifling black leaders must stop telling; and black people must stop being gullible enough to accept this lie if they want to stay the hand of the black assassins roaming our streets murdering our sons and daughters, sometime in cold blood.

And when it comes to the problem of race in America, there have always been three types of white people: those who think that blacks have no right that whites are bound to respect; those who think that blacks have some rights whites are bound to respect; and those who think that blacks should have the same rights and privileges and responsibilities as whites.

Those in the third group have always been an ally; those in the second have always vacillated, and those in the first have always said that they shall not be moved. And since 1968, the year the fratricides of blacks began reaching over one a day in Detroit, I have seen very few blacks who want to revert to Jim Crow and his tenets or to slavery. Though racism is prevalent today, most blacks agree that it has been more so in the past.

Yet we did not murder ourselves in acts of criminal violence in nearly the numbers then as we do now. One observes with interest the educational opportunities blacks had before 1968 and the ones they have had since. If two main educational instruments, popular culture and schools, are viewed, we find that in the 1950s the popular black TV programming was basically one show, *Amos 'n' Andy*, which was one-dimensional slapstick. But since 1968, we have seen a variety of blacks on television, including the *Bill Cosby Show*, the *Oprah Winfrey Show*, and the crowning of black beauty queens in the Miss America Pageant.

And in the school system of Detroit, during this same period, we have seen the rise of black professionals to dominance at all levels of the system as members of the board, as superintendent of schools, as principals and as teachers. These advances did not, however, result in a reduction in the dropout rate of black students nor was there a rise in the academic achievement of black students.

These black academicians, once advanced, did not, under their leadership, create a situation in which the classroom was so charged with their imagination and ability that it ignited in black students an ardent desire to learn. They did not fill them with curiosity so magnanimous that they were drawn to the classroom because something was going on there that they would just absolutely refuse to miss.

Most, I believe, will agree that it is the duty of the academicians to set the moral tone and social decorum and academic standards for the whole school system, to create a congenial atmosphere that is fit for the academic achievement of black students and to sharply dissipate the credibility that one hears in such expressions as "cesspool of crime," "battleground," and "war zone" to describe the schools and their environs.

And since the academicians and the students in the system are predominantly black, the main factors are not merely a lack of educational opportunity. They are, it seems, that these black academicians cannot, or refuse to, teach black students or that black students cannot, or refuse to, learn. This last situation, if true, presents a whole different problem than that of a lack of educational opportunities. This circumstance presents a situation in which horses are led to water but they refuse to drink. The problem then is no longer, "Is there plenty of water, or are the horses at the trough?" the question then is simple: "Can, or will, they drink?"

It is certain that the educational opportunities for blacks are not as good as they are for whites. But they have been infinitely better since 1968 than they were before. So, to many people, the claim that blacks murder blacks in such high numbers because they lack educational opportunities has to it a very hollow ring.

SHELTON VAUGHN

To complain about irresponsible parents is possibly correct, but parents do not set community standards. Think about it; even with the lack of parental guidance, there is an attitude within blacks that is guiding them to murder themselves in high numbers but not whites whose prejudice they profess profoundly to resent.

Parents are not the community any more than a person is a family or a cell is a body. So as the example clearly shows, aside from those of an individual or family, the community itself has interests.

Now the challenge is to instill in the group the attitude that also values the lives of members of the community. This, if done, would end the current pattern of self-slaughter and effect a quick and sensible level of peace and calm tranquility to a community and a people that have bled far too much far too long.

Of all the excuses one hears as to why blacks murder blacks in such high numbers, the claim of economic deprivation is by far the most specious. Nobody, to my knowledge, has ever proven that the pattern of rapacious murdering of blacks by blacks causes an economic boon in the black community or that it creates upstanding jobs for the murderers.

When opening the 1989 National Convention of the NAACP (National Association for the Advancement of Colored People) in Detroit, Benjamin Hooks, executive director, made it clear in his public remarks that the income of the thirty million blacks in America was over three hundred billion dollars annually and that if it were a separate economy it would be among the top seven on earth.

The census shows that Detroit, during the decade of the 1970s, when it was gaining its reputation as the murder capital of the nation and making credible the tagline black on black crime, had the highest average household income of blacks in America's ten largest cities. The census also shows that the per capita income of blacks for the same period in Detroit was $5,490 and that over 758,000 blacks were counted. These conservative facts show that the aggregate income for blacks in Detroit for the period was over four billion dollars per year. The lesson is that the lack of money is no doubt a problem for us, but what we do with the money we have is a far-bigger problem.

I looked into something: crime is not free nor cheap. It costs nothing not to murder, but murder is expensive. To buy guns and ammunition costs money. To bury the dead costs money. To track down perpetrators costs money. To prosecute and defend the accused costs money. To buy security apparatuses costs money. And to try to mend the broken heart of a grieving mother, of a demoralized people of a community overrun with the blood of self killing costs more than money.

It is going to be darn nigh impossible, therefore, to convince anybody that blacks are all that poor when they carry on (and have continued to carry on since 1968) the expensive activities of fratricidal murdering well over a person per day on average in Detroit, when the alternative was—and still is—not only better but free.

So, even more than money, we need men to form agreeable imaginations that will secure the cooperation of the people in opposition to our murdering habit. We need men to stimulate and move us out of lethargy, stupidity and ignorance. In short, we need men with the ability and skill to organize and guide our community to safety, cleanliness, and prosperity.

I say men, not to exclude women. I say men because I believe that we as people would rather our mothers, sisters, wives and daughters be respected. I say men because men determine the path people will take; it was men who beginning in 1968 turned our community into a killing ground, into a place of criminal savagery unbounded. And when the century closed, the group with the largest percentage of increase entering the penal system was the black female, thus reinforcing the axiom that women will follow men wherever they lead even into the bowels of hell.

So turnabout being fair play, if we train our sons to be constructive and productive, the descriptive words in their songs referring to the females of their world would change from bitches, whores and sluts to baby (soft), sugar (sweet), and honey (a flowing, never ending stream of quintessential beauty).

The Guilt of Du Bois and The Genius of Washington

Du Bois was guilty of never understanding the needs of black people, of never seeing the opportunities in their midst, and of missing the mark, therefore, by a thousand miles.

"In the wee wooden schoolhouse, something put it into the boys' and girls' heads to buy gorgeous visiting-cards—ten cents a package—and exchange. The exchange was merry, till one girl, a tall newcomer, refused my card,—refused it peremptorily, with a glance. Then it dawned upon me with a certain suddenness that I was different from the others; or like, mayhap, in heart and life and longing, but shut out from their world by a vast veil. I had thereafter no desire to tear down that veil, to creep through; I held all beyond it in common contempt, and lived above it in a region of blue sky and great wandering shadows. That sky was bluest when I could beat my mates at examination-time, or beat them at a foot-race, or even beat their stringy heads. Alas, with the years all this fine contempt began to fade; for the worlds I longed for, and all their dazzling opportunities, were theirs, not mine. But they should not keep these prizes, I said; some, all, I would wrest from them. Just how I would do it I could never decide: by reading law, by healing the sick, by telling the wonderful tales that swam in my head,—some way. With other black boys the strife was not so fiercely sunny: their youth shrunk into tasteless sycophancy, or into silent hatred of the pale world about them and mocking distrust of everything white; or wasted itself in a bitter cry, Why did God make me an outcast and a stranger in mine own house? The shades of the prison-house closed round about us all: walls strait and stubborn to the whitest, but relentlessly narrow, tall, and unscalable to sons of night who must plod darkly on in resignation, or beat unavailing palms against the stone, or steadily, half hopelessly, watch the streak of blue above." W. E. B. Du Bois. *The Souls of Black Folk*, 1903.

"In my early life I used to cherish a feeling of ill will toward any one who spoke in bitter terms against the Negro, or who advocated measures that tended to oppress the black man or take from him opportunities for growth in the most complete manner. Now, whenever I hear any one advocating measures that are meant to curtail the development of another, I pity the individual who would do this. I know that the one who makes this mistake does so because of his lack of opportunity for the highest kind of growth. I pity him because I know that he is trying to stop the progress of the world, and because I know that in time the development and the ceaseless advance of humanity will make him ashamed of his weak and narrow position. One might as well try to stop the progress of a mighty railroad train by throwing his body across the track, as try to stop the growth of the direction of giving mankind more intelligence, more culture, more skill, more liberty, and in the direction of extending more sympathy and more brotherly kindness . . . . I tried to emphasize the fact that while the Negro should not be deprived by unfair means of the franchise, political agitation alone would not save him, and that economy, intelligence, and character, and no race without these elements could permanently succeed . . . . Nor should we permit our grievances to overshadow our opportunities." Booker T. Washington. *Up from Slavery*, 1901.

The deceptive distinction Du Bois makes in the top of his narrative about himself and his commitment to wrest opportunity from whites in their world, and the bottom when referencing the so-called sons of night, he thought, no doubt, appeared to be true and genuine but the bottom is in reality an unconvincing effort to make there be two entities, himself at the top and the so-called sons of night at the bottom, but arguably both are about himself the bottom being how he actually sees himself as a black man, about how he hates being black. Speaking not of himself as a hopeless son of night, he becomes so rarefied in the top that he holds all the white world in "common contempt." This rejection, however, is brief and momentary. And in a turnabout, he embodies himself as one of might and power; "All opportunities," he says, "I would wrest from them." Seeing no opportunity in his world, in a turnabout, he longed for theirs, not his. After the turnabout, he seems to say that if it was not for the sons of night whites were identifying him with, he would be just another white person for the resignation he sees in the so-called sons of night is in actuality a badly disguised presentation of his own unsuccessful resignation from the race, as he says, God made an outcast. That bespeaks a man resentful of what God made him but God did not make him an outcast; God made him a man and black people human beings. Denying that affirms the tone of a somber, pessimistic and caustic attitude toward what he was, and the turnabout identifies and affirms what he wanted.

His embitterment and extreme hatred of what he was tainted his spirit, causing him to be incapable of facing the challenges of his life in the race intelligently. The insult of the girl marked him for life; it ripped out his center. Something rushed in at that instant and destroyed his potential ever fully to be a man; he was forever fixed by the insult of a child. She discarded his significance with less regard than she would a cockroach and with a social might and authority against which he could not appeal. He was never able afterwards to find his center again. The center of a man makes him seek and find his own opportunities, not try to wrest from another man his. Without a center, he floundered through life, becoming famous but not beneficial. Blacks who flocked to him were the laziest and most trifling and the easily misguided, weak headed, of the black elite who preferred pretense over substance. The insult packed a double whammy for how she rejected him impacted his tender life as much, or more, perhaps, than the act. Rejection is hard; it puts one out of the circle. But to be so peremptorily is like being kicked out and having the door slammed and locked. Though he lived a long life, he never understood her power over him; being without this essential knowledge left him defenseless and helpless before the might and power of a girl and her mates whom he could outperform in academics, outrun in a foot-race, or whose "stringy heads" he could whip in a fist fight. He saw, therefore, his abilities being in academics, pugilism and footracing, not for his nor his people's social development.

What is meant by "different"? If it is that he knew not that he was black, that he was of a different race than whites, that would tell volumes about a downside in him: What kind of person he was or the people rearing him that he would not know he was black and his white playmates were white? But that is not the difference, I don't think, of which he speaks. And though he never says precisely in the piece what exactly the veil nor difference is, he implies in blissful and carefree ignorance it to be racial, not social, as he indicates explicitly elsewhere. The girl's action taught him in one quick lesson, which he never learned, that the difference was social, not racial. Her social scene, not her race, was superior to his in politics, religion, economics, and civic affairs and lacking the requisite intelligence, he knew not how to recognize nor develop these forces in his social scene nor therefore how to make it superior, so he longed for hers instead of his own. This was wasted ambition, which led essentially to a wasted life for he did nothing honorably heroic and though he lived a long life and wrote many monographs, he said nothing that would light the future path of men. Why long for the other fellow's when, if intelligent and not mentally and socially lazy, you can demonstrate that you are socially astute by being about the business of making your social scene become what it ought to be? A tree is known by the fruit it bears, not by the fruit it wrests from others. If he had been a man with a center, a man of imagination, production and social initiative, he would have seen far more dazzling opportunities in his race, as Washington did, than he could ever have seen in hers. Not seeing his opportunities made him a social cripple, a retard. Being socially lazy, he did not want to build what she had; he merely wanted it. He thought, no doubt, that the difference between them was race and color but it was not these; it was a compendium of forces affirming her race's excellence in politics, religion, business and civic affairs, and a lack thereof in his. When she refused his card, she affirmed the feeling held in her race that their social scene was superior to his in each of these elements and affirmed also her contempt for lack of similar or more advanced social development in his for all human power and progress flows from the social ability and initiative of men to form unions that meet their common needs. Without the ability and initiative to congeal socially, men are nothing more than a collection of individual specimen with less care for one another than dogs and cats. The girl's action, though swift, was potent and powerful and struck to the core of his being not because she was white, as Du Bois would want to think, but for being of a race well rounded in social intercourse and humane development, while his, in her view, obviously was not. By then, he had not learned her lesson, and sadly there is no evidence that he ever did.

The blue-sky metaphor shifts from his commitment to personal achievement to the blue sky blue above, or to airy nothing, when referencing what he calls the sons of night, ignorant, it seems, of the fact that black men are not the sons of night, though black but are the sons of the living God. This obscene and vicious attack against his people did not stop there: He implies that the veil that shut him out was a veil of his race and color. Washington saw it as ignorance, policy, attitude and sentiment, all changeable. Thus, rather than whine and yelp endlessly about the immovable of race and color, he instead opted to lift the veil of ignorance from his people. Du Bois spent a great portion of his energy maliciously attacking Washington, beating up on the psychic of his race, and convincing a great portion of his race that the abuse of his race by whites and horrible and despicable condition of his race were so, not in part because of the poor social policy of his race, but because his race was black. This banal ignorance blinded him to the real reason for the condition of his people. Seeking to resolve the real reason required a measure of intelligence, imagination and initiative, Du Bois never demonstrated any evidence of having at any point during his life. This is how the improper assessment for the cause of the condition of people can cause one to go so grossly wrong. He thought the veil was a veil of color due to his race and color. They being unalterable caused him to see walls unscalable.

Seeing dazzling opportunities in his race, Washington took people who had served as chattel for 246 years and as free savages, as certain whites called them, for thirteen, and transformed them from the station of an illiterate savage people to a learning people. There is no other feat in history that can match this. Any man then or now saying there is no opportunities in the black race, when practically every human need cries out to be met has to be either an idiot or a fool, or both. Not seeing dazzling opportunities in his race, though they are there for any one to see, Du Bois being socially lazy and intelligently trifling did not want to engage the process of building the good life for blacks; he wanted to "wrest" the good life whites had gained for themselves from them. This means simply that he would have been satisfied if they had pretended that he was not black and had just let him drift in, around and among them like an animal taking no initiative and having no responsibility for any thing. And that is basically the way he ended up living his life. That Washington took people whose most touted academic of the day saw their future housed behind walls unscalable and led them to build the greatest and most significant property ever in American history by black intelligence, imagination and initiative is absolutely astounding, is like pedaling forward while those supposed to be helping are pushing down hard on the brakes.

Du Bois' initial desire not to tear down the veil was a desire of wanting to be missed, of wanting to prove that they were no better than he, that he too was important but that strategy did not work, because he, unlike Washington, did not know how to make his social scene important did not know what the veil was, and did not know how to remove it. With that strategy not working, and being socially lazy and intellectually trifling, he wanted whites to accept him in their world, and never saw any real opportunities in building his world, and, in that attitude, he turned against himself by turning against his people and began longing for white opportunities; by doing so, he missed a grand opportunity to grow in a process of developing himself and his race to greatness. It was at that moment he lost his center and soon came to the strange, destructive and delusional conclusion that he was never able to see the "dazzling opportunities," as Washington did, in his race. And he died at the full age of ninety-five not knowing where his dazzling opportunities were. Thus, he fought and studied all his life to attain white opportunities and not his own, not knowing even where they were. Not ever knowing where his opportunities were, he cast them aside in tasteless sycophancy, silent hatred, bitter cries, and an impudent question: Why did God make him an outcast in this world? Never understanding that God made him man, not an outcast, and human with great potential, not an idiot who would turn against himself, his people, and his maker. Thus, he sort not to form a social bond with his own people and to seek opportunities among them, but instead he sort them among hers.

Social bonding teaches men how to make proper use of academic training to advance themselves together for the common good. Ignoring the need, lacking the ability to understand the need, or just willfully neglectful of the need for social bonding made Du Bois oblivious to the fact that the Whiteman cannot set the Blackman totally free: The type of bondage white had black in was physical; he had full possession of him; he bought and sold him like farm implements, and bred him like farm animals or household pets like cats and dogs. There is no doubt nor question about these facts. Black had no rights as human; his humanity was not recognized except in form which itself was physically evident. He had, therefore, no rights as human nor citizen. Now in all these matters, white can free black. White can free black from physical chattel; can cease buying and selling him like a cat or dog or a mule, a cow or a horse; can recognize his humanity, and accept him as a full-fledged citizen. But white cannot free black to form social bonds that meet the common needs of men as civilized human beings.

There is a correction inside of us that we the black people of America must make—a correction only we ourselves can make before we can ever be totally free. Social bonding between us must take place by us. That feat will only be accomplished when we do it. If we cannot, it will never get done. If we can, but in peevish opposition, refuse, the result will be the same. A complete lack of racism cannot make this happen, and all the racism in the world cannot prevent it. This responsibility belongs to us alone; it cannot be delegated nor transferred. And as long as we are not free to build our community to what we want it to be, we are still not free. And this is a freedom white cannot give to us; only we can give it to ourselves through the willful and deliberate act of social bonding.

Du Bois went down to the grave never knowing this, and Washington understanding it wonderfully well built a great institution to prove it.

The Andrew Young Dodge

A decisive look at the significant role that key words by Andrew Young in the foreword to Dr. Martin Luther King Jr.'s last speech have played in crippling the social growth and proper civil development of black people in the black community since the death of Dr. King.

"It was awesome, and the response of the people produced what German theologian Dr. Rudolf Otto described in his classic *The Idea of the Holy* as a powerful spiritual transcendent religious moment via the '*mysterium transmondum.*' God was in this place." That is what Andrew Young emphasized in his introduction to Dr. King's "I've Been to the Mountaintop" speech of April 3, 1968, the night before he was assassinated, in Memphis. Young said this in 2001 in the book *A Call to Conscience: The Landmark Speeches of Dr. Martin Luther King Jr.* and on the CD by the same name. There are two things very troubling with that focus: It does not address the aim nor reference the focus of the speech. Dr. King made a policy speech that night; the heart of it was "we are saying that we are determined to be men. We are determined to be people." This "means that we've got to stay

SHELTON VAUGHN

together." These quotes capture the policy of the speech. Yet Young treated it not as a policy speech; he treated it as a sermon, and being a preacher and a colleague, he was certain it was not. Ignoring the stated policy and treating it like a sermon, he chose to quote a German theologian rather than the policy espoused by Dr. King.

The purpose of the speech was not to awaken the spirituality of the people; it was to awaken and cultivate in them a high level of cohesive social consciousness. It called the people to be steadfast and the leaders of the Southern Christian Leadership Conference to stay together and lead the people to build the beloved community. Being well trained and highly educated and a key leader at SCLC, Young's choice to ignore the focus of the speech and to place it in a different context had to be willful and deliberate. If he had stayed with the focus of the speech, its effect could have led to blacks' continuous social growth and progressive civil expansion. By shifting its context, he led them down into a dank and dreary pen of slaughter and murder; and nipped in the bud any possibility of black social development led by SCLC. By changing its focus, he readily severed SCLC from being a forward in blacks struggle for upward mobility in the social skills of communal living.

I want to explore this angle of treachery with the reader so we all can see that the destructive path, deadly and bloody, black society chose after Dr. King was assassinated, is a direct result of the destructive action Andrew Young, as the face of black leaders, took against black people specifically and the nation and all mankind generally; for when you have done it, evil, against the least of these, you have done it also unto Me, saith the Lord.

We know that with a slick and crafty subtlety, he changed the context and the focus of the speech. And we know the bloody mess the change created in black society. What we need to know is his cause. Was it intentional or natural? Why would he scuttle opportunity to lead his people to greatness? Thirty-three years later, we see in his own words how he/they just simply ignored King's message to stay together.

It is disconcerting that a man as educated and trained as Young would use those skills to hoodwink people with puff language in a dodge. This is evidence that the best-educated black leaders in the main use their training against the people, not on their behalf, not to lead them to greatness. That he almost got away with it shows that we black people have not yet developed a language for judging our leaders. Except that my lookout for what black leaders are saying and doing that is taking our community in the wrong direction, he would have escaped notice for such ghastliness. Therefore, they choose to pull a dodge as he did and we accept it as praise for Dr. King and not as a heinous and vicious insult in a complete commitment to drag the race down, while pretending to compliment a beloved leader with whom he has served but for whom he obviously has extreme hatred, because you do not treat a friend nor a respected colleague nor any body else like that. If your child has diabetes, you do not stuff him full of ice cream because it taste good, because it could kill him. Likewise, you do not shift the focus and the context of what someone you love say. On a matter so great, you should not only not change it, you should repeat it with contagious excitement often individually and mutually till the whole black community is obeying the call to be men, to be people and to stay together.

And because of this failure, many thousands of blacks have been slaughtered and murdered by blacks in black society. This evil man and all evil men must come to know, however, that man has no ability to defeat truth. If the leader's message is be determined men, determined people and to stay together, you do not change it to mysterium transmondum, a foreign language, nor from a social call to a grand-sounding religious motif. Not if you have any respect for the person, yourself, the people or above all for truth.

In that collar, now some inane blacks are saying we have got to demystify King; he is not a god; he is just a man. I was in a general discussion, as some of the race's most learned men discoursed about him. Some said we can't sit around waiting for another Martin; he was one of a kind. Some said we put too much emphasis on him, making him seem too big to live up to. While this empty headed nonsensical noise was being spouted by these learned souls, a fourteen-year-old boy said, "Any of us can do what Dr. King did." Then he said, "What did he do?" Then he said, "He did the best he could." Then he said, "Who among us cannot do that?" Then these black learned men were mute on that point.

Since, on Young's watch, the human personality of black people has been hacked into a bloody mess, his and the whole cadre of black leaders' popularity should be discharged without honor. Popularity is not the full measure of a leader; Adolf Hitler and the southern rebel rouser were popular. The proper measure is does he uplift human personality by providing the input that causes all people to engage life respectful of one another?

It is obvious that Young's dodge was willful—nobody made him do it—and deliberate—he put thought into it.

Now I am going to look at the cause, was it intentional or natural? This discourse could not have been written, if I had found his behavior to be natural, because that would mean there is no hope for black people: that we as people are condemned by nature to wallow in squalor all our days. But what gives me not only hope but makes me optimistic is something else Dr. King said in his speech that night: "We as a people will get to the promised land:" the beloved community. He believed that we can and will build that community. That prophecy is in the sentence next to the last sentence in the speech. And I believe with every fiber of my being that we as people will get to that promised land.

Young's action was intentional because he knew too much for it not to be. And we can be certain that he saw nothing wrong with what he did and we can be just as certain also that those who roam about in the sanctity of the community murdering even in cold blood see nothing wrong with what they do. Our community today is in the mess it is because our leaders have led us there. Who would have thought that Young would have been so demeaning, seemingly, without conscious, like we should expect that of him. Well, we should not. If we are men, we will see the wrong; if we are people, we will acknowledge it; and if we stay together, we shall stop it.

If we get away from the language of puff and fluff and dodge and engage the language of being men, of being people and of staying together, there is no problem in the black community we with the goodwill of others cannot solve.

Young's dodge, though obvious to the trained eye and perceptive mind, is ingrained in the black elite, and they use it with devastating effect in language disguised as complimentary and positive and in actions appearing worthy. Who at first blush could fault his run for a seat in Congress, mayor of Atlanta or accepting appointment as the United States ambassador to the United Nations? The answer, of course, is any one cognizant of the need blacks had at the time and his position in the struggle. Doing these things is evidence of a lack of level headedness on his part. That behavior proves there was no thought in him for binding and mending the lives of black people. Is there joy for him in this neglect, fraught with such massive killing of his people, a fratricide? It would have to be a weird, sick joy, turning reasonableness on its head, a form of joy had by a person without a proper social conscious. He along with others was expected and actually promised Dr. King they would continue to build SCLC strong in cultivating black people to brave intelligently the new challenges they were about to face as a free people unbounded by the shackles of Jim Crow. His desertion of the people gives to the destruction of SCLC the, "and you too Brutus," effect. King's life example was that when your choices are many, choose the one that calls to conscious first the well-being of those broken. Do not ask, if you leave SCLC, what will it do for you? Ask, if you leave it, how will that departure hurt the race?

We have no language in media, white or black, to counter this malevolence in black leaders that points to it and calls it out, whenever it is written, spoken or performed. To do that requires diligence in the study and reporting of this phenomenon. There is a conscious, aggressive, vicious and evil resistance to black progress in the very character of the Talented Tenth, built up in them over hundreds of years that must be countermanded. The label Talented Tenth was given to them by Du Bois, but a minimal read of black history gives us to know that this phenomenon goes way back in African culture (Du Bois was more full blooded than he thought). They did not decide on the spur of the moment when the Europeans came to African's shores to be brutal and to mistreat their fellows.

Currently, black media deals in surliness and happy talk, and white media poke fun at blacks, saying, tongue in cheek, "What fools these coloreds be." This behavior comes up in white media when interviewing a black mayor of Newark, Philadelphia or Detroit, etc. They look the mayor straight in the eye and, with all sincerity, say, "What is causing this spate of killings, Mr. Mayor?" The mayor then shuffles from foot to foot, and say, "Well, it is a combination of things . . . ." Then that media person is off to file his report in a White Paper broadcast or on a regular newscast, giggling on the way for he has just seen a black in over his head and don't know anymore how to improve the situation than a man with no arms knows how to throw a ninety-five miles per hour fastball across home plate for a call strike. And he is going to get to show this idiot to the world on television, while saying to himself, "Comedy does not get any better than that."

The question the media should ask is, "Would you like to see this behavior curtailed in your city, Mr. Mayor?" And in the same instance he says, "Yes," ask him, "Why?" This approach may not get the savvy reporter many belly laughs, but it will began to build a language of calling black leaders out, with the results of saving tens of thousand of lives. That question gets on record his thoughts of why he wants it ended, and it is hard for a man to think about why he wants something that important done while in the position to do it and not do what is necessary to get it done. It also sets a path for other relevant questions: "What can or will or should you do to stop the killing and reduce high crime in your city? Do you believe you have the mental ability and level of insight and vision necessary for building a public policy that would bring out the best social traits of your fellow residents?"

If white media go for belly laughs when dealing with incompetent and inapt lazy black mayors and other black leaders, black media is a barrelful of laughs in and of itself for if it is a so-called militant type, it fills its voice with diatribe about racism; if a moderate, it is filled mainly with nonsensical babbling happy talk that a black is heading a Fortune 500 company, is appointed head of a great university, and elevated to a high political office, elected or appointed. It makes no report on how well or how badly the black is performing the duties of the office in terms of making the black community a safe, clean and prosperous place in which to live, raise a family and do business.

Thus, black leaders with awesome power and responsibility are left unchallenged by the media to do their duty to cleanup in America a camp of mayhem and human slaughter unparallel in history. Black people began to lose their grit in 1915 when Booker T. Washington died. It picked up again forty years later in 1955 with the advent of the Civil Rights Movement. After the Civil Rights Movement got advertisers to place lucrative ads in black media, it began to strive mightily to become irrelevant except destructively. Not having to respond to the needs of black people in neither black nor white media, black leaders in high politic positions and elsewhere in black society get a free ride. That should not be endured in a nation with a free press.

All media should know a dodge on sight or hearing, no matter how slick or sneaky and they should challenge it. Then look out for it; they should know its markers as thorough as we now know the racist markers, and they should challenge them with just as much vigor. Watch white men, even the most crude and petulant racists, when constantly challenged over time by both their white and black brothers, they expose their stripes less often and less viciously. They should cut nonsensical gibberish and cease fun poking and craft instead a language that gets black leaders to do their duty. And in time, they just might fall head over heels in love with the honorable execution of the duties of their high office.

Why The Blackman is Called Inferior?

Realizing no white man nor any group of them had ever raised a hand against a black person nor black people in general because of their race and having gained understanding that allowed me to see that we have been and will be abused and discriminated against by whites because the abuser chooses to do evil and because blacks are too weak socially to prevent it, I had to find why at this late date the black man is still called lazy and inferior and the white man industrious and superior. I had to find why the more education, position, authority, money and opportunity of every kind members of the black race accumulate, the labels of lazy and inferior become more and more creditable, not less and less, as one would want to think.

As one listens to the hopes and desires of black people, the belief that education is our race's way to peel these labels from us is expressed very distinctly; yet the denial of our hopes is enforced not only by others but also by us with a constant and unrelenting vigor.

For thousands of years but most especially during the past five hundred years, and most dramatically since 1968, the labels of lazy and inferior have retained an attachment to us that will not let go. Yet most of us, if asked, "Are black folk lazy and inferior?" say, "No," to both questions. But after seeing a black woman with a PhD go to white men in the media to beg them to stop her sons from calling her bitch, slut and whore in their songs, I went further than merely saying, "No." Instead I asked another question. Why do these labels so consistently attach themselves to us? It seems that the more education, money, freedom and fame we get, the more aggressively they, instead of falling away from us, become more and more creditable. Including the example of the woman here, we are held today by the people of the earth with greater contempt than ever before in history. In America, Haiti and Africa, we are begging the sons of former slave owners and sons of former colonial masters to stop us from disrespecting and killing us. It is hard to see how any people can ever become more contemptible than that.

A great many of us know there are two physical features, the heel and thumb, which distinguish man from animals. The heel permits him to stand upright and the thumb to manipulate most efficiently. What is not so well known is that superior man has a specific mental characteristic that distinguishes him not only from animals but also from inferior man. And it is in this realm that we are called lazy and inferior. We have teachers in our race. Some are retired and some are still active, and most of us have been to school. In school, and teachers as authorities can attest to this: If a test of a hundred questions is given and each question is of equal value and seventy is passing, if one student gets thirty right and another student gets all one hundred right, the student with thirty right gets an "F," an inferior grade; he flunks. And this is true if he is as white as a sheet. And the student with one hundred right gets an "A," a superior grade. And this is so even if the student is as black as the ace of spades. That is good to know. Now we know that superior and inferior are not based on color nor race, but grades.

The challenge for me at that point was to find the test we were failing, the test which by failing were marking us an inferior and lazy people even though we say, "No" and academically are receiving the PhD from Harvard and other major colleges and universities. I found that our shortfall was in performing the abstract thought in the social context. We, therefore, are called inferior people because we do not pass the test of abstract thinking in the social context; and nonperformance of the abstraction makes us lazy, and not understanding that to be the case makes us stupid. As strange as it may seem, "lazy," because it, in this context, implies ability, is in a way a backhanded compliment. It implies ability but lack of will; stupid implies lack of ability.

Deficiency in performing abstract thinking in the social context is the reason we are called lazy and inferior. Abstract thinking is that mental characteristic that separates not just man from animal but superior man from inferior man; and the process of the abstract thought has three main stages that separate inferior and lazy people from superior, industrious people. The abstract thought in the social context, unlike academic training, an individual pursuit, cannot be performed by oneself. As a matter of fact, in academic training, one can get one's own good grades in school; but the abstract thought in the social context corrals, determines and directs the thoughts and actions of a body of people through three main stages before they, as a body, can be called a superior people. The first stage lasts till the last of the founders have passed on; they are the pioneers. The second stage supports the founders till the last one of them has past from the scene and it lasts till the last one alive when the idea began has passed away. The third stage is that period when no one living knew the founders nor their supporters.

Now I think we can begin to see that our real problem is that we do not sustain an abstract idea in the social context across generations. There have been only two people of national statue who have tried to build a solid base of black communal development. They were Booker T. Washington and Martin Luther King Jr. Both of these men were viciously attacked by the best-educated blacks of the day. The vicious attacks, mostly verbal, against Washington are legendary and were by those blacks led by Du Bois and the Talented Tenth, who were not supportive of his effort to improve the lives of the mass of black people. But the ones against King were both verbal and active. The verbal attacks came against him mainly from old line civil rights organizations and the leading clergy, especially the head of the

National Baptist Convention, USA, Inc. But the deepest cut of all was from those closest to him. Their opposition was not verbal; it was action, and even blacks understand and know that actions speak louder than words. "The minute," as one observant lady put it, "racism assassinated him, Niggerism destroyed the Southern Christian Leadership Conference as an effective agent in building the beloved community."

Niggerism and racism: Niggerism is an evil in blacks directed against themselves; and racism, the most monumental evil ever to infect human personality, is an evil in whites directed against blacks. These are the twin-headed monsters. Each of them working in his own way to assure forever the credibility of the labels, lazy and inferior. The best-educated class of blacks assure this in two specific ways: One, they, unlike Washington and King, by moving out of the black community into a community where they have no roots, create the conviction in some that they are worse than lazy; they are stupid and lag headed; this weakens the race. A tree limb not connected to its trunk is fodder for something or for nothing. As a resource for racial growth and development, such behavior is more than worthless in terms of advancing the image of the race; it digs a deeper pit.

The other way is the raw and unmitigated predatory practice of Niggerism by the best-educated blacks living in or outside the community. A woman tells of a pastor in a mainline church who before he can make the one and one-half to two steps from his big chair behind the podium to the lectern he is already happy. He urges members to tithe. "Give it to God," he shouts as he bucks a bit before he settles down. After service, pleased with his swindle, he heads to his expensive home in a posh white suburb still able to pay the note. So they give up any hope of ever having the black race become a superior people while choosing deliberately and willfully to be lapdogs in the outhouse of another people's community. Thus, they give credence to the axiom: There is no other fool bigger than the black educated fool.

The challenge facing us today is can we or will we perform successfully the second and third stages of the abstract idea started by Washington and restarted forty years after his death by King in 1955 and make our race a truly superior and industrious people and toss aside forever the labels of lazy and inferior from our resume? Till we do this, no matter how much personal achievement we may have within the abstract thoughts of others, we shall never lift the shamefully descriptive labels of lazy and inferior from us as people. Moving into a white neighborhood, being paid billions of dollars, achieving fame, earning the PhD, as we can now see from our experience since 1968, will not remove them. A young black man, interviewing an internationally renown black male opinion making, and a possessor of the PhD, asked the interviewee this question: "Now that we are producing the college graduate, including the PhD, in such high numbers, when will the black community begin to benefit from these individual and laudatory personal achievements?" This man, though professing loudly the desire to improve the status of blacks, had no answer to the question. He twisted and screwed around in his chair like a little child; he had no answer. It was obvious abstract thinking in the social context had never occurred to him.

It was, and still is by some, thought that education would shed from us these labels; but as we can see, that's a fallacy; education is only a tool, is only a form of training; dogs and other animals can be trained. There was a television show called Lassie; the dog was popular and the show was popular. It is the will and coherence of people that determine the level of their superior intelligence; education determines the level of their training. An animal can be trained, but only superior men will cohere and sustain man's highest ideals for hundreds or even thousands of years. Many people including some blacks like to quote Jefferson's inspired revelation "All men are created equal" clause in the first part of the Declaration of Independence but we blacks neglect the pledge at the end. It says, "We mutually pledge to each other our lives, our fortunes, and our sacred honor." We can only wonder what SCLC would be like today if those chartered with the mantle of its leadership at the death of King had mutually pledged to each other their lives, their fortunes, and their sacred honor to sustain and guide it in leading black people in building the black community, in becoming the anchor for advancing the beloved community. Based on their behavior after Dr. King's assassination, it is obvious they had no concept of the abstract thought he had spent thirteen years with their help developing. Though educated, some with the PhD, their willingness to turn from SCLC and its quest to build the beloved community shows, their involvement with it was not in the context of the abstract thought but solely for the removal of those affronting and in your face practices of Jim Crow. We can only wonder what the nation would be like today if its founders and those at its head had done as those with Dr. King did when he was assassinated; if they had deserted their posts in the new nation and went off to engage personal agendas, America's place in history would have been no doubt diminished significantly.

SCLC leaders' departure from it reflects or highlights the fact that they had been with it because they in the main were against Jim Crow, and not because they were for building the beloved community, for transforming the black community to reflect the best in black intelligence. It was most important however for them to have been for something, for building the beloved community. Not being in it for something allowed them, it seems, almost without conscious to drift away from it like subhuman animals or very unfocused, inferior and lazy, though highly educated persons.

We should not be impressed because a black has a PhD, a high political office, elected or appointed, heads a Fortune 500 company, a great university complex and the like. What should impress us is will they use their education, position, gifts, talents and money as Washington and King did to infuse directly the black community continuously with the can do ideals of them both? Understanding that Washington affirmed our humanity and that King led us to accept the color of our skin, and that the question facing us today is, what are we going to do with our humanity? Are we going to use it to uplift human personality, yes to build the beloved community?

CHAPTER 9

Of Flying the Confederate Flag in Public

THE CONFEDERATE FLAG is divisive. This symbol stood against freedom and for the perpetual enslavement of certain people. Its stance rent the country, thus creating two nations—the United States and the Confederate States—and two belligerent sections—Northern, which valued the supremacy of the Union, and Southern, which demanded the assurance of the spread of slavery to the territories or it would leave the Union. Though the United States, in its effort to appease the South, offered a constitutional amendment guaranteeing the perpetual enslavement of certain people in the slave states, it was unwilling to allow the spread of slavery to the territories. Whereupon eleven states (South Carolina, Mississippi, Florida, Alabama, Georgia, Louisiana, Texas, Virginia, Arkansas, Tennessee, and North Carolina) then withdrew from the Union and formed themselves into a new nation called the Confederates States of America. The United States said the secession was unlawful and that the Union was a sacred bond, indissoluble and indivisible; and President Abraham Lincoln said that he would, therefore, enforce the laws of the United States in all the states, including the seceded states.

When the president sort to do this with a shipment of supplies into a seceded state, the intended recipient, Fort Sumter, in S.C., was attacked, on April 12, 1861, by Confederate Armed Force and forced to surrender. The seceded states were now in a state of armed rebellion. And this meant only one thing: War had come between the two sections.

Early on in the fight, the North was not for ending slavery; it was for saving the Union merely. The two, however, were incongruent. One had to go: the Union or slavery. The North chose to save the Union; the South chose to save slavery. The North was victorious; the South was defeated. The Union was saved, and slavery was ended in the United States of America. It went, therefore, from its longest and darkest hour to its brightest day for on December 6, 1865, every American for the first time was free, not yet to pursue happiness nor to enjoy the blessings of liberty, but at least from the bondage of chattel slavery.

Lincoln said at Gettysburg that the nation should have a "new birth of freedom." Displaying the Confederate symbol is disrespectful of those, and their descendants, who were delivered freedom at the new birth. Some say they fly the Confederate Flag out of Southern and rebel pride, a way of celebrating the glorious heritage of the South. It is true that belligerence to expand slavery to the territories is a part of Southern Heritage, but to call that part of its heritage glorious is a stretch, is like Germans calling the Nazi period glorious. That part of it then should have no place of honor anywhere in America, nor in any American who wants liberty and justice for all. The American Flag is a symbol of liberty, for its drive and struggle from its birth has been a hunt for liberty and justice for all, striving to become a more-perfect union.

The new nation chose the old nation's bad feature to expand, but did not attach to itself any of the sparks of light and hope sprinkled about in the framework of the old nation: Words like "all men are created equal," and "to form a more perfect union," and "liberty and justice for all" were omitted.

The war was brutal; it is the bloodiest America has ever fought. They fought on the water, in the woods, on the planes, and in the fields. When it started, the Northern forces fought to save the Union. As it moved along, however, they realized that to save the Union, they would have to end slavery. They realized that a state of slavery is inconsistent with the concept of liberty and justice for all. The strength of the knowledge of this inconsistency drew them to the concept of a nation without slavery. And the Southern forces began to realize that if they lost, they would not only have no right to expand slavery to the territories, but that they could end up loosing their human chattel at home. Each side fought bravely for its cause. But in the end, the South's cause became a lost cause.

It is true that America was born part slave and part free. But neither in the Revolutionary War nor in the Civil War did she fight to retain or to expand slavery. It was ironic that in the Revolutionary War, the colonies, while fighting for their freedom, independence, and liberty, were themselves holding certain human beings as chattel; and that, though the federal government was not willing to fight to end slavery in the Civil War, it was forced to end it or dissolve the Union.

That the rebellious states would break a sacred bond and fight to spread the agony of human bondage shows the depth of human depravity present in the Confederates. There is no doubt that they thought that to fight to hold human beings as chattel property was proper; that their cause was right and honorable; and that that was a way to build a glorious heritage. But there is also no doubt that their cause became a flaming inferno, burning itself out in an ignominious defeat.

The South, albeit in a different aspect, recognized perhaps before the North did that, in a nation not accepting of slavery everywhere, there may come a day when it would not be accepting of it anywhere. For it was so intent on spreading slavery to the territories, it refused to accept an amendment to the Constitution assuring the permanence of the institution in the slave states. It chose instead to sever its sacred bond to the Union and to create unto itself a free and independent state. But it didn't realize that it could not break the bond, nor that the very idea of a slave state being free and independent was an impossibility, for in actuality no slave state is truly free, because no crime is perfect. It did not understand that, while every crime is perfect in the sense that it was not prevented, no crime is perfect in the sense that no retribution is ever paid.

It had no way of knowing at the onset of hostilities that its intended crime was about to be prevented and that the United States was about to pay partial retribution for her crime of slavery—was about to fight, as Lincoln said, "Until every drop of blood drawn with the lash, shall be paid by another drawn with the sword."

Devotees of the Confederate Flag fly it because, though they lost the war, they say it is a part of their glorious heritage. Well, to those who would raise it on public property must be asked these questions: Would you want white women *forced* to bear yellow babies as your ancestors, including Thomas Jefferson, *forced* black women to bear yellow babies? Would you want blacks to declare you to be a subhuman savage to be bred like cattle and bought and sold at auction? Would you want to be stripped of every shred of your human dignity and forced to work without pay for the sole satisfaction of your owner? Would you want that tyranny to be defeated in war, only to see its flag raised again in your midst in the claim of idealizing a glorious heritage? Answers to these questions should be given in the affirmative before the flag is raised because there was no honor in their cause and by continuing to fly the flag, they are trying, it seems, to prove that there is no honor in them.

The flag, therefore, represents division and defeat and is an emblem of shame and disgrace—not of glory. It is shameful because it dehumanizes human personality. When the policy of the state is pitted against the very humanity of people, such a policy can't help but drag all mankind into the path of devalued humanity where no man is free to be just. The victim submits under the bludgeoning force and power of the policy and the policy makers think that because of their power to plunder, they can ignore justice and commit the perfect crime. When this thought becomes primary, they lose sight of a better way.

It is disgraceful because it exposes a pathology in them that should be cured already. When the principle of "do to others as you'd have others do to you" is considered, the disgrace in the Confederate cause pierces the conscience of all civilized people. They understand then that the Confederates' cause is honorable to them only because they think they are immune to having done to them the atrocities they fought to perpetuate against certain people. Yet it is Lincoln's words, "with malice toward none," that should reign today.

But instead, today, there still are those who want to squelch an ebullient spirit in black people, to deny them their rights as citizens, to crush their humanity to the earth, and to oppose every opportunity for them to thrive and learn and rise to the fullest possibility of excellence. That is not glorious; that is evil. The United States fought to save the Union but the Confederates fought to retain and expand the institution of slavery.

Proof that the urge to fly the Confederate Flag springs from the seed of an evil spirit is this: I have never met nor read a Confederate who wants blacks to do to whites what the fighters under that flag wanted to continue doing to blacks. So the ultimate question has to be: what does the flag stand for and what did those who fought under it fight for? Theirs is not a glorious but a demonic heritage whose folly bespeaks them to be crows from hell ready to pick the carcasses of what is dead, not angels from heaven willing to give life to dry bones.

To hail the legacy of slavery as glorious is like clawing into the bowels of skunks or like drinking brew from the cauldron of evil spirits.

Flying that flag is hurtful and insulting to blacks. It hurts because it seeks to limit their excellence. Paul Robeson became the best-known personality in the world because his father, born a slave, was freed in that mammoth overthrow of the institution of slavery. And it insults because it demeans human relationships, makes dirty what should be clean, contaminates the well of hope, and removes the cushion of social graces, thus causing the races to come before each other with bare knuckles and harsh, shrill and biting voices, speaking to each other not as friends and neighbors, but as hostile enemies who like Achilles and Hector must oppose each other to the final end.

It has to be a measure or form of pinhead insanity to hold on to what should be relegated to the ash bin of history and set into a vase of shame to be seen only when someone chooses to visit the scrap heap of evil deeds.

Without the light in the words, "all men are created equal," nor the brilliance in the phrase, "to form a more perfect union," to guide and inspire them, the plunderers, if victorious, would have plunged mankind into a period of almost complete and total darkness. Complete because there was no ray of hope for them nor their prey for since their main intent was to keep their prey down, they would have had to stay in the ditch too. And total because since there was no light, they could see no way out.

So the Confederates should devise a symbol showing pride not in the fact that they fought that fight but in the fact that they lost it. But never mind Confederates, that symbol, the American Flag, has been devised already. And it should be sufficient.

Some Confederate devotees today say their cause is for more than the desire to retain and expand forever the institution of slavery. I have found no other issue but if there were others, in their view, slavery was dominate. And as the swastika should not be honored because the Nazis made the trains run on time, the Confederate Flag should not be in a place of honor because there is a claim of other issues.

As the swastika should be reviled today by civilized people everywhere because it symbolizes a policy of extermination, the Confederate Flag should be pegged an evil marker by anyone who loves freedom and liberty, because its main motivation was to retain and expand the institution of slavery.

There are hooded souls who gather and march in the streets today to support flying this flag on public property. But ducking under the cloak of hooded sheets does not hide the wrongful deeds of evil men. To behave thus says two things about such marchers and those others who support flying the flag anywhere in public but especially on public property. It says that they are proud of slavery and regrets its ending or that they are fools. Neither choice compliments them. The former shows extreme depravity, and the latter shows a lack of shame.

CHAPTER 10

The Crown of a Noble Life

The legacy of one of America's greatest sons—a humble life honored by his fellow citizens and by the Congress and the president of the United States.

THIS DISCOURSE DISCUSSES my father, Willie Vaughn, in three main categories—family, community and church—and how, because he did these three things so extraordinarily well, his fellow citizens, Congress and the President crowned this humble, committed and dedicated life of service with a great honor. Not because he was a brainy student of renown—though I think it will be shown that he was a brilliant man. One day, when he had passed one hundred years, one of his granddaughters with a bachelor's degree in engineering came by to go over the Sunday School lesson with him. When she came out, she was asked, how he was doing. She said with a bounce of enlighten joy in her voice, "He is still teaching." So his wisdom was reaching down to all generations. He was not a soldier in the armed forces; he was too young for WWI, too old for WWII, though he had family members in WWI, brothers in WWII, and sons in both the Korean and Vietnam wars. He was not an eminent national figure but he was a good neighbor, a good citizen, and a good friend to all. His father had two habits that affected him deeply. He drank, but he had a sturdy character with a strong bent for doing the right thing by people. My father rejected completely the drinking. I never saw him smoke nor take any form of strong drink, not even a beer but he wore his dad's other feature like a fine suit. That feature would define his life to the end; he had an abiding friendship for all people.

Let us start now from the beginning, Willie Vaughn was born the grandson of a slave couple, Madison and Cillar, who were born in the 1840s. He was born the son of Thomas and Mattie, who were born in the first generation after slavery in the early 1870s. Slavery ended December 6, 1865. Willie Vaughn himself was born Wednesday, April 20, 1904, in Thomasville, Alabama (Clark County). His mother died in childbirth in 1916, when he was twelve years old. In 1917, because the ravenous bole weaver ate their corps, his father and other family members including his grandmother, Cillar, and a host of friends and acquaintances pulled up stakes and moved to Parkdale (county of Ashley in Southeastern), Arkansas. In 1918, his grandmother passed away. In due time, he met a beautiful young woman, named L. C., he fancied much. One thing led to another and on October 27, 1927, this young man of promise and she were joined in the bond of holy matrimony, a bond that lasted until death parted them, during January 1990, more than sixty-two years later. In 1928, in mid-September, their first child (Sadie), a daughter and the first of seven children, made a noisy debut on the stage of the world, and because of that wonderful event, the cosmos is still buzzing with much excitement and pleasure. In 1929, his father died, the bottom fell out of the stock market, and the United States economy went to pot. During the 1930s, as his children were being born, times were hard. But he and his thrifty and industrious wife, like so many others of that day, made it through with the help of almighty God for they always had a plenty for a growing family to eat by raising hogs for meat, chickens for meat and eggs, cows for milk and butter, and by cultivating a richly endowed garden that provided a variety of fruits and vegetables. We plucked many a watermelon there and discharged the seeds with the force and power of giants. That period in history is called the Great Depression.

Of the seven children of my mother and father, the second born, a son, Thomas died between three and four years of age. The others, three boys and three girls, grew up to be adults. In 1979, one of the grown children, a son, (Andrew) died of cancer.

In 1952, his wife's side of the family began a family reunion. The first gathering was held at his house. There has been an annual gathering of this event every year since. As time rolled on, those of his generation on both sides of the family began passing away one by one till there came a time when only two were left, my father and one of my mother's sisters. We called her Aunt Bunch, a name of affection. Though Aunt Bunch was small in stature, she was tough as nails and strong as steel. We would go to the reunion, and there you would see Dad and Aunt Bunch sitting, talking, reminiscing, and sharing memories.

In terms of community, the greatest accolade, compliment or tribute that can ever be paid to any man is that he was involved with mankind for its betterment. That can truly be said of my father. I remember as a child, people coming to our house anytime, day or night, not to invite him to a boogaloo party but because they were facing the challenging issues of life. It could be that a spouse was sick or dead or a child. They may have wanted his assistance to help get the sick to the doctor or to help make arrangements to bury the dead. But in the main, they came because they knew in him they had a friend. My father truly was involved with people. He was not on the sidelines of life loose lipping, pontificating, and running off at the mouth. He was down in the trenches among the moving and mingling crowd, helping whenever, however and whomever he could.

The reason he was able to be effective as head of his family and as a community leader is that the center of his life was the church with God at the head of all. It is believed that Madison, his grandfather, was part of the colored part of the Methodist Episcopal Church South, when slavery ended. We know that the Christian Methodist Episcopal Church was formed out of the Methodist Episcopal Church South in 1870 as the Colored Methodist Episcopal Church. Before leaving Alabama, my father had already joined the church of his fathers, Miles Chapel Christian Methodist Episcopal Church. Once established in Arkansas, his father, who could neither read nor write, went to a white man and asked for a prime plot of land to build a church, which was built in 1922. If I learned anything from my parents, I gained from my mother a keen desire to learn and study and I learned from my father the importance of focus and purpose. Every day of his life was filled with purpose. He saw the church in three main parts—laity, clergy, and property—and he supported all three with time and money. His home was a host for preachers. My mother was a sister who could low moe cook. In today's nomenclature, you could interpret that to main: "The sista could through down in the kitchen." Her soft-to-the-palate, piping hot biscuits, chicken, rice, gravy and a variety of other culinary delights have fed the belly of many a satisfied reverend. And we children never resented the preacher fearing he may eat too much, because there was always a plenty. My father not only helped to build the church but, over the years, also held most if not all of the key leadership roles of steward, trustee, and superintendent of Sunday School, a position he held for more than fifty years. If asked, he would say he got to the third or fourth grade, but these positions were not just titles; he studied and knew the book of Discipline, the book of rules for the CME church. In addition, he studied and knew the Bible. When we were growing up, he took and read the daily paper. I remember him from time to time reading aloud a comic strip, called Hambone. I would just roll with laughter. He himself had a great sense of humor. He loved giving and raising money for the church. When taking a collection, quite often, he would break the ice so to speak with a joke, feeling perhaps once their funny bone was jarred, they would think of how good God had been to them causing them to give generously.

The greatest noted or public achievement of his life is he, as an officer of the Annual Conference and a delegate to the General Conference in 1954, in Memphis, had the opportunity to vote to change the name of the CME Church from Colored to Christian. That was a marvelous opportunity after eighty-four years. His name shall forever be part of the official record of that vote.

Before my father passed February 4, 2006, at 101 years of age, his lifetime of service to his country as a family man and a church and community leader was honored with legislation passed by Congress and signed into law by the president of the United States naming the Post Office in Parkdale, Arkansas, the Willie Vaughn Post Office.

He saw the legislation passed by Congress in October 2005; he died, however, before the dedication took place on Sunday, August 6, 2006.

This action was initiated by Congressman Danny K. Davis, a Parkdale native, who went to Chicago, earned a master's degree and then a doctorate, got involved in politics, got elected to: Chicago City Council, Cook County Commission, and Congress.

Congressman Davis grew up in Parkdale, and when he brought the idea to my father's Congressman Mike Ross he said he asked Danny, "weren't you born and raised there? And wouldn't that be an honor fit for you one day?" "No," Danny said, "if it had not been for Uncle Dude, I would not be in Congress today."

When this honor came, all my father's contemporaries, black and white, were deceased. So it was the children and grandchildren of his contemporaries, black and white, who grew up knowing Willie Vaughn, who took this action. The Parkdale City Council and the mayor unanimously in formal succession approved the resolution for the honor and sent it to Congress. At the dedication ceremony, in addition to Congressmen Mike Ross and Danny Davis, people came from all over the country—judges, bishops, law makers, educators, business owners and above all just plain folk.

So on the banks of Bayou Bartholomew, in a sleepy southern town in the last county down Highway 165 going into the State of Louisiana, history was made. It was said at the ceremony that the life of Willie Vaughn reflects the highest ideals of America's greatness.

CHAPTER 11

The Pathway to Greatness

1. Accept our blackness, recognize our beauty, and attain excellence.

*I*N *NOTES OF a Native Son*, 1955, James Baldwin states this about his father: "He knew that he was black but did not know that he was beautiful." That gap in nature was closed in 1966 when led by Stokely Carmichael; we finally taught that black is beautiful and screamed it with an articulate voice in a tone black folk heeded. Learning that we are black and beautiful, however, we now know by painful experience, is not all we need to lift us to our rightful place among the people of the earth. To climb to that proper perch, we must first as people reach for and attain excellence; we must create by our own initiative, imagination and intelligence a unifying, coherent and working public policy somewhere on this planet that produces, not excuses but, a first-class, first-world—not third-world—world-class society where people including us try hard to get in, not scramble hard to get out.

In the midst of many false, we need true leaders, gang rappers, and killers our hearts yearn to know and to perform this third bar of which has to be for us our holy trilogy needed for us to play our best music here in a strange land or anywhere else in the world. The holy trilogy is accept our blackness recognize our beauty and reach for and attain excellence. The first two, we have pretty much come to grips with; it is the third bar that holds what might yet be for us our greatest challenge. Our primary struggle right now is not to lose sight of the bright beacon light of hope.

Accepting our blackness was not easy. Nothing worthwhile rarely is. Unaware that "Negro" in Spanish means black and thinking perhaps that the word described us without identifying our color, some of us resisted being called black vigorously by saying we are all colors—brown, yellow, red and, because of the thoroughness of the way whites bread us, yes some of us are light enough to pass for white, all of this in the mistaken assumption that to deny a fact changes it. Over the years, those facts notwithstanding, the song of our blackness has been recorded: cynically by W. E. B. Du Bois's *The Souls of Black Folk* 1903 and positively by Richard Wright's *Black Boy* in the 1940s; but in the main, we still resisted being called by our color, because we thought it was the problem.

An example of resistance is shown in an incident one night in 1963, when a white man was approaching a jet-black man in an ally in the dark. The white could see only the form of a man and unable to make out who the person was he called out and the black who had beautiful white teeth laughed. Recognizing who the black was, the white said that because of darkness, he could not see any of the black's features till he laughed. This sent the black into a tizzy, for not only did we in that day not want to be called black, but also we did not want to be in any way associated in terms of our race or skin color with darkness or blackness. (The mantra at the time was if you are white, you are right; if you are brown, stick around; if you are black, get back. The quote to come was if you are black, join the pack; if you are white, get right; and if you are brown, don't clown). The white apologized and said that he had inadvertently broken a taboo that may not be acceptable in, perhaps, a thousand years. The taboo, like a house of cards, tumbled three years later in 1966, when blacks in a thunderous roar and with a mighty shout said we are black and we are proud. In the 1970s, James Brown told us all in a song to say it loud, "I'm black and I'm proud."

It took a long time for us to know we are black and some time further to know black is beautiful, and in a little while yet, we as people will achieve the rightness of excellence. In excellence is meant a community built on our initiative and intelligence that is prestigious, clean, and prosperous where because of our industry and brilliance, our streets are safe, our homes are secure, and the gaiety in the voices of our children is heard around the world.

To achieve this goal, we need a vehicle to get us there. We need to establish by our own initiative and intelligence a unifying, coherent, public policy that will take us to where we want to be. Its function would be to determine need or issues and set and achieve goals.

In community are general issues on which most members will agree: saving the lives of children, the most basic responsibility of any human society, is an example. Determining issues then is relatively easy; the difficulty is in building that public policy that molds agreement into an indelible plank in the standards of the community, making it so strong that no outside enemy nor an individual predator or hostile gangs inside of it, no matter how evil or contrary, can ever uproot and destroy the consensus of the people represented in the plank. This sense of purpose will be passed on from generation to generation.

It is because our failure to mold a unifying and coherent public policy that effectively protects us from ourselves and others that we have failed ourselves, our children, and our community. Our leaders, by not guiding us in devising such a policy, have failed to lead us in the way we should go; they have led us backward instead of forward.

That an individual, a group or gangs inside the community would find it impossible to destroy the plank is easily understood. But the effectiveness of the plank against an outside force, such as racism, is more of a challenge. This is so because whites have dominated us for hundreds of years; and because we submitted to their domination, we might think that we are totally incapable of building for our children a community that is safe, clean, and prosperous. We may think our competence to rear our children to be civilized human beings is an ideal further from our ability than the East is from the West. We may think that a powerful outside force such as racism may be too large and overwhelming. Even if a force such as racism is large and seems overwhelming, it can never distort the indelible quality of the plank; it will still hold; it is therefore indestructible. It would be then an intricate part of the character of the people. As long as the community itself lasts, the safety and the well-being of its children to the extent that it is humanly possible is assured.

SHELTON VAUGHN

Realistically speaking, whites are the cause of all, some, or none of blacks problems. There are some problems blacks have that whites play on but on close examination, the evidence shows that not one problem of substance of blacks is caused by whites. To conclude that, two assumptions must be made: blacks are human beings and whites are not God. Once these two assumptions are made, one ultimately sees a partnership of sorts emerge between us and whites; in it is niggerism in us and racism in whites and in a way each of these balances off the other. Eliminate black niggerism and white racism will have no host. Viewing the race problem from this perspective one sees us not so much as victims of white brutality only, but also of black niggerism; and one sees whites guiltiness being the crime of overreaching or racism. The Africans were fully capable of being brutal, but showed absolutely no facility for developing a public policy of being purposefully civil, for organizing themselves under a single banner to defend their honor instead, it was they who rounded us up, brought us to the shores of Africa and sold us to the white buyers. They acted as though they had no honor to defend or knew what it was. Noticing in essence this lest than human trait in us, whites took advantage of this condition, which they viewed as an obvious weakness and exploited it with as much arrogance and contempt as they could muster.

History is filled with examples of black niggerism. One of these occurred during the Revolutionary War when blacks showed by their actions that they did not want liberty because it was what they wanted but that they wanted liberty because it was what whites wanted. And in the end, whites got liberty and retained blacks as slaves. Blacks fought for white liberation from England. Whites in their fight for their liberty had on their side their own great ability as well as that of blacks, so in time, whites obtained their liberty and maintained blacks as slaves. Blacks' desire for their own liberty had no one fighting for it, not even them; so they were forced by arrogant whites to carry the burden of slavery to the end of the Civil War. And the insult of Jim Crow for another hundred years after slavery and the affront of racism and their own niggerism are still malignant parts of their daily fore. Remember the admonition of John Brown to Frederick Douglas: "Douglas," he said, "You say you are willing to fight to end slavery in America; but you know something, I'm not only willing to fight, I'm willing to die to end slavery in America." If blacks had had as much fire in the belly for their liberty as whites had for theirs or as the white Brown had for blacks, they would have fought against their oppressors with as much vigor as whites did against theirs. Whites saw that black behavior as a sign of stupidity, a lack of intelligence.

Determining the issue and learning what to do lead to the most daunting task of all—how to build the plank: Who should head the effort and why, what should the goal be, how to develop the public policy, and how in other words to reach and maintain the set goal?

There are tens of millions of us in the United States and hundreds of millions of us worldwide. Yet, wherever we are, we are considered to be a poor and powerless, third-world people. Some say this is so because we are black; I contend, however, that the difference between whites and blacks is behavior, not skin color. The reason whites dominate us is not because we are black but because of an almost complete lack of coherence and unity among us, and an over abundance of coherence and unity among them that advances their cause. In other words, whites have a coherent, unifying public policy that affirms their humanity and meets their needs all the time, and blacks do not. This is made evident in the Nat Turner rebellion during slavery when black slaves who, once their owners fell in the rebels' fight, were free but rather than joining the rebellion, they ran instead and alerted whites to the danger. Once whites were alerted, none of them (the whites) joined the rebels. They instead joined together, formed a posse, called out the militia, and began to hunt or wait in ambush to kill or capture the rebels. After the rebellion was put down, those slaves that betrayed it did not retain the freedom the rebels had won for them; they were reentered under the yoke of slavery and still retained as chattel property. And whites saw the traitor's actions as proof that enslavement was their proper lot. Said Thomas R. Dew, a professor at William and Mary College, "slavery was not as evil as Jefferson's generation had tended to believe, but was a necessary stage of human progress." "Moreover," he said, "from sheer practical considerations, the institution was an indispensable means of regulating Negroes, who were 'not ready' for freedom. Indeed, Negroes were 'vastly inferior' to whites and should not be liberated." Because in his view, free blacks would not work unless made to do so.

Today, because the action comes from within the race, the situation is more insidious, because a black with education, money, position or fame will take those resources and move out of our community where they are sorely needed and into the white community where they are not needed, and where most often he is not wanted. Such a move brands us more as an inferior, impulsive savage people than as an intelligent self-respecting people; for it conveys the sense that we lack intelligence needed to build a civilized community, and that the only way for one of us to experience the joy of living in a civilized community is to move out of ours and into the white, if they will let us.

SHELTON VAUGHN

Why, when there are so many of us, did we let whites enslave, segregate and, in other ways, abuse us? There is strength in numbers, but there is power in unity. We, our numbers notwithstanding, let whites enslave, segregate and, in other ways, abuse us, because we had no coherent, unifying public policy of our own to prevent domination. If there is no coherent, unifying public policy guiding our behavior, our strength of numbers can be used to make us serve the will of others, and that is what happened in this case.

I am hearing now from some black ministers and social scientists that we are a "we" people and that whites are an "I" people. They say that whites focus on the individual thus creating a society of self-centeredness. That is obviously not true, because it does not explain why whites are so powerful and we are so powerless, because "we" is more powerful than "I."

The strength of people is not in the individual; it is in their institutions. Without institutions to give their individual strength coherent power, they as a group will be forever powerless though they may have educated, wealthy, talented, and/or famous individuals. It is one thing to join whites as an individual; it is another to forge a coherent public policy, as Washington and King did, to lead blacks and whites to join together and work cooperatively for the common good.

We must develop positivity and discard negativity. The litany—whether we are educated or not, rich or not, famous or not, in a position of high authority and leadership or not—it is not uncommon to hear us say "Nobody speaks for me. I speak for myself. All blacks do not think alike. We are not a monolith." This in and of itself is a huge monolithic statement. There is, however, a perverse truth in the statement in that it does not speak for us, but it certainly does with a poisonous tongue speak against us. If thinking alike means we are monolithic, we are then a monolith, albeit negative. And here is a way to prove that we think alike; ask the next ten or the next ten thousand blacks you meet, liberally selected from each option in the litany, if they speak for all blacks, every response will most likely be the same, "No." If that is true, then we do think alike. The question becomes then not do we think alike but what kind of thinking alike we do, negative or positive, negative being against us and positive being for us? The unanimity of our views causes us, the leaders and the led, to act out in some very strange and dangerous ways against our best interest as people. The basis for this kind of thinking is not only spoken but written. In the book, *On Being Negro in America*, 1951, by Saunders Redding, he says, "When one presumes to speak for me he must reflect my mind so accurately that I find no source of disagreement with him," (if he had ended there, he would have made a good point; but he continued.) "to do this, he must be either a lack-brain parrot or a god." He, a black educator and author, sums up black sentiment, sums up the way most of us think and we think the way we think because that is the way we are taught. There may be many ways to test the veracity of his view. But it is both dangerous and erroneous. Its danger lies in its rigidity. Leaving no grounds for flexibility, it pens us each into our own little isolated space, preventing an openness for one to speak for all. It is erroneous, because there are times when one of us can and should speak for all of us most certainly on broad, general public-policy issues and concerns.

It also reduces us to the level of the animal saying essentially that our role is merely to eat and sleep and do what we are told by whites, because somebody has to think for us if we can't think for ourselves.

Why can't one of us speak for all? Why do we find it possible to thus speak negatively, and not positively affirming toward the race?

We generally answer such questions by saying that if someone has not spoken to us, how can one presume to speak for us? If one were to say that all blacks are human beings, would that offend him? If one would say that blacks would rather their children live than be killed, would that offend him? Thomas Jefferson said that "all men are created equal," Did that offend him? It is likely that he would be in full agreement with each of these statements and would not think the speaker to be a lack-brain parrot nor a god. Now there certainly are times when what a person says should only be for himself or for a limited number of people he is authorized to represent. If someone invites him to a party, he or his representative should be the ones to accept or reject. So it is not all or nothing. Putting it simply, there are times when one should speak for all and there are times when one should not. But because one might presume to speak for you when one should not, that error should not mean that no one, except a lack-brain parrot or a god, should ever presume to speak for all of us on any subject at any time.

And we see this concept of one speaking for all exercised readily among us by whites. We hear them say the American people want this or that—that Europeans prefer this to this; that whites are a civilized race, a superior race. And at any given point in time, one might find a white waxing well about the principles of western man, meaning white. In the Declaration of Independence, Thomas Jefferson said, "All men are created equal," and again, some black say meaning whites. In none of these examples has the speaker spoken to every white. Yet in each of the instances, he chooses to speak for them. Evidently, they recognize a positive in speaking for each other. And we do not see the danger in speaking against each other and are too lead headed to know there are positives in speaking for each other.

It may be true that the "positive" Jefferson said, he said for whites but because he said it, even though he said it for them we can claim it too. Positivity, therefore, helps all. Negativity on the other hand hurts all. Positivity helps the positive most, and negativity hurts the negative most. Whites benefit more from Jefferson's positive assumption than blacks, and blacks are hurt more by their negative assumptions than others. Whites thought enough alike in the positive vein to enslave us, and we thought enough alike in the negative vein to let it happen. We must stop presuming not to speak for all blacks and start presuming when it is appropriate to speak for all blacks as well as for all mankind.

Sometimes, we put blinders over our mental eye when a light of truth is turned on. A lady, a very vigorous, energetic and high-achieving lady (the fact that these adjectives accurately describe her), make me tremble for the future of our people; but then in a minute, I think of the white man's thoughts in the ally of a thousand years ending in three, and it gives me hope. But this lady said to me that she had asked an individual white if he spoke for all whites and that he had said, "No," also.

And I told her about two women who were invited to a wedding. One of them had more than twenty-five hundred dresses, gowns, and frocks, and thousands of pairs of shoes for practically every occasion under the sun; but upon receiving the invitation, she said, "I don't have anything to wear." The other woman coming in from a field trip, her house had just burned to the ground, and the only clothes she had were those torn, dirty, and sweaty ones on her back. Her response upon receipt of the invitation was, "I don't have anything to wear." Each of these women used the same exact words, but had they said the same exact thing?

In the Declaration of Independence, there are three very telling words: savage, barbarous, and civilized. We know that the framers of the founding documents of the United States called us savages; but in the Declaration of Independence, the adjective used to modify savage is barbarous. They used the phrase "barbarous savage Indians." We know that they made a sharp distinction on how they treated our humanity and that of the Indians. They did not count the Indians, so they essentially were zero. They counted us as three fifth human. This for us, however, was a negative count, which in effect made us three-fifth less than zero in terms of our humanness. The three-fifth count was not to get representation for us in the Congress at a lesser rate; it was to assure more representation in the centers of power and authority against us. So since they called both us and the Indians savages, but gave to the Indians a higher status than us, and used the adjective phrase "barbarous savage" when referring to them, I sought and found the adjective they used to define us. The phrase they used to describe us was "impulsive savage," just the opposite of reasonable man.

In the view of whites, impulse not reason is the dictate in us, and in themselves, they say it is reason. Impulse is baser than reason. Reason is on a higher realm than impulse. Reason therefore is superior to impulse. A reasonable people will rule and dominate an impulsive people.

In the Constitution, the framers had no problem joining us in speaking against us: "Article I Section 9: The Migration or importation of such Persons," meaning us, "as any of the States now existing shall think proper to admit, shall not be prohibited by the Congress prior to the Year one thousand eight hundred and eight, but a Tax or duty may be imposed on such Importation, not exceeding ten dollars for each Person." As we do not think it unreasonable to talk against us, they joined us in exercising that sentiment.

Since I cannot be everywhere and cannot hear everything said about me, I have no problem having all other blacks to speak for me on those broad public-policy issues which assert the quality of our humanity. I would rather have them speak for me than against me, which has been our pattern historically and is still our pattern today. If we had granted each other such permission earlier on, it is unlikely that the slave trade would have occurred, because the resulting unanimity of our strength and level of our sophistication would have equaled or exceeded that of those who enslaved us.

History defines three levels of human development: savage, barbaric and civilized. Savage is discussed above. Barbaric people are in the main careless and brutal, but do what they do for a reason, they lack the refinement of the civilized men. Impulse is an animalistic subhuman trait.

2. The Importance of the Black Church

It is hard to pinpoint exactly when deterioration of the black church began. All we know is that we woke up one day during the past forty years and our streets were red, our homes and families were in shambles, more babies were being born out of wedlock than in the bonds of holy matrimony, more children were having babies than women, and that the black church had let it happen, for it and it alone had the admonition of the scriptures as its basic guide.

Pastors blame members and others and members blame pastors and others. And because of the blame game progress may be a long way off.

What is in its favor, however, is that both pastors and members want to restore the family to health, stop the flow of blood, and make life in the black community a joyous experience.

Here are some suggestions for pastors since they head congregations and by the position they hold are considered to be leaders: They should form a general ministerial alliance for the sole purpose of devising and implementing policies that restore the family to health by making it whole again, by making it clear that where children are concerned an unbroken family has a husband and a wife and at least one child, and that any other arrangement where children are concerned is a faulty or broken home, no matter the reason. The reason for the brokenness should be explained, not ignored. The three main reasons for broken or fractured homes are (1) out of wedlock births, (2) separation and/or divorce of father and mother, (3) or death of the mother or father. They should get the most current statistical data on out-of-wedlock births and the number or percentage of families with only a mother or father in the home and set as a minimal objective of reaching the goal of restoring the family to what it was in the 1930s when 80 to 85 percent of black families was headed by a husband and a wife in the home.

They should seek to develop a level of respect for life strong enough to cause a complete reversal in the high-homicide and suicide rates now entrenched in our community.

Some, the cynics, may say that I have too much confidence in pastors, because today they are too bigshotty to cooperate in such alliance. I do not know about big shottiness, nor even stiff-necked pastors; but I do know something about the black church.

In the novel *To Kill a Mockingbird*, by Harper Lee, are these words: "Negroes worshipped in it on Sundays and white men gambled in it on weekdays." The "it" is the "First Purchase African M.E. Church," so called, "because it was paid for from the first earnings of freed slaves. It was the only church in Maycomb with a steeple and bell." If a black pastor and his congregation can re-sanctify every Sunday a place white men desecrated by gambling in it every week, there is no doubt that the pastors and their congregations can, if they choose, restore our homes and families to health, stop the blood letting, and make the church once again a tower of confidence and a moral compass in black society.

3.   A Season in Montgomery

It was an interesting time, when we were on our way to our first truly, massive victory in history, coherent in a common cause to benefit everyone. Now we had a man comfortable enough in his blackness, grounded enough in his training, determined enough in his purpose, and capable enough in his abilities to lead us and all the people of Montgomery and of the United States of America to a proper resolution of a lingering problem and an immediate crisis.

The problem went back before the foundation of the nation, to a time when whites ruled over us with complete and unquestioned authority, to a time when the Supreme Court, itself, said we had no right whites were bound to respect, to a time when we were bought and sold by white gentlemen who traded in the flesh of men on the auction block in the market place, and to a time when whites told us that they owned us body and soul.

And while our limited rationality told us the claim of owning our soul was not true, we made no attempt openly to disprove the claim. But we did wonder if they owned our souls, who owned theirs. Because when they came to died, they had no more control over their passing than we did over ours. They could send us to fetch things; they could be brutal to our bodies, and they certainly tried very hard to crush our spirit, but an order to die for one when his time came was curiously never given. And if it had been it would have been to no effect, for somebody else was in charge of both of our souls. So the claim of owning us body and soul was merely pompous, rhetorical bombast.

The crisis was brought by three things: the refusal of a black woman to get up and give her seat to a white man, the arrest of her for the refusal, and the response of the black community to her arrest.

Kicking blacks off buses or making them give their seats to whites was nothing new; it had been going on for a long time. It was something of a ritual, a black would get on the bus and take a seat in the black section. A white would get on after all seats in the white section was taken; the drive then, if the black in the forward seat did not jump up on his own, would order the black to get up and give his seat to the white. If the black refused, the driver then would order him off the bus. If he refused, and some did, the driver then would call the police and they would come and arrest the black.

So ordering blacks out of their seats and off the bus and arresting them was nothing new; the new element here was the unified, coherent response the black community made under committed leadership to the arrest, which of itself was routine. The unusually coherent and purposeful response of the black community lifted a quiet, dignified, unassuming black woman returning home from work on a city bus from obscurity into the bright high beam of history. Little did she or her adversaries know that they were about to write a page in history, that her return home that day in Montgomery was to be anything but routine.

Blacks' response to this arrest demonstrates a powerful lesson, for it not only defines racism, but it also identifies its cause. Racism is an evil in whites direct against blacks. The feed for racism is an ineptness in blacks that let whites practice it against them. Racism is not a natural phenomenon, and nor is this ineptitude. They are behaviors and attitudes manifested in each race. In this encounter, the black woman stood up by staying seated and forcing whites into the stance of bully. By standing up she showed blacks' unwillingness to accept the refusal of whites to let them ride the bus in dignity. Whites recognizing a lack of ineptness on the part of blacks and, therefore being without blacks' permission to bully them, open up the bus to first come first served. Victory came for the blacks because they struggled united and dignifiedly, and respect came from whites when they saw in blacks not ineptness but something closely resembling coherent human intelligence. This tells blacks that their problem is not color nor race but ineptitude, a.k.a., niggerism.

4.   The Leadership

Blocked by slavery, Jim Crow, and self-flagellation, blacks' trip to greatness is yet to be. Slavery ended in a ball of fire in Sherman's March through Georgia to the sea, and Jim Crow ended with Dr. King's lead of determined marches in the streets, and self-flagellation among us is still a raging storm. Realistically speaking, whites are the cause of all, some, or none of blacks' problems. To make our trip successfully, we must harness our rage and use the force of the storm to speed us on our way. The race problem is rooted and manifested in both races. Dr. King was right: A man cannot ride your back unless it's bent. We not only let white ride our backs, but we have now bent our backs to make his ride more comfortable. In whites, it is racism; in blacks, it is ineptitude or lack of initiative; whites dominate; blacks submit. Submission is the effect of ineptitude or lack of initiative in blacks, and dominance is the result of racism in whites. Racism is an attitude generated in whites, after observing certain careless behaviors in Africans toward each other. This behavior created a conviction in whites that made them think that they could not only do anything they chose to Africans but they could also make Africans do anything as well; and that because they are inferior to whites, whites have the right to discriminate against them. A racist is any white who feels or thinks that way. In this context, all racists are white, but all whites are not racists. There is no form of human life more evil than a racist. Any human being with the ability to reason and exercise judgment earnestly, should understand that racism is evil and vile. It is evil because it harms human personality in both the perpetrator and the target. It is vile because it affronts the dignity of man, and distorts human relations. It makes what should be normal grotesque and what is beautiful criminal. It gives one race the status of a god and denies the humanity of the other. But, on close examination, the evidence shows that not one problem of substance of blacks is caused by whites. Even so, racism is the most evil reality ever to infect human personality. To reach this conclusion, two assumptions must be made: blacks are human beings and whites are not God. These assumptions make each race responsible for its own choices.

Ultimately then blacks are more the victim of their own ineptness than of white brutality. It is their ineptness that gives whites license to commit against them the crime of overreaching or racism.

Racism in whites and ineptness in blacks faced off hundreds of years ago on the shores of Africa, when African chiefs, kings, and potentates rounded up their tribal brothers and sold them to white buyers. As each encountered each, one gained dominance. And their relationship of dominance and forced submission has ebbed and flowed continuously in its intensity over the years. In the early years, blacks were treated as indentured servants; efforts were made to Christen them; they owned property; and whites saw themselves as English, German, etc. then slavery, then Jim Crow, then post-Jim Crow.

This is an inviolable law rooted in the principle that we teach people how to treat us. What will we accept? Slavery? We will be enslaved. Segregation? We will be segregated. It, perhaps, would be nice if there were a people who, on their own, would not do evil things, and would be nice to us because they are nice. But that is not the dictate in nature's laws. By its dictate, we must first respect ourselves. If this is done, that very fact alone demands that others do the same. When this principle is adhered to by a people, others feel bound by their choice and will adhere to it as well. Violation of this principle against a self-respecting people is cause for the violator to be concerned.

For centuries, blacks have left the choice of being nice to them by whites to whites. That is like giving the choice to suck eggs to a suck-egg dog. If the choice is left solely to the dog, he will always suck the eggs. If the choice whether whites abuse blacks is left solely to whites, blacks will be abused by whites forever.

The odd thing is, however, that over the centuries, whites have been for better to blacks than blacks have been to themselves. And blacks reward them with gratitude in many ways. One way they do it today is by trying to get under their rule, for it is from Africa and from the islands of the sea as Haiti that blacks try hard to get to America and under the rule of whites, and blacks in America, once they get money, position, or education, or fame, try hard to move into white areas and, once they have done so, think that they have made a move up.

The Africans were fully capable of being brutal, but showed hardly any facility for developing a public policy of being purposefully civil, for organizing themselves under a single banner to defend their honor; instead, they acted as though they had no honor to defend. Noticing this quirk in their nature, whites exploited it in the past and still do today to a lesser degree, with as much arrogance and contempt as they choose to use.

A prime example of black ineptness occurred during the Revolutionary War when they showed by their actions they did not want liberty because it was what they wanted, but because it was what whites wanted. And in the end, whites got liberty and retained blacks as slaves. Blacks fought and died for white liberation from England. Whites in their fight for their liberty had on their side their own great ability as well as that of blacks, so in time success was theirs. Blacks' desire for their liberty had no one fighting for it, not even them, so they were forced by arrogant whites to carry the burden of slavery to the end of the Civil War and the insult of Jim Crow for another hundred years after slavery, and the affront of racism and their ineptness they still carry to this day. Claud Anderson, EdD, in *Dirty Little Secrets*, 1997, draws a comparison between Frederick Douglas and John Brown, a white man, who died for blacks' freedom; "History suggests that Frederick Douglas did not mind being a black hero, but he did not want to be a black martyr." If blacks had had as much fire in the belly for their liberty as whites had for theirs or as John Brown had for blacks, they would have fought against their oppressors with as much vigor and unity as whites did against theirs. Whites no doubt saw that malady in black behavior as a sign of stupidity, a lack of intelligence.

5. Intelligence and Race

If blacks say they are as intelligent as whites, but it is blacks who are enslaved by whites, and it is blacks who are always dancing to the orders of whites, pretty soon the claim of equal intelligence began to sound like a phony claim, especially to whites.

To the question, whether blacks are as intelligent as whites, most blacks say, "Yes." And there the discussion generally ends. But the question being asked here is, if blacks are intelligent as whites, why are whites more powerful than blacks? Because to the question, are whites more powerful than blacks, most blacks answer, "Yes." The next question is one most blacks do not ask, which is, is not the degree of people's power evidence of their level of intelligence? To this question, a "yes" or "no," most blacks feel leaves them where they are already, behind the eight ball. But I do not see it that way. I think posing the question and dealing with it openly and earnestly is a sign of a maturing people. It gives them a chance to express points of view that cannot help but enhance their understanding of how best to elevate their standing in the world.

First, there has to be a comprehensive, working definition of intelligence in the context of human development. One definition of intelligence in this context is how well people treat themselves as a group as well as each person individually, looking at those actions they take to enhance or diminish their humanity.

Superior intelligence is of two types, proven and unproven. Whites have proven theirs; blacks must yet do so. It is in this chasm where hope for black development resides. And it is also where the real dispute is between whites and blacks. Whites say that because blacks have not yet built a world-class community, they are therefore a lazy, sully and stupid, impulsive savage people designed by nature to be in subjugation to whites.

Whites and blacks define intelligence differently. Whites define intelligence more broadly than blacks. Whites say it is the ability to set a coherent public policy that works for the common good; blacks say it is merely the ability to get good grades in school. So when a black goes to Harvard and graduate summa cum laude, he thinks he has proved false the charge by whites that he is stupid. But he has not. He has merely proved that he can absorb academic curricula. To prove, when he comes out of college, he is intelligent from a humanly social prospective, he must demonstrate that he knows not only what to do but also how to use what he has been taught in academia to cause, as whites do, his community to cohere as a unit of human civility. The sign of human intelligence as defined by whites is not if a being can be taught. They pride themselves on their ability to teach many types of animals, including horses, cats, dogs and now there is an industry of sort around elephant art. Whites, view of intelligence is comprehensive; they see it as a desire to achieve academically, true; but they see it also as an opportunity to serve, to accumulate wealth, to build complex economy, to build world-class, top-of-the-line community and the ability to build abstract social systems—political, religious, economic, civic and educational—that work so well that others beg for permission to enter them. In this matrix of intelligence only one item is looked at with any degree of seriousness by blacks, and that is education and this only by a few blacks. Whites know intelligence of a people is for more than mere academic absorption or the accumulation of wealth by a few individuals. So knowing this and knowing blacks do not, they will educate blacks academically and still tell them what to do, when to do, where to do, and how to do. Seeing blacks as lazy, meaning they lack initiative and stupid, meaning they do not know how to set among themselves a coherent public policy that raises the standards of their community to equal that of whites.

Whites would not dare teach them why things are done. Whites' thought is that an intelligent people do not need to be taught why. And that to teach a stupid people why would do no good and would be a waste of time.

6.   The Bravery of a Black Pastor

There was an educated young Methodist minister in the 1930s assigned by his bishop to a church in Oklahoma. The structure of the church was very dilapidated. The members said when it rained, it rained in the church and leaked outside. Upside-down washtubs were used for steps. Windows had long ago lost their glass; sticks were set in crosswise to reduce warping; pews got soaked when it rained; when dry, they formed creases that made sitting not only uncomfortable but also hazardous, for one ran the risk of being stuck by a splinter.

It was in the face of the need of the repair or replacement of this physical structure that the youthful preacher took charge with great hope, when one day he got a congenial invitation from a leading white citizen of the city. He received the invitation not with excitement. His apprehension was well founded of course. This was the decade that saw the blowtorch lynching in Winona, Mississippi, of Roosevelt Townes and Bootjack McDaniels.

But he kept his appointment. The citizen was pleasant. And after a moment of pleasantries, he got down to business. He had noticed the disrepair of the church, and he wanted to be of help. He then pulled from his desk draw a large, neatly folded canvas, opened it, and asked the preacher to inspect the image thereon. On the canvas was the image of a beautiful red brick church with a concrete walkway leading from the road to the entrance, windows trimmed in white, and a steeple for a bell tower, and a layout of the inside was also very attractive and just as elaborate.

"Do you know what you see, Reverend?"

"I see the image of a marvelous church."

"But that's not all you see. You are looking at your church."

"Well, no sir, this looks nothing like my church."

"You are talking 'bout your old church. This is your new church."

At that instant, he remembered a lesson from his father: Nobody gives anything for nothing. Then he asked the citizen what did he have in mind. The citizen offered to build this church for the preacher if he would vote against Walter White, the man who had proved to be the greatest anti-lynching fighter in American history. How could he possibly vote against Walter White who was doing so much to help save the lives of colored people?

He was caught between a rock and a hard place. If he rejected the offer, it could upset the citizen. And the upset citizen could kill him or have him murdered and be considered a hero for having killed a colored. And yet if he were to accept the offer, he would go against the teachings of his father, which was to never do anything that would bring shame on his people.

When he opened his mouth, God spoke for him. He said to the citizen, "You do not want me with you if I vote against Walter White, where will I go?"

The citizen looked amazed as though he had just seen the preacher as a human being for the first time, as though he thought he was dealing not with a "nigger boy" but with a man God blessed with enough sense to have self-respect, though his skin was black as tar.

A year later a man trained in masonry at Tuskegee Institute came to town. The pastor got to know him and talked to him about building a church; and, he then went back to the citizen and let him know about what his congregation would like to do, if it would be okay with him. The citizen not only gave his wholehearted approval but a hefty donation to help out.

SHELTON VAUGHN

7. The Killing of a Good Grandfather and Hope

A man who had done it all right. He had been a good youth, a husband and father, and now he was being a good grandfather on the day, which was to be his last. This day, he had come to visit his daughter and to spend sometime with his six-year-old grandson, who, according to both his mother and father, had been a good boy around the house and had received good grades in school.

And it was for these reasons and because he wanted to spend some special time alone with his grandson, the grandfather decided to take the young fellow to the corner store for a treat. That trip turned out to be fatal for the grandfather.

They walked to the store, man and boy, grandfather and grandson. They went into the store; the man paid for the treat, they came out of the store, and less than one hundred feet from the entrance to the store, the man was shot accidentally by a stray bullet, killed in a crazy act of random violence, by a man in the drug culture shooting at someone else.

While the body was still lying on the sidewalk, on lookers began to gather. The media, the police and emergency medical ambulance came in that order. After stating that drugs were sold on this corner daily and that there were drug houses around there in all directions of the campus, north and east, south and west, the media man pushed a microphone in the face of a citizen and asked, "Why do you think this happen?" The citizen answered with one word, "Crack."

When I researched this response, I found that most blacks thought that was a good response.

It seems ironic that as blacks, during the decade of the 1970s, were making certain gains, crime was drowning out the glory. Homicide reached its peak in several ways: While during that decade in Detroit, the first black took office as mayor and appointed the first black police thief, and African Americans became dominate in politics and education. We gained a majority: on City Council, the school board, and as principals and teachers. And we took over the position of superintendent of schools. Yet the 1970s was the deadliest decade Detroit has ever had; and, 1974, the year the mayor took office, was the deadliest ever, upwards of eight hundred homicides. The city has averaged well over five hundred homicides per year from 1968 through the end of 2003.

In Dearborn, homicide ranges about one in thirty to fifty thousand; in Detroit, it ranges about one in one to two thousand.

I believe that with the formula that follows, we can bring Detroit in line with Dearborn. This means that we can reduce homicides in Detroit from over five hundred average per year to twenty to fifty per year at most.

W. E. B. Du Bois, though excusing it for blacks, said over a hundred years ago, "The greatest deterrent to crime is the public opinion of one's community."

Surveys show that African Americans in Detroit, to the question would you rather your sons and daughters live than be killed, answered not only with statistical numbers as high as the residents of Dearborn, but also their "yes" response was offered with stamina and vigor.

When I found this to be the case, I then began to look for the cause of the big disparity between the two communities, Detroit being mostly black and Dearborn being mostly white. Why with such similar views about this issue, the reality in the two communities in terms of safety was so vastly different?

The potential for success is in that reservoir of desire. My research in the sample that follows will in effect show Detroiters how to make their desire for safety a reality in their community.

Here is one example of what I found: In 1981, Detroit had just come through the bloodiest decade in its history. Homicides in the city had been occurring at the rate of over one a day since 1968. In deed during the 1970s, Detroit gained infamy in the title, "Murder Capital of the Nation." This was true, despite the fact that my research showed that blacks and whites, at that time and now for the past the thirty odd years, have done essentially the same things for their children. In politics in America, blacks like whites have ascended to practically every position from top to bottom, both elected and appointed, except only one, the presidency of the United States and it is likely that will be obtained one day.

In education, blacks like whites have seen their sons and daughters graduate from Harvard, Yale, Princeton and other major colleges and universities. And these graduates have earned degrees in these school's bachelor's, master's, and doctoral programs. Blacks have had their children ascend to the presidency of major colleges and universities. In athletics blacks have received huge salaries for displaying their talents in their chosen athletic activity, plus huge amounts in product-endorsement contracts, which some times exceeded their salaries. In entertainment, blacks have reigned as most popular recording artist in Michael Jackson and the most popular and top quality television programs in the *Cosby Show* in prime time and the *Oprah Winfrey Show* during the day. In the movies, Eddie Murphy,

SHELTON VAUGHN

Denzel Washington and others as actors have gained top credits. Spike Lee, John Singleton and others as producers and directors have reached the top in their fields.

In business, Reginald Lewis, in the Beatrice Foods buyout, has pulled off at least one multibillion-dollar deal. In religion, blacks like whites have pastors with earned doctoral degrees from leading divinity schools and theological seminaries. And according to the Church World News Service, a greater percentage of blacks go to church than whites, 52 percent for blacks to 39 percent for whites. In civic endeavors, especially in Optimism, which came to blacks in Detroit in 1968, blacks not only offer black children the same optimist activities—oratorical, essay, etc.—as whites, but black children also speak and write on the same subjects and win a fair share of the same prizes.

Yet though blacks and whites during the past thirty plus years have done essentially the same exact things for their children, the result, as reflected in each of their communities, is vastly different. In the white community, for instance, is found social hope and civility; in the black community is found social despair and criminality. In the white community is found moral health and vigor—more babies born in the bond of holy matrimony than out and more babies born to women than to children.

In the black community, it is just the opposite. In their community is found infamy and moral depravity: More babies are born out of wedlock than in the bonds of holy matrimony, and more babies are born to children than to women. This condition has caused one loving black woman in a sense of moral outrage to say, "We are bastardizing the black race." In the white community is economic abundance and a high level of safety and prestige, which blacks are begging to get in. In the black community is economic devastation and a high level of crime and danger, and blacks are begging and scrambling to get out. If the list of achievements and desires of blacks is true and the facts are unarguable, this vast difference within the two communities, for the most part, is found not in what they teach or do for their children, but in why.

In other words, whites teach their children for one set of reasons and blacks teach their children for another. Whites do, for instance, for their children because they see in them qualities of civility that allow them to carry on a pattern of productive social discourse. They pride themselves in being able to discuss, accommodate, compromise and resolve issues relative to the well-being of their community.

During white America's discussion whether to send troupes to feed the starving black Somali people, I heard white Americans from the president down to the white man on the street, say America should carryout the mission because Americans are civilized people. I heard that mantra repeated at least ninety-two times in a period of ninety days. I can truly say that I have never heard a black leader refer to black people as civilized people.

Whites do for their children because they see in them the ability to solve problems. White people go about daily in their community looking for problems that need solutions and, once they find a problem whether it is crime, a lack of morality or a lack of good, quality business outlets in the neighborhood, they pull together and find a solution for the problem. Blacks, on the other hand, lacking a language of safety, go about in their community looking for ways not to improve it but to get out of it and into the white community. The scramble to get out makes them who leave feel slimy and those who stay, trapped.

Whites do for their children because they see in them the ability to build a desirable community; they see in them the ability to build community that is safe, clean and prosperous. Blacks, on the other hand, do for their children, and this is the heart of the matter because (1) they want to keep them off the streets (2) they want to keep them out of trouble and (3) they want to keep them off drugs.

And ironically it is for these reasons (problems in the streets, trouble in the neighborhood and dope heads) that blacks have a bleeding persona, a bleeding family and a bleeding community. However, others say blacks are bleeding because they are lazy and stupid and depreciate the value of property and point to where ever they rule in the world, whether on the continent of Africa or in the islands of the sea, such as Madagascar or Haiti or in the black enclaves in America, as proof that blacks fail to manifest the basic human intelligence necessary to build a community whose tenants are safety, cleanliness and prosperity.

(Here is an aside: a sixty-seven-year-old upstanding widow lived in her niece's well-kept home in a floral setting including azaleas, petunias, daffodils, sunflowers and more. With her husband gone, except for a sorry son who came occasionally, she was basically alone. But she had been active in the community in civic endeavors, so she had a lively circle of friends. This day, she had a few friends over for brunch and some chitchat. Crime had hit twice on her block during the past twelve months. One homicide occurred mid-block and another next door. Now it is reasonable to fear when that kind of criminality strikes so close, but what she said scared the living day lights out of me.

Someone said black leaders, judges, pastors, school teachers, in other words, our best-educated, able and moneyed folks were moving to the suburbs.

This lady said her pastor lives in the suburbs and she was glad he did, and if she could, she would too. Yes, she was so beaten down by these people—her leaders—that she expected no leadership from them in improving the social condition in the black community, while sitting in misery wishing she could move out with them to the suburbs. The other voices chimed support of her wish. The person raised the point clammed up and said no more.

Then I thought what kind of people are we really that our leaders would treat their own people so neglectful that they would expect nothing of them, while filled with an empty wish that has as much chance of success as a snowball in hell. When I realized that the role of leaders is to inspire their people to greatness, I must say I saw in that scene one dark hour).

The black challenge today is to build desirable community, to build community that reflects black initiative and intelligence and black genius, to build community that is safe, clean and prosperous. Till we do this, individual black achievement can never be glorified, can never have a place in which it can properly reside. The inevitable question is, can we do it? Can we do it!

The proposition is the toughest request ever asked of black people in more than six thousand years. It will seem to go against the molecular stretcher of black DNA; it will seem also to go against every fiber in black bodies, but it is worth doing. And if done, it will pay great social benefits and untold economic dividends. The request is that black people never again offer their sons and daughters opportunities in life to keep them off the streets, out of trouble or off drugs. Let us instead extend opportunity to our children for the exact same reasons and expectations as whites and then watch the black community bloom and blossom with safety, cleanliness and prosperity, thus reflecting the intelligence and genius of black people. I know there will be some blacks and perhaps others who will inevitably resent the fact that blacks would no longer have to beg to move into the white community to feel safe and to be in a prestigious neighborhood. But to that sick and despicable drivel, I say, so what.

The Bible says, the truth will make you free, and James Russell Lowell put it in poetic terms when he said, "Truth forever on the scaffold, wrong forever on the throne, yet that scaffold sways the future, and behind the dim unknown standeth God within the shadow, keeping watch above his own." Can we do it?

I shared the essence of the findings presented here with members of an optimist club. To a person, each of them was not only very impressed, but they also admitted using these negative reasons with both their own children as well as those they serve in the community.

What really sealed for them the validity of the argument was when, during Q and A, I asked them this question, "Which would you prefer, someone say, I will give you a full scholarship to go to college because I want to keep you off the streets (from becoming a whore or a pimp), out of trouble (a thief, a killer, etc.), or off drugs (a dope head); or I will give you a full scholarship because I think you are intelligent and smart, and that once you graduate, you can apply your knowledge to help transform the hood, as a leader in business, politics, religion, or civic affairs?" The former is slimy; the latter is edifying.

There are literally thousands of such faux pas expressed by blacks daily to their detriment while earnestly thinking they are helping their cause; but when in actuality, they are digging for their community a deeper hole of crime.

People then are basically the language they speak. We must begin to speak a better language in our community. I believe that we can learn and speak the language of excellence. And we need now the opportunity to learn it. I believe that once we learn it, we will speak it and speak it wonderfully well.

8.   False Leaders

Webster's Dictionary defines impulsiveness as a "propensity or natural tendency, usually other than rational" and reasonableness as "possessing sound judgment."

After having taken the mantle of leadership from the guidance of Dr. Martin Luther King Jr., it was the duty of Jesse Jackson and Andrew Young and others to lead us forward, to help us set and reach goals, and to help us learn and cultivate some of the basic qualities of civilized people, which are self-respect, trustworthiness, courage and fortitude.

Teaching us respect for ourselves would have developed in us a center core of decency that would have brought out the best in us, instead of as it turned out, our worse after Dr. King's death. As a virtue, respect has no bounds when it is properly focused. So once we had learned it, it would not only have improved our attitudes toward each other individually, but the whole race. And once we had learned this virtue, we could have then applied its principles to all people and things deserving it. This would have helped us build goodwill among ourselves and in the hearts of other people.

There is a difference between helping the race write its headline than using the race to help you write yours. If Andrew Young, for instance, had used his mantle of leadership inherited from Dr. King properly, he would have helped us write our headline of virtue, which would have said that the black community in Atlanta is the safest and cleanest in the whole Atlanta area and he would have benefited from such a headline, as well as the greater community of mankind: result: a win-win.

But by using us to elect him congressman and mayor of Atlanta and his accepting the office as the U.S. representative at the U.N., he gained personal achievements that made headlines for him, while the void left by his lack of leadership in the black community wrote a headline not of honor but of horror, death and slaughter, headlines in the murdered blood of the sons and daughters of black people.

Likewise of Jesse Jackson. If he had by carrying forward the work of the Southern Christian Leadership Conference by helping us write our own headline of excellence instead of seeking merely to write his own, perhaps, over 90 percent of the black males in prison would be leading productive lives as husbands and fathers as heads of their households. But instead, he used his blackness to help him write personal headlines, when both he and Young, using the mantle of leadership inherited by them from Dr. King, could have followed the example of their mentor, Dr. King, and helped us write positive headlines for the whole entire race and the nation.

9.   Dr. Martin Luther King Jr.

Dr. Martin Luther King. Jr. came armed with the philosophy of nonviolence, the force of love, a strategy for action, and a compendium of various tactics, including marching in the streets, all for the purpose of transforming the jingling discords of the nation into a beautiful symphony of brotherhood. He had studied whites very carefully, for he knew to be successful he would have to know what makes them tick, their strengths and weaknesses. To help him in this process, he reviewed their record, including their major actions of the twentieth century, two world wars and the cold war. After much analysis, he looked forward to the future, thinking of what it had in store for America in general and for us in particular for in his analysis, he had learned basically that whites want three things—love, money and power—and that we wanted to stop scratching when not itching and laughing when not tickle. We wanted also to learn to respect ourselves and to be respected by whites, and his great lesson to us was that for us to achieve these goals we would have to rise to our best potential as people created in the image of God and build the beloved community. This stance was very credible, for he was indeed a man of faith, a minister and a pastor.

The analysis showed the strategy of nonviolence was not new to America for she was using it effectively in the cold war against the Soviet Union. He knew in the history of America was a violent Civil War. So he decided to use her current example of a nonviolent war with the Soviets to reduce the arrogance of whites and to infuse blacks with hope. His analysis showed that a lie cannot last forever and that truth trounced to the ground will rise again.

He wanted whites not to confuse fear with respect and, therefore, he wanted to get through to them the point that it is in their best interest to allow blacks some hope before the long campaign of fear began to fail and began to be replaced with hate. Because when feared you can control, but when hated you cannot. His choice to them was to be loved or hated.

So instead of having another civil war of violence, he led a civil war, called the civil rights movement, of nonviolence. And again, like the first, the right side won. And a grateful nation honored him as the lone American born citizen with a red letter day on the calendar. The honor is most astounding when men, some of whom once considered themselves to be the vilest and the most vicious reprobates against us ever born of woman, voted this honor upon him posthumously in the Congress of the United States, and the law providing this was signed by the president.

Integration is not putting dogs with cats or cats with people. It is putting people with people or, in this case, race with race. It is about two groups—one white and one black—finding a way to mutually benefit each other.

Obviously, this cannot mean only physical closeness, because we cannot be closer physically to whites than we were during slavery. Because then they were in our vaginas continuously if heterosexual, and our anus if homo. And by the laws of nature humans cannot get physically more closer to each other than that. But not even those blacks rushing into white neighborhoods today are calling that closeness integration. I have heard more than one call that closeness, under the circumstance, rape.

Integration then is yet to be defined, or is it? I think there is a proper definition in the example of the life and leadership of Dr. King. For sure integration is not merely physicality. And it certainly connotes something of equal or relevant value of both parties. It then is not all one way; it is

SHELTON VAUGHN

an intermixing. If the effort is all one way, it is not integration; it is an invasion. Before, therefore, a black moves into a white neighborhood, he should have acted to cause a white to move or want to move into a black neighborhood.

In my research, both in reading and listening, I have never found one person who understood Dr. King's definition of integration taught by the example of his life. Though it was obvious and there for all the world to see, it still escaped most of us, because as I have said it requires something of us; and it was refused by whites because they saw him as an anomaly who once off the scene would see us revert to our old ways of kicking each other, rather than reaching for excellence in the cooperative spirit of building the beloved community, which had been the hallmark of his journey here. They knew that his definition of integration was being missed by us and that certainty suited them, because then they knew when he was off the scene, they would be at liberty once again to kicking us around with our help. They held to their assessment that we were born to be kicked, to be hews of wood and carriers of water, and that we were getting antsy to get back to that level of depravity.

In terms of reverting, the record shows that we did with a vengeance. As the saying goes, "We lost it." In 1968 the year he was assassinated, for the first time in history, we in Detroit alone killed each other at the rate of more than one per day, and the homicides to date have not averaged under one a day since. But this point is not about the horrors we all know about; it is about hope given to us by a man brave enough to give his life for the cause of justice, for the cause of integration, which is mutual respect between the races.

Why black preachers especially pastors after the great example of Dr. King would dabble in politics is a told mystery to me, unless they are not really ministers and are just claiming that to glean its prestige. If that be the case, that would certainly be a perversion of that office.

His definition of integration is basic, simple, not complicated at all; in short, it requires something of both blacks and whites, for instance, in Montgomery when we had no right whites were bound to respect, when on the bus whites felt no need to respect our humanity. They called us black apes, fat cows, nigger and any other word of insult they felt like at the time. Our seat was never secure though we had paid full fare. The driver could at any moment at his own whim order us off the bus; he could make us get off, once we had entered at the front and paid the fare, and walk along the side to reenter at the rear, if he did not drive off and leave us in the street in route to the rear; he could make us get up and let whites sit. That is what precipitated the struggle in Montgomery that has become known as the birth of the civil rights movement. A forty-two-year-old black woman, named Rosa Parks, was ordered to get up and give her seat to a white man.

With all of the weight of these insults heaped upon us, his view that for integration to take place, each party must bring something to the table, seemed on the face of it irrational. It was because it seemed typical black lunacy that whites did not take it seriously, and it was because it was not black lunacy but black genius that made it work for blacks and whites. By the time whites figured out that it was not black lunacy, it was too late for them to stop the struggle by scaring the pants off two or three strategically placed lag-headed blacks in the community, who would then babble idiocy till the struggle would have collapsed like dominos.

What he showed them they had to bring to the negotiating table was their human dignity, yea, but they do not see us as humans, yea, but we are, and remember now the rules have changed; they are no longer about how they see us; they are now about how we see us. We also must bring to the table a willingness to insist on fairness and a specific attainable goal.

Before this, we had been leaning solely on the goodwill of whites to see the rightness of our cause from their perspective, never giving thought that we could show them the rightness of our cause from our perspective. Once this perspective was made clear to us, the fact that whites saw us more as apes and baboons, or buffoons, became irrelevant. We would go with a committee and tell the office of transportation and other responsible city officials of the abuse; they would listen attentively and promise to have the drivers do better, and no change would occur. So with this pattern in place, whites saw us as idiots without brains. And our behavior certainly had us thinking that was all we could do since we had no rights.

The insight King brought to the issue was that despite the fact that under the system we had no rights whites were bound to respect, we did have something to bring to the table. He understood that whites thought we were apes, fat cows, and monkeys, (one of the common names they called him was Martin Luther Coon), but he realized that just because they thought that did not make that way of thinking right, nor true. He saw a need for us not to think of ourselves as they thought of us, but to develop our own way of thinking about ourselves. That was revolutionary; it is probably the second-most significant revolution ever in human history, for there has never been a people declared by the state not to be human but to be of some substratum approximating more of apes and monkeys than man.

And in an instance, we were transformed not in whites but in our eyes from apes, fat cows, and monkeys to full-fledged human beings with God-given rights that no state, no people, nor any man not even the white man could deny. Booker T. Washington was the first, for he affirmed our humanity, but King brought us to accept it.

Armed now in the cloak of our humanity, having developed our own correct way of seeing ourselves, we went to city officials not to see what they would do, but to let them know what we were going to do. By the revolutionary change in our attitude, the Whiteman was forced to change his attitude about us, thus bringing a change in how he would treat us.

10. Du Bois's Two Big Mistakes

When reading Du Bois in my twenties, I found two of his contentions very troubling; but not wanting to rush to judgment on this truly great man of letters, I put my concerns aside, not away however. Needless to say the concerns were not allayed with further study. Now history and additional passing of time make clear the correctness of my first impressions.

His concept of the Talented Tenth and his limited view on what constitutes intelligence have served mainly to misguide blacks. Till the concept of the Talented Tenth is examined critically, it has that something about it that will tend to sucker in the weak headed and the evil hearted. It was advanced as a means of developing a body of black talent that in turn could inculcate the masses, thus advancing the whole black race. But instead of this concept advancing the race, it serves more as a mark against it. It pays homage and honor to a gift or talent rather than to service. So for, too often, a black with talent thinks he should be celebrated because of a gift given to him by God, not for service rendered by him for the betterment of the black community. He tends to act as though he thinks he is better than the black community.

His view of what constitutes intelligence has proved to be a monumental trap for blacks. His whole emphasis regarding intelligence was around book learning. If a black goes to Harvard and finishes summa cum laude at the head of his class, that to us means that he is smart, that he is intelligent, that he is very astute, and that that level of black academic achievement makes a lie of whites' claim that blacks are not as intelligent as whites.

Needless to say, blacks today still labor under these two misguided and very unfortunate concepts. They are misguided because they miss the mark, and they are unfortunate because we labor in them to the detriment of the black community. What whites look for and what is absolutely necessary for blacks to claim equal intelligence is that they build a civilized, industrious community and build there their own Harvard, not just go to the Harvard whites built, and this is crucial. Because otherwise what blacks are saying is that building a civilized community that builds the school, writes the books, and builds the course equates with merely attending class, left with that stupefying concept; it is a wonder more blacks are not in jail.

There is a significant difference between an academically educated man and a socially intelligent man. An educated man is one who has absorbed an academic curricula merely; a socially intelligent man not only absorbs academic curricula, but he also knows what to do with what he has learned: He uses his education to build the preferred community. There is the possibility that an educated man is not socially intelligent. Not only does Du Bois' concept not make this point clear, it does not address the point at all.

Blacks' greatest need is more social intelligence not mere academic education; blacks in America today are, in the main, educated people, but we are proving that we do not have enough social intelligence to know how to use our education to make our streets safe, our homes secure, and the gaiety in the voices of our children heard around the world.

We are finishing high school and many of us are getting college degrees, but we do not know how to use them to build the family, the neighborhood and the community. The Du Boisian concepts did not prep us for a life of that kind, for a life of discipline and self-control. It prepped us to insist that whites not control us but left us in the lurch on how to discipline and control ourselves on what to do with the college education. While recognizing that blacks did not want to be controlled, it ignored an immutable law of nature that man will be controlled.

There are two lessons whites have learned all too well, but blacks have not. One is that man will be controlled. That fact is not arguable. The question is, who will control him? Will he control himself or will others control him? People who control themselves will not be controlled by others, but will control people who are too lazy or too stupid to exercise self-control. They will enslave them, segregate them, drug them, or do anything else they choose to do with them. The choice is theirs.

Ignorant of why this fact is so, many blacks today talk of the fact that we developed businesses and built families and exercised for more discipline when we were under the control of Jim Crow. Under Jim Crow, for instance, upwards of 85 per cent of black households were headed by a husband-and-wife team. Contrast that to Detroit today where we are left to control ourselves, more than 70 per cent of babies born to black females are out of wedlock births.

The concept of the Talented Tenth also has about it a high degree of pomposity. It says "I," the talented one, speaks to the white for the poor, down-trodden black masses. That is arrogant and in the main stupid. It should not be that way; it should be all for one and one for all. When a black speaks to whites on behalf of blacks, he should speak not as a big shot, but as one of them, not as one apart, but as though he is speaking for himself. And the truth be told, he really is. And it is the concept of the Talented Tenth that blocks his understanding of that fact, thus making the concept an impediment in the path of black progress. And thus, it should be cast into the cesspool of arrogant fools never to be remembered or used again for we have now a superior model: the example of Dr. King. We see in King the creative genius of an exceptionally gifted individual working for the common good of all, always displaying a full understanding that all includes himself.

11. Majority Rule

The black struggle is not about majority/minority rule. It is about superior intelligence ruling and dominating inferior intelligence. During slavery, there were counties in the United States where blacks out numbered whites more than ten to one. And in Africa, during colonial times, there were places where blacks outnumbered whites more than a million to one and in South Africa when whites ruled, blacks were the overwhelming majority.

To talk numerically of majority/minority respecting the race problem does not lend itself to the possibility of addressing the problem. There is no way to hit the bull's-eye when the shot is not aimed at the target.

In race, the majority/minority issue is about superior intelligence and inferior intelligence. If history has meaning, one white has more intelligence than a thousand or even a million blacks. The Street Philosopher says based on past experience, one white can take full control of a million blacks and get more done in a year than a million blacks on their own can get done in a thousand years.

That may sound bombastic and hyperbolic till it is realized that under colonial rule in Africa and slavery and Jim Crow in America, blacks advanced more than they ever had during the many thousands of years before on their own. And now that colonial, slavery and Jim Crow control have ended blacks in many ways are reverting back to the impulsive and savage brutality that marked their character before the days of white control came upon them.

12. Blacks and Religion

We say we are religious people; if that is true, where and what is the African religion? This claim contrasts to the summation of black reality, which shows it was a lack of a unifying belief system that caused our kings, chiefs and potentates to round us up and sell us into slavery and that it is a lack of belief in any dignifying philosophy today that causes our community to be a cauldron of crime and despair.

Black ministers today know how to be preachy but not how to preach effectively the admonition of family called for in the Holy Scripture. They, therefore, have lost the ministerial authority they had under Jim Crow.

CHAPTER 12

Some Special Research Findings

Studying Black People

WHEN STUDYING BLACK folk, two points stick out with very sharp edges: We as a people refuse to develop a public policy that makes community a first-class, first-world, world-class place in which to live, raise a family and do business; and we reject outright, with an almost vicious resistance, the American system of self-governance. From America to Haiti to Africa, we show hardly any evidence of human genius in these two areas as a means of guiding our thoughts and actions for making the black community a preferred place. Individual pride is etched in the notion that when one of us succeeds in an individual endeavor, whether in athletics, entertainment, accumulating money, education, or being elevated to high public office, elected or appointed, and is allowed to move in among whites, he has escaped slum, he has made it, he is out of the ghetto. This results from the thought that slum is geography, not personal and cultural.

There are four words that sketch the broad skeletal frame of American governance: common, practical, rational and reasonable. America makes credible the notion that the common man's intelligence is practical, rational and reasonable enough for him to exercise the discipline needed for self-governance. Whites take pride in proclaiming themselves to be civilized people, a key ingredient in the ark of self-governance. The point that black people are civilized people is a point I have never heard expressed by a black leader. I made this point known to a black doctor who had just wrapped up a presentation on how busy the coroner's office was in his town sorting the dead bodies of black males slaughtered and murdered by other black males in the black community. After a thoughtful moment, he said that he had never heard a black leader say so either. He told of a terse response of an assistant referencing a body on the table: "He was viciously brutal, mean, big, tough, and black and now he is dead. The bigger they are the harder they fall. And this is so common now, the black community sees a murdered or slaughtered son or daughter as just another nigger dead."

Three Necessities for Black Humanity to Thrive

When researching black people, I find the community to be unsafe, unclean and un-prosperous. Safety, it seems, has a low priority there. Though we have now blacks in politics, business, civic affairs, religion, and education nobody ever in a coherent approach takes the mantle of leader and drives home the idea of safety so firmly and with such engrossing excitement that it catches on and becomes the spark in the social suit that becomes the choice the people choose to wear to reflect the image of their community and their humanity. Instead of this, my research has brought to the surface evidence of a willful neglect in those who have accepted the charge of developing a coherent public policy that would interlink the people in their pride of person each to the other so completely that their community would be so thoroughly transformed that safety in it would be on par with other communities. With that level of deliberate development of themselves, they would have something about themselves to look up to and it is commonly known and broadly acknowledged that when a people look up to themselves, others will also look up to them. That is the reason whites are looked up to.

When I do a survey of blacks, they overwhelmingly say they would rather live in a clean community than a nasty, junky one yet the reality I see when traversing it is trash of every kind in the streets, in the alleys and on the sidewalks. Trash cans, even when there, are in many instances ignored. This makes the streets and the alleys themselves look more like trash bins and junk heaps, than thoroughfares for self-respecting people to traverse in their acts of going out and coming in. This condition screams out two things; neither of which is complimentary. One, that scene does not reflect the image of an industrious people and two, it is evidence that we do not have those individuals manifested in our race whose clarion call awakes in us a will to act together that generates in us a keen sense of pride, that develops in us a view of ourselves that would not allow us to litter and make our space a junk heap so messy it seems almost unfit for human habitation.

When I probe for prosperity in the black community, I make the shocking discovery that in the main, the wealth generating mechanism, which is business, is in the main conducted by people other than us. In addition to jobs, business provides a community with the products and services necessary to keep its people alive, as well as those things that, once the basic needs are met, make for the good life such as entertainment, recreation and athletics.

Not generating wealth means we are economically dead. An economically dead people is like an actually dead person. We understand that if a person is dead, it matters not what is put in the body, on it, or where it is put; it is still without life. Likewise with prosperity, it matters not where we live or how much money, education and other economic resources available to people or a particular individual among them may acquire; if they are economically dead, it is utterly impossible for them to prosper. We have the same natural and physical resources available to us that other people have. But until we use them wisely, until we do like the corpse being taken from its house to the funeral home, when it rose up and asked the driver what day was it, we will continue to flounder. In addition to scaring the driver most seriously, the speaker ceased being a corpse and was alive again. If we have superior human intelligence, we should breathe into our community the breath of economic life—meaning opening grocery stores, clothing stores, construction companies and providing first-class, first-world, world-class products and service. We shall then see the sparks of prosperity begin flickering the radiance of a brighter pathway in our economy. Prosperity is not only about how much resource people have, it is also about the efficiency of its use. Often a black will say our children don't have anything to do.

That mindless bit of loose-headed drivel ignores the fact that black children have as much to do as other children. The problem is that black adults do not open business outlets in the community and thereby provide jobs for youth, thus building pride and character in them and wealth and stability in the neighborhood. Dr. King asked us to build the beloved community. He would not have asked that of us, if there was any doubt whether we could do it.

The theologian Reinhold Niebuhr enforces the same idea: "Nobody . . . lacks courage when convictions are strong. Courage is simply the rigorous devotion to one set of values against other values and interests" *Leaves from the Notebook of a Tamed Cynic*, 1957.

Why More Black Managers are not in the Pros and Level-One College Athletics?

I still hear sometimes a black being interviewed on radio or television asked, why there are not more black managers in the pros and level-one college athletics? The response, as does the question, usually implies that it is due to racial discrimination. However, I think the answer to that problem today is twofold; it may be tinged a bit with a smidgen of racism. But when considered fairly, it could be due mainly to the fact that the black race has very few world class managers functioning within the black community for that decision to draw from. Look around in the black community today and see how many blacks are managing anything on a world class level. Institutions in the black community run by blacks are generally run into the ground. They are not managed in ways that make the black community a first-class, first-world, world-class place in which to live, raise a family and do business. Blacks would rather crank out a batch of excuses to explain this problem than develop a coherent public policy to solve it.

Since managers tend to come out of people whose community has a high and abiding level of self-respect, respect for the community and for individuals, this facile question will likely go on being asked forever. Because when a community of people, as I hear so often, say they do not need managers (leaders if you please), the question becomes why would they want some other people to make them leaders, when their culture teaches that leaders are not necessary? Black culture does not nurture and develop leaders for neither the black pastor, politician, civic leader, the business owner nor educator by his behavior sees himself as a leader. He sees himself as having a job that pays enough to pay the bills, not as some one possessing the intelligence, skill, power and responsibility to have his community reflect his level of intelligence in a vision keen enough to make it safe, clean and prosperous.

If headhunters of pro teams were to look for black managers, on what basis would they do so among people whose view is that managers are not needed in their own society, where resistance to basic rules of civil conduct is rampant? Where would they look and on what basis would such a community claim to have some one fit for some other people to pick to be a manager? There is only one basis on which a claim could reasonably be made—charity. That from the start would put him at best in a very tenuous position. This would make such a manager's presence on the field shaky.

Sometime when I hear the interviewer asking the question and listening to some one trying with a straight face to answer it, if the situation was not so pitifully pathetic, I would laugh at it as a comedy and wish them success on the road. While that question is holding space, it should yield to another question, why are black folk not managing the affairs of their community in a first-class, first-world, world-class manner? That is the question for the black politician, pastor, educator, civic and business persons today.

Is Affirmative Action a Curse or a Blessing

The affirmative-action idea has proved itself to be detrimental for black people, and here is proof. Before it blacks tried to improve themselves in the black community, keeping the family together, promoting education, cleaning the neighborhood (Neighborhoods were not the best in the world, but were far better than the crime-laden cesspools they are today.) and being brotherly. Today, the black family is in almost complete disarray; education is used by the learned to be slick in dodging responsibility, not as a friend to help us out. Black folk, it seems, have lost the spirit of cooperation or, at least, refuse to train their children to be the best they can be. They have switched from that philosophy; now they teach them to be the worst they can be by committing constantly pernicious murder of each other. In this throe of death, the community is known more for crime than for the proper use of education. And if cleanliness is next to godliness, black folk are a long way from God. Brotherly love is no longer a hallmark of black humanity in the black community. Let us look now at how the affirmative action idea first began.

The idea of affirmative action was first used in a discriminatory context by President John F. Kennedy in 1961. In Executive Order No. 10925,

President Kennedy indicated that federal contractors should take affirmative action to ensure that prospective job applicants and federal employees were treated in an equal manner without regard to race, creed, color, or national origin. In this order, President Kennedy was advocating equal access and equal treatment for all individuals, including blacks. In 1965, President Lyndon B. Johnson created decisive affirmative-action policy with Executive Order No. 11246. After that President Richard M. Nixon expanded the affirmative action executive order by establishing goals, timetables, and specific guidelines for companies to follow in order to comply with federal regulations governing affirmative action. All of this is filled with good intentions and sounds good but the affirmative action idea has been hijacked by the Talented Tenth and they, being a vicious enemy of the mass of black people, have made the idea the focus, not equal opportunity resulting in the black community being a safe, clean and prosperous place on the ground throughout the neighborhood.

As Affirmative Action has unfolded, it now asserts passivity. It implies that you are convinced you cannot think nor act for yourself and that black leaders are too deficient mentally to take initiative and actively participate in the affairs of men on an intelligent, reasonable and rational basis. They must wait, therefore, for somebody to take them by the hand and lead them around by the nose like they are lag-headed, moronic idiots or very small minor children.

The struggle for equal opportunity requires action from the party denied till his grievances are met and once they are, he ought to use every brain cell he has to make certain the community reflects just how intelligent he is in terms of making and keeping it a safe, clean and prosperous place in which to live, raise a family and do business. In the case of black folk in America, it is incumbent upon us to act as an intelligent body of humanity who will make and keep our community as safe and clean and prosperous as other people keep theirs. Affirmative Action is not having that effect on black folk in the black community. If there is any encroachment upon our right to do this as men and as citizens of the United States of America, we should cry out in unison in a loud clear voice saying, help us America, help us people of the world and do not seek to hinder us from keeping our streets safe, clean and prosperous. As long as we have all the physical attributes of man, given to us by God, we can keep our neighborhoods safe, clean and prosperous by resisting the impulse to be negative.

Therefore, what is passing as Affirmative Action is not affirming us; it is killing us. It has turned the black community into a slaughter house has made it a killing field has made it a hell hole of death, while the earth drinks the slaughtered blood of our sons and daughters. First of all, we should know affirmative action has been changed and has been tampered with really; it has been twisted from an intended positive to an assertive negative by the Talented Tenth. It is now the updated version of the Talented Tenth idea. Its effect is to block access to opportunity in American by the mass of black people. Affirmative action has become to the civil rights struggle what intelligent design is to the creationists. The creationists could not get creationism into the science classroom, so they reconfigured it and submitted it under a new title, same message, new package. Commonsense did not buy it in 1925, and commonsense did not buy it eighty years later in 2005. The element in black humanity wanting to be something other than black, influenced by W. E. B. Du Bois, hatched up something called the Talented Tenth idea back in 1903, claiming white folk should train them and put the care for training the mass of blacks into their hands; the Talented Tenth idea did not stop black people under the leadership of B. T. Washington from trying to secure education for their children. The Talented Tenth, undaunted seeing opportunity to twist the affirmative-action idea to hurt blacks, jumped for it like a ferocious dog for raw meat, corralled it against us, then committed to it with energetic vigor to block black progress, and now for nearly forty years not long after its inception under presidents John F. Kennedy's and Lyndon Baines Johnson's Executive Orders, it has seen the slaughter and murder of blacks in their homes and the streets of neighborhoods in numbers greater than have died in battle in America's major wars. The American Heritage Dictionary defines affirmative action this way: An active effort to improve the employment or educational opportunities of members of minority groups and women. Affirmative action puts the well-being of blacks, like its predecessor, squarely in the hands of the Talented Tenth, the most vicious enemy black humanity could ever have. The Blackman's struggle in America is for equal opportunity. To get that requires concentrated, united action on the part of black people in general and all people of goodwill. Affirmative Action as advanced by the Talented Tenth gives blacks the false notion that human progress, their progress, is to be had with no sweat. As claimed by the Talented Tenth, Affirmative Action sounds like somebody is going to get something for nothing and is going to scale the ladder of success without paying due diligence, without putting in some sweat equity. Dr. Martin Luther King Jr.'s life teaches us that that is a lie.

We must burn the midnight oil; we must study night and day; we must direct our actions to improving our community, to having it reflect the best in our humanity, by keeping our families intact and strong, by keeping the father in the home with wife and children and when the marriage does not last, keep the children protected by staying responsible in the neighborhood, and not becoming fodder for the prison system.

Here is what I will guarantee without any fear of contradiction in results on the ground in the black community that if Affirmative Action is pulled from the American scene in every form and guise and ditched in the ashbin of history, and replaced with the blacks' struggle for equal opportunity, and blacks take those steps necessary to make their community equal in safety, cleanliness and prosperity, the murder rate among blacks will shrink to or below the level of that in the general population. Now here is the first claim that will be trotted out by affirmative action advocates. Yea, but the equal opportunity caveat is the opening for my escape. Now notice, their response was to equal opportunity, not to saving the lives of black folk. But I will go beyond that; I am certain that the academic level of achievement among blacks will rise to the level of their intelligence. These are the two things, the Talented Tenth idea crowd, now guised the affirmative action crowd, uses to insure that black folk will keep performing at subhuman levels, as well as continuing to murder, slaughter and kill each in high numbers while pretending to be on their side.

Affirmative Action holds out the false promise that somebody else is going to do something for you. The struggle for equal opportunity requires and demands that every black person join the struggle and seek collectively and individually to secure a place of achievement in American society. Good intentions are not enough; proper results are all that count.

Is the Fight for Racial Equality Bogus?

After talking literally to hundreds of black people—some white as a Norse blueblood, some black as ebony, and some between; some highly educated, some moderately educated and some hardly educated at all; some men and some women, I found the two questions: Do you think you are inferior or equal to whites? And do you think the black race is inferior or equal to the white race? They all said they were not inferior but were equal to whites, and the black race is not inferior but is equal to the white race. But yet I heard some of these same people say blacks, including themselves, are fighting for racial equality. But if we are already racially equal, is that a bogus fight, a noisy clatter merely? If you are already racially equal, why would you fight to get something you already have? In short, what is the fuss all about? If this black unity of sentiment is true, it seems the Blackman is fighting for something, but he does not know what it is. And the question cries out, saying if you do not know what you are fighting for, how can it ever be achieved? As long as he fights for something he says he already has, the world cannot but look on him in his miserable state and wonder what is wrong with him.

I have never seem an article or a book in which a black person laid out any proof to back the claim they are racially inferior to the Whiteman, therefore, should be made equal to him. Yet the main thing, instead, that flows from them in this regard is the claim they are fighting for racial equality. This, when taken literally, means obviously they are fighting to obtain something which by their own admission is already firmly in their possession. But it is not difficult to find books by black authors proclaiming blacks' fight for racial equality. If you have in your possession what you claim you are fighting to get, is that a form of Ebonics?

This kind of sloppy, muddleheaded mental dexterity is a use of language that does not help our cause. I think therefore we should either rethink the claim of fighting for racial equality or stop claiming we are equal. This murkiness of purpose makes clarity of purpose impossible. If we rethink the claim and eliminate one or the other, we can then focus on the one chosen and strive mightily for success.

If we choose to fight for racial equality, we must resolve what makes us inferior. Is it for instance physical—size of hands, feet, lips, nose, ears, eyes, toe and finger-nails; the shape of our head, size of brains, length of neck, arms, legs, hair, tone of skin? Once this is done, it would then behoove us to make known which of these features are inferior and to say exactly and precisely what we are going to do or what can white do to make these physical characteristics in our race be equal to those in the white race. If we take the choice that we are indeed inferior to whites, our fight for racial equality then would not be with the Whiteman, but with God. So since we say our body parts are equal to whites in every way in shape, size, length, number and color, we do not have to fight for racial equality even with God.

There is a difference between the races, but obviously, it is not due to the physical characteristics of the races; it is cultural. There are four words that identify the core value of the American system: reason, rationality, practice and common. America is formed on the premise that the common man is reasonable, rational and practical. These are concepts blacks do not believe in, especially the Talented Tenth and, therefore, refuse to adhere. Blacks believe in something, never defined, advanced by the Talented Tenth, called "wise leadership." No defined purpose places us in an inferior position. To define our purpose is our responsibility; the expression, "wise leadership," without definition makes it nothing more than verbal gibberish expressed by the cleft palates of fools, not reasonable, not rational, and not practical.

If a child is yelling and howling and, when asked what is the matter, he says he wants a Baby Ruth candy bar, and he has one in his hands clearly at that point, you need to look further into the cause of his crying. If people say they are fighting for racial equality, but at the same time say they are racially equal, clearly that is an impractical, convoluted, illogical and loose-headed, nonsensical statement needing careful investigation.

The struggle is for equal opportunity and to be treated fairly. To say Jackie Robinson fight was for racial equality would be wrong. He was equal to his white team mates. What he and his race sought was equal opportunity, not racial equality. To sue to use public facilities on a first-come-first-served basis expresses the desire to be treated fairly not to make the race equal, which it already is. Further, as was proved in the bus struggle in Montgomery, blacks when treated fairly can sit in a bus seat with as much efficiency as whites.

Detroit Elections

We have just elected a mayor, council and school board. The mayor is responsible for developing a public policy that makes the city a safe, clean, and preferred place in which to live, raise a family and do business. The council's role is to participate productively in formulating the policy. The school board is responsible for establishing a policy that makes Detroit Public School system second to none in the nation.

These are the things these entities must do to reverse the trend of people leaving, thus decreasing the city's population. But from none of these entities did I hear a plan to increase the population of Detroit. Thus, with the need the city has for bringing out tens of thousands of angels on angels' night to watch property to keep those who would from torching it, if no plan is executed to stop the exodus, in a few years, people will have to be imported to the city to put the fires out on angels' night.

I never ask whether black policy makers intentions are good; I look mainly at the results their policies produce. After more than thirty years of continuous population decline for the city on the river, is it not reasonable to ask if black policy makers are able to develop the policies needed to get the job done, to make the city a safe, clean and prosperous place in which to live raise a family and do business?

SHELTON VAUGHN

Individually, blacks can perform under the auspices of white folk. But can these people just elected formulate policies without a manifest plan for achieving the objective? Can they break the pattern of the past thirty odd years of failure? With a plan, it would be tough; without one—well, it is something to think about.

Can Black Folk Make Apple Pie?

There is a keen, apparent, innate depravity in the character of black humanity. I say apparent, because on close examination, it is not depravity but undisguised indifference that draws this description of him. His character is not depravity and it is what it is. It is seen as depravity because he acts depraved, and one then shifts the adjective to a noun and practices that so long it becomes in the mind what it is called, instead of what it is. Strip depravity from his character, and it can stand alone, pure and untarnished.

Certainly, evil pervades blacks, but that is not their essence. Evil gets attention because it is odious, and his indifference to it makes no sense. It is because of this that when a black, with his PhD, his billion dollars, and his fame, moves about in the world, people tend to shun him, causing him to beg for acceptance into their society, while they haughtily cast him in contempt and call him lazy, and tell him he stinks and that he is stupid.

A mantra black militants preached while trying to destroy the effective, nonviolent civil rights movement was violence is American "as apple pie." They became violent, but provided the world no apple pie.

Whites are evil, true but they are not indifferent to it. And it is for that reason that Africans, Haitians and blacks in America all try to get out of jurisdictions run by blacks in Africa, Haiti and America and into those run by whites. This phenomenon is not lost on anyone. In the 2000 census, Detroit's black population declined. Blacks do not try to get to and reside in jurisdictions run by whites because whites are not violent but because in addition to being violent, they also make and sometime share delicious, social apple pie.

Blacks can clean up their character real fast if they would begin to make for themselves and market to the world some really good, mouth-watering social apple pie in the form of safe, clean, pristine streets, and prosperous, beautiful jurisdictions where they are trying to provide governance. People then would begin to ask, are these those blacks we called lazy and stupid?

If they would for instance make Detroit the safest and cleanest city in Michigan, do not use habits that damage it, but look for and develop ideas for causing and creating harmony, they would then be making the best of America real in their own environs. They would, in other words, be making authentic social apple pie.

Honored Memory of Rosa Parks

When Rosa Parks died much was said of how she moved a recalcitrant nation to do the right thing, but nothing of how she failed to move her race to do so. In Detroit, the house she was molested in by a young black male should be lifted from obscurity and the site made a shrine to her legacy so that blacks, and others, shall never forget how cruel we allowed her to be treated among us by us. Her legacy is not complete without the full story. Unless the full story is told, by omission, that lie will fester and infect us with rot within and its stench shall never cease. Unless headway is made on this matter, the world will still and forever be a dark, dank and dreary place. And the children of Africa shall stay in a long night with no end.

Having not been trained adequately by their culture to respect her greatness, a black male in Detroit entered her home and robbed and beat her. It was black males who in song and movie maligned her good name. The white system abused her in Montgomery; the black system did so in Detroit and in Hollywood. The black system's actions against her were particularly offensive because it was on behalf of blacks she toiled so determinedly to improve their internal fiber, sense of dignity, and fair play, as she appealed to whites to cease oppressing her people. But her people, like the snake, bit her. And to heal that wound, we must tend it. To do less will say only the evil done to us by whites matters. The facts should be told over and over in every household to every generation to come.

As we show her sitting defiantly on the bus, refusing to give up her seat to a white man, we should in her senior years show a young black male, sneaking into her home to rob and beat her. As we see white men arresting, trying, and finding her guilty of breaking a Jim Crow law, we should show black males in their actions of disrespect of her.

Pictures of the shrine should hang in the Charles H. Wright Museum of African American History in Detroit and in other museums in America and throughout the world. The facts of her life should be taught in every home and in history classes in every school that teaches human history.

Her life tells us that we have two problems: one with whites and one with ourselves. If her legacy is to matter more than a pitch of empty breath, if it can effectively call forth from all of us our best, then her life will not have been for naught. When life is threatened with two fatal diseases, to cure one is not enough to save the life. We must, therefore, gird ourselves and put on the full armor of courage and work just as hard to cure ourselves internally, while continuing to cause white oppression to cease, as she did. With quiet strength, she went to court to stop white oppression and to stop black males from smearing her name, and to send the robber to jail. So with a clarity of need, we should consecrate the shrine in her honored memory.

Failure of Detroit's Mayoral Debates Was Big

It was an attitude of hostility not civility that made the mayoral debates a bad scene not merely the promises the candidates did or did not make. You cannot accomplish desire, if blinded with hostility, even if victorious in the election. In population today, Detroit is less than half the city it was fifty years ago, because hostility has it on a death march.

The question, say something good about your opponent, is really a fat, softball question for the astute politician sufficiently lacking in self-absorption. A discerning candidate should always be ready, willing, and able to say there is good in every man; my opponent is a man; therefore, there is good in him. And this is my short list of good things I see in him. Then tick them off with firmness, clarity and a resonant conviction. The headline would cheerfully report the compliments and ring up boundless joy in the hearts of many.

The laws of nature cannot be violated, for instance, you cannot be in two places at once; share nor give what you do not have. If you cannot see good in your opponent, how can you see it in the aggregate? The laws of nature are not toys to break but to obey; they are not merciful; they are what they are. Therefore, if you don't have civility, you can't sell nor barter it. You cannot carve a path of civility, if blinded with hostility. Every person has good in him. If you cannot see it, take the blinders off. As good as the great Ray Charles was, because he was blind, he had to be led by someone with sight. No politician should be so self-absorbed that he cannot see good in the humanity of the opposition. These candidates appeared to be so self-absorbed that they talked as though the campaign is about them. Though it is their campaign; it is not about them; it is about us.

The win should be pursued vigorously, unrelentingly and determinedly but never at the expense of not seeing the dignity in all humanity. That price is too high to pay for the attainment of any political office. We all have humanity in common. One should pursue, court, engage and marry civility and never leave home without it. If each candidate would see the good in the other, they could use the campaign to carve a pathway of civility, and thus lead by example. Seeing good in others may not by itself qualify one for dog catcher but not seeing it in the opposition is an absolute disqualifier. Because if victorious, one would inevitably become a slave to truculence. This would drive light out, nix hope and smear further the image of the whole city. This consequence is not petty.

The main purpose of the campaign should be to inspire us to be our very best. If the campaign does that, even if you do not get elected, you would have been part of a winning process. Failing to inspire, even if you win the election, you still lose.

Seeing nothing good in the opposition is to say you have discharged dignity and that, for you, a decent respect for mankind is impossible. That level of hostility is a crime against self big enough to implode the city. Reason teaches that that level of hostility means that one is over the edge and is dedicated alone to death. The solution to this? Change it. Cease hostility close the chasm of division that makes us hostile, and use every opportunity to be civil. With that great softball question, the candidates had a chance to do this, but instead of that, they chose to insult, demean, diminish and deny the very sanctity in their fellow man.

I, like others, have cried myself dry many times because of hostility performed in the city since 1968, but knowing one of these men will be elected mayor for the next four years, I went to well one more time. Water was there; it sprang up till my ducks filled with tears and now once again, my eyes have become a flowing stream. Why can't we see the good that is in each of us and express it in no uncertain terms?

In the end, the winner did not win. In the third year of the four-year term, he was driven from office for violating the public's trust, and sent to jail a convicted felon.

Assessing the farewell Speech of Kwame Malik Kilpatrick

Mayor of the City of Detroit

Mayor Kwame Malik Kilpatrick made a blunder insulting the governor for no justifiable reason. She did not perform misdeeds in office. He did. That insult shows strongly that his head yet rests in one dark place. She was carrying out the constitutional responsibilities of her office. If he had done the same, he would still be in office and not headed to a cell in jail, a convicted criminal.

That lack of character says he is unrepentant and does not understand that what he did was wrong. Bluster will not salve nor heal the mess he is in. He said Detroit is his city. Each resident makes her his city too. She is not his city alone to do what he wants. He should not abuse her, lie to her, nor soil or sully her good name.

I wrote him when he had that lavish thirty-six year birthday party, and told him it was foolish to do so. And if he was going to have a party, it should have been a public fest celebrating family, honoring women and encouraging men to engage in rearing children. I tried to get the letter published but found no takers. Included also in the letter was an article on America's system of governance, which could have been beneficial to the people of the city in helping them understand that the office of mayor is a perpetual trust belonging to the people, not the occupier. They may know that somewhere in the back of their heads, but some things are so fundamentally important they should be brought front center from time to time.

During the governor's hearing, somebody said the mayor is an intelligent man. There are two types of intelligence, good and bad. He used bad intelligence to get into trouble and to insult the governor in his farewell speech. He boasted that he was proud to be his father's son and that he was proud of both his parents then promptly insulted the very essence of their humanity by not taking full responsibility for his criminal acts. When a son betrays the public's trust, that dishonors his parents and he should come before them with no boast or bluster but in a sea of contrition, regretting that he has brought shame on the family. That would have been evidence of good intelligence. He would have done this if he was mature and was dealing out of his good-intelligence bag. There is no growth in him; he continues, instead, to show extreme retardation, a malignant retrogression, a predilection for using bad intelligence.

Much was made in the media about his philandering, and while the circumstance makes the matter serious and he was found to have perjured himself about it, that was not his most damaging act, which was, to cover his misdeeds, firing a good police officer. Women and men have been chasing each other and bumping and grinding in the rhythm of life a long time with no end in sight. That was not the crime that cried with bells in the ears of civilized men with a need to boot him out of office. Breach of the public trust in abuse asserted against a lowly worker to exercise the might and power of one's high office in that way for personal reasons is heinous and criminal in every view imaginable.

Yet as every civilized human being should, I am sad today to see the young mayor who had a bright future leave office a convicted criminal.

No Black Person Should Long for Jim Crow

A hue and cry is sounded over certain things whites say about blacks, as Bill Bennett saying that crime would go down in America if all black babies were aborted, the people of Livonia not wanting a Walmart store because it would attract blacks, Jimmy the Greek's conviction that breeding blacks during slavery developed in them a strong athletic gene, the Japanese that blacks drag down educational scores of America, and Al Campanis' view that blacks are not bright. These are some of the things white folk say about us that scratch our craw.

Now here are some things we actually *do* that hurt us: In the 2000 census, blacks joined the exodus from Detroit, a black-run city, murder each other in for too great a number; complain about what others say, but neglect measures we should take to help our cause and improve our status in the world. When given a choice of finding something negative a white said, or doing something to help the race cooperate to solve the problems of black on black crime, inferior community standards in education, poor entrepreneurship and the like, we take to yakking about the white comments, thus leaving the black community unaided in the throes of continuous and unrelenting despair (meaning social laziness), with no concentrated effort to help it out.

Instead of taking proper advantage of opportunities granted under desegregation, some of us look back to the days of Jim Crow with a sincere longing, saying, falsely, that black folk then had a coherent, egalitarian community, where the doctor, teacher, preacher, numbers runner, drug dealer, pimp, prostitute and entrepreneur all lived in the same neighborhood; and that the youth, therefore, saw a variety of possibilities to choose from. What blacks lived in under Jim Crow was not a developed community. They lived in a social pressure cooker controlled by whites. When a black male acted up, whites would come in, bust his head and lynch two or three others for good measure. That scared the hell out of the clan, and they then would hunker down and somewhat behave themselves not because they had chosen to exercise high human intelligence but because they were quivering and shaking with mortal fear till desegregation allowed them to show their face. Before then they were cowed by the sheer brutality whites would mete out to keep them in their place.

Jim Crow is a horrible system. To get some sense of it, one should read the book *Soul Sister*, 1970, by Grace Halsell. No black with good sense should want that nor long for it. It is a system where blacks have no right the white man is bound to respect. It is generally the black female expressing regret that it has passed away. She cannot control the black male, and he refuses to control himself. Thus the black community stays in a continuous state of turmoil, with him stealing, raping and murdering black people, often children, in the black community with a predatory propensity that tells much about him. And about all of us.

The Three Greatest Statements Ever Made

The theme of today is what are you giving back? And though I had nothing to do with its selection, it is a question I use in my research, and by using it, I have had many astounding breakthroughs in learning about black people. I like it because it has multiple applications. The first and the most basic, of course, is what are you giving back, to your family, your church, your neighborhood, and your city. But other possible applications are, what are we giving back to family, church and city. Then a third application is, what is my family giving back, what is my church giving back, what is my city giving back, and then the great big one, what is my race giving back.

I am going to put two questions before you, and, as I go through my remarks, just let them hangout with you; and I will answer them later. Was Jesus on the cross a victim? Do our experiences of slavery, Jim Crow, and other abuse at the hands of whites make us a victim?

Now for my remarks, I am going to speak briefly of what in my view are the three greatest statements ever uttered in all the annals of human history. And they are as follows: The truth will make you free by Jesus Christ; all men are created equal by Thomas Jefferson; and no race that has anything to contribute to the markets of the world is long in any degree ostracized by Booker T. Washington.

The parable of the two sons gives us to know that truth is more than what is said for each son did the opposite of what he promised. This parable makes understandable that truth also is what is right. Truth then is shown in at least two ways: in what is said and in what is done. In this example, truth also has two qualities: right and good. In the case of the two sons, the question was not who told the truth or who did what he said, but who did the will of the father, which means who did the right thing.

It has often been asked if a Nazi had asked, was Anne Frank in the house? If the person had answered, "No," would that answer have been a lie? Before answering, ask two questions: Is it right to say no and is it good? The question then is not did the person lie. It is did he do the will of the father or did he do the right thing?

I am going to bank what I say with beauty and truth. Truth is eternal; you cannot destroy truth, and beauty is everywhere; you cannot be, therefore, where there is no beauty. Now you may say, "wait a minute, brother speaker, there is no beauty nor truth in me nor black people." I will differ strongly with that claim, for there are beauty and truth in you and likewise in all black people. And you might with some justification ask how is that so?

Let us now discourse the Jeffersonian revelation. I have heard many black people, some with the PhD degree from America's most prestigious colleges and universities, say in seminars and speeches, on television and in personal conversations that Jefferson did not mean us. But the question, what did he mean, is not the first question one should ask. Upon hearing these words of Jefferson, the question one should ask first is, am a man? There is no way to say "Yes" to that question and still say earnestly that Jefferson's words did not mean you. Once that question is clearly understood, one can then go on to what did Jefferson mean. Certainly, he did not mean that all men are created with the same size, height, color or mental acuity. So what did he mean? To find the answer to that question, one has to look at the problem he was addressing at the time, which was the divine right of kings. In that right, the king could do no wrong. On a fit of impulse, he could have his queen beheaded or anyone else in the kingdom and the life of the common man was of less value than dirt. So the Jeffersonian declaration had a double effect: It struck down the divinity of the king idea and lifted up high the status of the common man. In short, he was saying all men were created human; the king is human; therefore, the king is not divine.

Now to Washington's observation. Let us look at what we blacks have offered to the markets of the world. The only really big splash we have made with consistency in the markets of the world has not been with something but with somebody, us. For four hundred long and torturous years, we rounded us up, brought us to the shores of Africa and sold us mostly to Europeans. There has been no other group who has done that to its people. While coming across the continent of Africa, we may have been sold several

SHELTON VAUGHN

times to other African traders before we got to the seashore to be sold to the Europeans.

Before continuing, let me tell how I came to study this. In the early 1990s, I read a book, titled, *The Fires of Jubilee: Nat Turner's Fierce Rebellion*, 1990, by Stephen B. Oates, a professor of history at the University of Massachusetts.

The Nat Turner rebellion was the most successful of all black rebellions against slavery; it consisted of a small band of committed rebels intent on killing mean slave owners, thus freeing their slaves. Now here is the thing that gave me pause; when a slave owner was killed, his slaves were then free but these freed men in the main did not join the rebels to fight to free more slaves to join their ranks; instead, they went and told other slave owners that there were blacks down the way killing white people. The fact that they chose to do this caused me to want to know what was in our past so horrible that we would go to other slave masters rather than join the rebels and fight as free men to help to free others. The answer came in 1998 in the book *Africans in America: America's Journey Through Slavery* (1998) by Charles Johnson and Patricia Smith as part of the WGBH Series Research Team. This book was a companion to the PBS Series by the same name. In chapter two, they say, "Half of the more than 20 million Africans captured and sold into slavery never made it to the ship. Most died on the march to the sea. It is impossible to determine how many more lost their lives during the crossing. Current estimates range from 1 million to 2.2 million." They went on to say, "African traders were extremely cruel to their captives. According to ship's surgeon Alexander Falconbridge: the traders have instantly beheaded them in sight of the captain." This was done to those the buyers did not buy due to some malady that would make them unlikely to survive the crossing.

I have highlighted Booker T. Washington who in truth has to be the greatest human being who ever lived. He asked a former slave if he was ever sold; he said, "Yes, my master sold five of us, three mules, my brother and me." Hearing this, Washington then, in the face of unrelenting and vicious attacks by Du Bois and his Talented Tenth, did two things: He lifted the veil of ignorance from his people and broke down, shattered and destroyed that sense of equivalence we saw in us to the mule. There has never been another human being in history who was faced with such an awesome task and made such a monumental difference. If black is inferior, white cannot make him equal for what *is* white, but a man? Further, as was proved in the bus struggle in Montgomery, black, when treated fairly, can sit in a bus seat with as much efficiency as white.

Ralph Ellison's book, *Invisible Man* (1952), intended motif was that white folk do not see the humanity of black people. But my research shows that black folk do not see their own humanity either. So just as whites mistreat us because they do not see our humanity, if we had seen our own humanity, we would not have killed us in the millions in the slave trade nor sold us into slavery and we would not have killed more than eighteen thousand people in Detroit alone, some as young as six months of age, during the past thirty-seven (1968-2005) years and the slaughter continues.

Earlier you were given two questions; now I will answer them: Jesus on the cross was not a victim; he was a victory and blacks are not victims for as the scenes here presented show, we are participants in these crimes committed against our humanity given to us by God.

We thought being released from the bonds of chattel slavery would free us; we thought ending Jim Crow would free us; we thought education would free us; we thought attaining good jobs that paid well and accumulating great amounts of money would free us; we thought holding high elective and appointive office would free us; but now we know that the truth alone will make us free and that we shall never really be free till we tell the truth; and then the beauty within us will shine with a glow so bright it will truly light the world.

In the civil rights movement, Dr. King, standing on the shoulders of Booker T. Washington, led us to accept our color. And he echoed Washington when he said the white man cannot ride the black man's back if the black man's back is not bent. Here is the continuum: Washington affirmed our humanity, and Dr. King led us to accept our color. Now we must come to accept and embrace our humanity and when we do, we shall then begin to provide resources to the markets of the world, and at that moment we will come to know the bounties of riches untold.

Let us begin. Thank you.

The Black Politick

Politick is the totality of a people, of what they and others have done for and against them. In the case of black people, it tells how in Africa during the slave trade, their kings, chiefs and potentates round them up, marched them—millions died in route—to the shores of Africa and sold them into slavery to foreign buyers, mostly Europeans.

In America, the first batch of slaves was bought in Jamestown, Virginia, in 1619. The importing of slaves continued through to 1808, and the system of slavery continued till December 6, 1865. After slavery ended, the former slaves and their descendants were put under a system of segregation that was codified into law by the United States Supreme Court in 1896 in *Plessy v. Ferguson,*

Those who bought us made two devastating charges against us. One of the charges is that black folks are lazy people. This charge we use quite often against each other. However when we use it, we are not speaking of ourselves; then it is those other blacks, those across the street or on the corner or those raunchy ones who are always a little nasty in appearance and manner. But those who make the charge mean all blacks without exception. In other words, they see the general condition of the black race—crime ridden, broken homes, massive starvation, utter despair and make the conclusion that black folks are lazy. But as off key as the charge lazy may sound to blacks in denial, when looked upon in real terms, it in a way is a backhanded compliment as it implies ability, merely lacking imagination, initiative and the will to do certain things. But there is a greater charge; this charge is completely negative and does not equivocate; it says that we do not have the ability in the race to perform the abstract thought. The abstract thought is like one coin with two sides. One way to perform the abstract thought is environmental or communal—that is, to transform our community from a den of laziness and despair into a safe, clean and prosperous place in which to live, raise our families and do business. That is develop a public policy in our community that cleans up the neighborhoods, and opens stores that provide products and services suitable for building a synergistic lifestyle that bespeaks us, superior people.

The comment we hear most often is that whenever blacks move in and dominate an area, property values go down. Now that is the environmental side of the abstract thought; the other side manifests itself over time. The overtime performance of the abstract thought requires that the idea be sustained with consistent vigor for centuries after the founders have passed from the scene. An example of this is the United States of America, born 1776 with the single idea that the common man is intelligent enough to govern himself.

What does the abstract thought do? It inspires people, it sings carols in the hearts of men, it controls their behavior for the good, it directs their path, it determines their feelings in matters of great importance and it, above all, demands that a body of people act in concert for a common and beneficial purpose for hundreds or even thousands of years for their own edification as well as for the edification of others. Those who gave birth to America in

1776, started a legacy of building the abstract thought over time; they have passed it on to their children and now every generation that comes after them must ask, "Are we superior or inferior?" And the only way to answer that question is by sustaining the idea, which in this case is the American system of governance. The founders were not only of superior intelligence but, though flawed, were a noble people because they reflected the best spirit of mankind.

The abstract thought cannot be performed by one person nor by the founding generation merely nor are college degrees necessary; its only abiding ingredient is superior human intelligence. The kind of human intelligence that can guide you to the burial grounds of your ancestors, and while standing at the tomb, you can feel their presence shut up in your bones and, knowing without doubt of your descent, be jubilant there in that knowledge. With less respect for our heritage than that despite our university degrees, we are nothing more than trained inferior beings to do jobs provide to us by others.

That in practice is the general opinion of mankind of what constitutes superior or inferior people.

While many may have heard the lazy charge, the notion of performing the abstract thought may be more obscure, because black scholars and black intelligentsia conspire to hide that charge from us, because that is how they cover their own laziness. So let us make absolutely clear what performing the abstract idea is not. It is not a matter of high academic degrees or scholastic knowledge and individual achievement. The first black PhD graduated from Harvard College more than one hundred years ago in 1896. At the turn of the twentieth century, only 6 percent of the United States—white, black, and other—had completed high school. Yet American was already becoming a dominate nation in human affairs and had built the cross-continental railroad and the Brooklyn Bridge, two of the greatest engineering feats in history.

At the beginning of the twenty-first century, about 78 to 80 percent of blacks in the United States had high school education and many with college degrees. Yet the proper assessment of the situation in the world during the past thirty years is that in terms of self-governance black folks have gone backward not forward. So whether in America, Haiti or Africa, blacks want to get out of where blacks rule and in to jurisdictions of white rule.

We have blacks running Fortune 500 companies, heading major universities, and running multibillion-dollar private foundations. Yet in all of these cases, we are running enterprises for others and are functionaries merely. But the test is not if we can run a business for others, but whether we can transform our own community from its blight today into an economic oasis that is second to none, that is so successful people clamber to get in rather than try in desperation to get out.

In Detroit, a quintessential black American city during the 2000 census, the black population went down for the first time during the prior fifty years and a scientific pole, taken a month ago, reveals that more than half of blacks in Detroit would leave if they could. Yet a black representative of the teachers union says that the teachers in the Detroit public schools are the best educated of any other school district in the United States. By best educated, she means they have the highest percentage with advanced degrees. However, the fall in black population was due mainly to black parents fleeing the city because of poor teacher quality. This is so because most members of the dominate black educated class think that the degree is enough. They do not know, it seems, as other folks do that the degree is merely a start and that they must take the degree and join with others in the community to make the community the best it can be, to make it the best in the world, and to make it second to none. Rather than do that, they try to run from the problem. But if we are not people of superior intelligence, running is not going to make it so. And if we are, we will stand up, stay put, work together and build a public policy that would make our community the best it can be.

Ida B. Wells, the little lady with the big voice that would be heard, back in the late 1800s, went to England to get the English to use their influence on their American brothers to stop lynching, because it was not reflective of civilized people. At one of her speaking engagements, a fellow raised the question of blacks stinking. She told him that question of concern was never raised when blacks were cooking in whites' kitchens, serving food at their tables, or when whites were crawling into the beds of blacks for sexual pleasure; that concern was raised only when we were suing for fair treatment under the law.

Now all of us know that white folk are intelligent, so we know that they know if they don't bathe, they will stink, so likewise with blacks. So when they raise the issue of blacks stinking, they are not talking about body odor; they are talking about the best-educated blacks. They are talking about blacks with a college degree, maybe even, a PhD shuffling around like lapdogs under their feet and so full of themselves they can hardly talk, pretending to think that they are as smart as the white man, who built the school, wrote the books, fixed the curricular, taught the courses, granted the degrees, and, holy of all holies, provided the jobs for the idiots. That level of stupidity, they say, stinks.

Superior intelligence is not taught; either we have and demonstrate it or we don't; it is like gender; we are male or female not because we are taught. We are male or female because of the physicality of our bodies. People are not of superior intelligence because they are taught; animals can be taught. *Evidence of people's superiority is shown in how they treat themselves and others in the community, and how well they transmit their heritage over time.* If they do these things poorly, that evidence highlights and makes plain their inferiority. If they do them well that is evidence of their superiority.

If a woman, for instance, has all degrees offered by all the universities on earth, she would still be a woman and conversely, if she not only has not gone to school a day in her life but also does not even know what a school is, she would still be a woman. This principle holds also for a man.

The Mayor's Challenge for Detroit

The challenge the mayor has is to build community. His duty is to develop a public policy that makes the city safe, clean and prosperous. He cannot do the latter if he does not understand the former. Some wonder why he did so well in the state legislature in Lansing, rising to leadership in that august body at such an early age. He was functioning in a developed system there. As mayor of a predominately black city, he has to formulate and develop a public policy that makes the city safe, clean and prosperous. The skills used being a functionary have little or no resemblance to what is absolutely essential for developing the black community. As a functionary you obey the established rules and look good, and may appear even to be bright. As the master builder of community, you must have a vision of civility so clear that it compels constituents to agree the vision is right not by fancy speeches full of empty promises but because the efficacy of the plan causes them to work the plan and plan to work till what is seen in the vision is reality on the ground.

They must see in his success their success, and they together stuffed with an inspired and joyful spirit must do what men have done through the ages when their call was to change the course of history and steer their destiny in a more amenable path. They will discharge the lifestyle of mayhem, clever dodge and casual murder for civil living. They will deliberately break the ways of the past and carve for themselves a future they can live in filled with practicality, optimism and hope. They will then be able to walk the streets of their community as the sons of men and lift every voice and sing till earth and freedom ring. They will never bow again to the tyranny of murder and bestial slaughter. Their understanding will accept the premise that community is not a person but a conglomeration of people bound forever to being that light in the pathway of progress in a place that is safe, clean and prosperous, where the gaiety in the voices of the children is heard around the world.

To be true to the call, all willful detractions must go.

GLOSSARY OF KEY TERMS AND WORDS

It took many years of study and analysis to determine reasonably the social value and meaning of the terms here listed as they revealed their meaning in usage in terms of whom precisely in the race or to which race they refer, and to what effect. Were they, in the main, emotional racist bombastic epithets pure and simple, meant only to insult and affront the most vulnerable and helpless or did there emerge some intended, descriptive logic in their usage? Finding it to be the latter, I continued to study and look for some depth in their motivation, because complicating the search was the fact that whites also called themselves many of these terms including lazy, stupid, barbaric and savage. Even the brilliant Thomas Jefferson called himself "savage." Plus there were hardly any names or labels whites call blacks; blacks have not been heard calling whites including the offending term of "boy." So if whites call themselves these terms and blacks call whites them, what is the big deal? Why do blacks get so over wrought when whites call them boy for instance, though they are over thirty-five? In the main, it is a matter of power; blacks mainly call whites these terms behind their backs like children, but whites call blacks them to their face. Blacks, ignorant of their own power and being too lazy or stupid, it seems, to its potency, in the face of such boldface power, feel helpless and intimidated. And in another sense, when all is said and done, blacks, no doubt, feel the stinging lash of truth upon them.

Some of these terms many blacks have heard referencing them by whites all their lives but have never understood fully their meaning, but must know their meaning if they are to understand them. Since the civil rights movement, many of these terms have been changed to euphemisms. But most know that calling a sow's ears silk does not make them be so.

I decided there is value in listing them when in a book study group, a member, who thought Thurgood Marshall was anything but lazy, was shocked when President Johnson in Juan Williams' book, *Thurgood Marshall: American Revolutionary* (2000)—when the president was considering Marshall for appointment as an associate justice to the U. S. Supreme Court—kept referring to his hero as lazy.

1. **A fool**—means a black who thinks black ghetto is geography and not the condition of the black persona of which every black is a part. A black who thinks he is not in the slums of the black ghetto because he heads a Fortune 500 company or an Ivy League University or graduated summa cum laude with a PhD degree from Harvard, is rich, or has some other high position of prestige and authority. Who does not understand that the so-called ignorant whites who called Dr. King, Martin Luther Coon, did so not because they had more education, money, position or authority than he but because white leaders had conceptualized and carried out a public policy that recognizes the basic humanity of every white person. And black leaders seem to be too lazy or too stupid to understand they must do the same for their major branch of humanity, before he can ever be equal. They must understand that every tub must sit on its own bottom; and every race, likewise, must stand on its own feet. They are too lazy or too stupid to understand that the white man may hold his nose and, with pompous contempt, tolerate them at his table; but that there are certain things no man, that is, no race, not even the black race, can delegate. If they are to have their own table,

SHELTON VAUGHN

built from their own intelligence, imagination and initiative, they must use them to do so. This will only happen when they develop the black persona to feel as keenly the sense of his humanity as the white man has done for his. A black who obtains education, money, fame, or position and thinks mere possession of these amenities makes him middle class is obviously a fool. This point is discussed under The Myth of the Black Middle Class.

2. **Barbaric**—means an elemental ability to reason, a creeping up from impulsive savagery, and though brutal, its movement is forward, toward civility.

3. **Belief**—means faith in the unknown no matter how elemental or basic. When one sits, he believes he will get up again.

4. **Bent back**—means a condition in the black elite that makes them rather be lapdogs at the white man's table than men who conceptualize and carry out a public policy with, perhaps, the cooperation of whites of goodwill that lifts the black race to greatness.

5. **Black elitist**—means that group of well-heeled blacks who seem to be more an enemy to black people than a friend; but who are needed most urgently to reverse their current stance against them, and move hurriedly and with all deliberate speed to lead them to greatness, but who so far have shown themselves to be too lazy or stupid to do so.

6. **Black ghetto**—means that degenerate quality in the black elite that will not let them break free of slovenliness and lapdogging and lead black people to greatness. It is more a mindset than geography.

7. **Black ineptitude**—means that quality in blacks that is the host for racism; it is a towering deficiency in black intelligence, for racism could not exist without a host. As long as there is a host for it, racism will exist, as long, therefore, as water will tend to run down stream.

8. **Boy**—means black leaders deficient in the will to lead black people to greatness. They lack, it seems, maturity and other qualities necessary for self-governance, which are self-control and the ability not only to see the true genius in the essence of black humanity but also to highlight it, tease it out, and develop it to its fullest potential.

9. **Civilized**—means skilled in the art of reasoning, is scientifically bent. The dominant force in a civilized people is their ability to think, to do things not on an animalistic impulse but for carefully thought-out reasons. Or can catch the essence of an impulse and give it direction

with discipline that leads to something great. I have never witnessed a black speaker or writer saying that black people are civilized people. Du Bois said civilization crushed black folk. That is a misreading of civilization. The proper reading is, civilization has been unable yet to lift black folk to greatness. In his book, *The Senator and the Socialite: The True Story of America's First Black Dynasty*, 2006, Lawrence Otis Graham, a devout Talented Tenther, says Booker T. Washington's inspired and uplifting, autobiography, *Up from Slavery* asks blacks to accept their inferiority. In this charge he adheres to the premise that if you are going to tell a really big, giant size lie, tell it with a straight face and a bold imprint. His imprint is evidence that the Blackman's long night is not over yet; and that, if the Talented Tenth has any say in the matter, it shall never end.

10. **Control**—means that which white has of black. Black resent this control of him, but is too lazy and too indifferent to the dignity of his humanity to prevent it by becoming noted for his own self-control.

11. **Dero**—means that person whose renown diminishes mankind. See also hero.

12. **Discipline**—means ability to control oneself and to instill the same in others. Disciplined people, if they choose, will control, enslave, segregate and in other ways abuse, demean and insult people without it.

13. **Discipline, lack of**—means black leaders are deficient in self-control; this deficiency in people makes certain they will be controlled by others.

14. **Empty headed**—means black elite void of communal qualities necessary for synergistic social intelligence, though they may have a PhD. from Harvard.

15. **Evil**—means that quality in the Talented Tenth so degenerate and so rancorously monstrous: it causes them to choose willfully and deliberately to act against the best interest of black people.

16. **Greatness**—means a safe, clean and prosperous community, the beloved community.

17. **Hero**—means that person whose renown enhances greatly the statue of mankind. See also dero.

18. **Idiot**—means an absolute fool to be pitied.

19. **Industry**—means hated viciously by Du Bois and the Talented Tenth. If they have their say forever, black folk will never be an industrious people. They will always be lag headed pretenders. The

Talented Tenth is as strong today as in the days when they were attacking BTW, and they are still lying about him. And are thus an ingrained evil in the flesh of black humanity.

20. **Integration**—means that there are laws regarding blacks that whites are bound to respect, mutual respect between the races. It does not mean living next door; the races lived next door and in the same house during slavery. It does not mean having interracial sex; there was interracial sex during slavery. There was no integration then and there is very little integration today, because there was none then and there is very little mutual respect today; but there is tolerance today. Tolerance is a step in the right direction. Blacks today do not respect the Whiteman; they fear him; this fear is rooted in the fact that blacks do not respect themselves; and the Whiteman, therefore, does not respect blacks; he alternates between pompous contempt and sniveling tolerance of them.

21. **Intelligence**—means if the black elite have conceptual, imaginative, and coherent intelligence, and each of these intelligences is needed for people to build a first-class, first-world, world-class community, they do not use them.

22. **Justice in the arch of the universe**—means an unintended consequence of an initiator of evil. An example of this is the Confederate States striking the blow at Fort Sumter, April 12, 1861, to preserve slavery forever.

23. **Lag headed**—means black elites have not plugged in to the forward march of mankind.

24. **Lazy**—means one has the ability but lacks the will. A black leader with the ability to conceptualize and effectuate a public policy that moves the race to greatness but is too lazy and trifling to do so.

25. **Loose headed**—means black elite not doing what is needed to move black people to full social development.

26. **Middle class**—means a group of people with the wealth necessary to pay for what they want or need, and the political clout and will necessary to get the job done. It is a set of social values infused into the persona of people that causes them to build a safe, clean and prosperous community. There is no black middle class today.

27. **Minority**—means deficiency. Wherever blacks are today, numerical ratio notwithstanding, they are too deficient in evidentiary intelligence to conceive and build the preferred (beloved) community that is safe, clean and prosperous.

28. **Miss education of the Negro**—means a misnomer. It is not that black is miss educated. His problem with education is he misuses it once he has it. Once he has his PhD summa cum laude degree from Harvard, he still stands around and waits for the white man to give him something to do and to tell him when to do it.

29. **Niggerism**—means an evil in black folk directed against themselves. A Nigger is a black male or female with an evil in him or her directed against one or more black persons, including the whole black race.

30. **Public policy**—means plan adhered to by a people that leads them to greatness or to degeneracy.

31. **Pretense**—means a condition and a practice in and of that portion of the black elite that is the black peoples worse enemy. It is essentially an excuse for them to do nothing to advance the black race to greatness, while pretending to be concerned, while in actuality doing evil against black people.

32. **Racism**—means an evil in whites directed against blacks. An evil perpetrated by white folk, industrious people, against black folk, lazy people indifferent to their own potential for industrious development. Racism is the most monumental evil ever to infect human personality. It is a flaw in the character of any white person who is so infected; for it is a claim that the white man has an absolute right to abuse black people. There is no other evil possible to be conceived in the minds of men that can be worse than that.

33. **Savage**—means human beings moved mainly by impulse not reason.

34. **Segregation**—means black has no right white is bound to respect. White feels that there is no law regarding respect for blacks that whites are bound to respect. Whites bully blacks because they (the whites) have the upper hand.

35. **Self-control**—means self-restraint. Uses reason rather than impulse; is fit for and capable of self-governance.

36. **Stupid**—means lack of ability. A black leader without the ability to conceptualize and carry out a public policy that moves the race to greatness.

37. **Talented Tenth** (TT for short)—means a view advocated by Du Bois which says that white folk would educate that tenth of blacks most gifted; and they, once educated would be the resource that would educate the other 90 percent of the black population.

SHELTON VAUGHN

It purports a role for themselves, but does not state the duty of the masses. This crackpot idea exposed more about Du Bois than he wanted known. So not changing his stripes, he abandoned it late in life. Then devotees of the concept abandoned him. TT is a highly educated, ignorant click of blacks who think they are less than whites but more than the mass of blacks; but this is really evidence that this black elite is too lazy or too stupid to conceptualize and carryout a public policy that leads black people to greatness. So instead of doing their duty, they concoct and adhere to a silly, demeaning notion that makes themselves look like contemptible, stupid, idiotic fools.

38. **Whiteman and Blackman**—mean capitalized because they refer to the composite persona of the race.

LETTERS

THIS IS A sampling of letters I have written overtime mostly to blacks with a public voice. Not one of these letters ever drew a response.

Dear Ms. Riley:

How are you? I hope these few lines find you in good spirit and feeling wonderfully well.

On Am I Right, Friday, July 6, 2007 here is the factor you did not consider in your end of show discussion about where the next black leader(s) is coming from. You said you told a group we don't need leaders, that each of us has to be one. Nolan happily and, rather, joyously agreed with your—and please forgive me—lead headed contention, because it fitted well in whites view of us as lazy dumb brutes.

The factor not considered in your congenial wrap-up is, why in black cities mainly anywhere in the world, in America, Haiti, Africa or elsewhere, they are generally places of despair (despair is code for laziness) and banal savagery, and almost everywhere whites rule, they are places preferred by both blacks and whites?

Whites know everybody can't be mayor or head of other major societal institutions that determine the standards and principles by which people shall live, and how well they develop and comport themselves with each other and among their fellowmen.

It is the no-leaders-needed philosophy you espoused that shall cause blacks to stay in their current nightmare a long time yet. Without leaders, it shall never end.

Looking at reality, assessing why it is thus, then devising means that effectively favor the whole body of the people requires leaders with a vision and ability to persuade the people to move to the path of excellence and civility, and away from the plane of savagery. As long as we claim we don't need leaders, we will never produce any; and we will stay in the bottomless pit forever.

Ms. Riley, I am going to share something with you. I know you are a brilliant person. You know how we talk about education being the way for us to advance? Well, here is a fact or two: at the turn of the 20th century only six percent of the total population of the U.S. had finished high school; yet America had built the cross continental railroad and the Brooklyn Bridge, two of the greatest engineering feats in history. These achievements could not have been wrought with a no leaders needed philosophy. Nolan knows this. So his joviality was at you, not with you.

At the turn of the 21st century, over 78 to 80 percent of blacks in America had a high school education; yet in Detroit, a city 85 percent black, with the no leaders needed philosophy, we can't feed, cloth nor house ourselves. So though we are educated, with our no leaders needed philosophy, we are as helpless as any pack of brute animals.

You can't state or teach what is expected of a leader if you say we don't need one. So instead of saying we don't need leaders, which, since we are humans, is obviously a lie, state what we need leaders to do: then the listener(s), be they youth or adults will begin to formulate and assess whether they will be a leader or a helper. And at that, we will develop a skill of evaluating the effectiveness of a leader with a sense of the role of the helper in the success or failure in the wellbeing of the community. But when, as you say you did, one says we don't need leaders because each of us is one: well that is not true; and that untruth

SHELTON VAUGHN

poisons the well of hope, make optimism impossible, kills opportunity, creates black society a mass crime scene of murder, killing and slaughter: where blacks in Detroit, Haiti and Africa try to get out and into places where whites rule.

The "terms" like lead headed and such are not personal; I am sure you are a fine cultured, highly educated lady. It is black culture I am trying to alert regarding the cause for black degeneracy. Black society is in the pit because of what our best educated people are saying and doing.

Sincerely,
Shelton Vaughn

Dear Ms. Riley:

I read (in the column of Wednesday, Oct. 25, 2006) with mild amusement your reflections on Jesse Jackson's runs for president in 1984 and 1988. I can understand your viewing at the time, being young and star struck, his idiotic antics as hopes not deaths for thousands of black sons and daughters by his and others negligence in the destruction of the Southern Christian Leadership Conference (SCLC). The mass murder of blacks by blacks was so complete throughout the black community in America, the tagline for the young of that time is, the lost generation.

Jesse Jackson, Andrew Young and Ralph Abernathy conjoined in one of the most evil action ever committed against black people. This is so even when slavery, Du Bois and his Talented Tenth, and Jim Crow are put in the mix. Dr. Martin Luther King Jr. had with commitment unceasingly led us with odds stacked against us by us and by others to bring an end to Jim Crow and to the acceptance of our color. The first physical attack on his life, with a stab almost to the heart, was by one of us, a black female, Mrs. Izola Curry in New York City; and we know a white man assassinated him. But in his life he showed what organization can do, even for an apparent scattered brain people like us. But these men were not merely scattered brain, they were evil rot to the core and, therefore, were having none of that "help the black race cohere and advance." They deliberately, therefore, ignored the value and importance of black life and went off in pursuit of personal agendas. This was a crime unforgivable.

So after King was assassinated, Jim Crow being essentially ended, they said: black folk be damned.

If given an aphorism, it would be: in King's case, never before has a man done so much with so little to benefit the race and the nation; in Jackson's, never has a man squandered so much for nothing.

To show how absolutely idiotic his runs were: nobody has ever been elected president having done anything to get there but to run for the office. Jackson had not only not done anything, but the one noticeable thing in his record was his participation in the destruction of SCLC after promising they would keep it going if something would happen to Dr. King.

Now that you have matured and are able to look on that time with sobriety, I hope truth will hammer at the cockles of your heart till it breaks through and that you will tell it even in your column. To see these men as any other than heinous vicious criminals is to say the blacks slaughtered at the hands of their negligence in destroying SCLC were not human beings, and that the grief of their black mothers' loss is of naught and counts for nothing. One of the mysteries we present to the world is why, when we get positions in white media and in black media, we do not articulate black savagery committed against us by blacks in power and positions of authority. These men were powerful, and should be held accountable for their neglect. We can wax well when portraying the evils of Benito Mussolini, Adolph Hitler, Paul Pot and other monsters for their crimes; but quietly ignore our own; or compliment them when in actuality they too should be hung.

Sincerely,
Shelton Vaughn

P. S. The engine that advance people is organization. Organization is where the strength of people is. Power is in numbers; there are millions of us; so we have power, but we have built no organization to manifest it. So when members of our race get to the top as these men did and act destructively of our best interest, we have responsibility to call them out as the Italians did Mussolini and the Germans, Hitler. There is no way we can accept the premise that we are human beings, thus able to have empathy with the black mother whose son or daughter is shot down routinely in our homes, streets and neighborhood by our own black sons, and not hold these men accountable for the slaughter.

Dear Emery King and Paul W. Smith:

I watched with sadness and tremendous trepidation about 10 minutes of your discussion, bridging the racial divide: your focus maybe unbeknownst to you was on a situation America had and struggled through in the 1950s and 1960s when Detroit had no black mayor, majority on city council, police chief, no superintendent of schools, no majority on school board, and no black dominance of principals and teachers in Detroit Public Schools. Gentlemen, that battle was fought and won under the leadership of Dr. Martin Luther King Jr.

What we need to know now is why with blacks in charge, the city is a crime scene, a killing field and a slaughter house of blacks murdering, slaughtering and killing blacks in high numbers in black neighborhoods, while blacks with money, education, fame, positions of authority and prestige seek to pimp it, but not lead it to greatness. (Why in others words would they rather ruin it, than lead black people to reflect their best intelligence, their superior human intelligence, why would they rather act like a pact of loose headed inferior persons)? The discussion you are trying to have now does nothing but produce rage in blacks, who lacking the restraint put on them by Jim Crow, while showing little or no will for self governance nor self respect, run around murdering blacks in their homes, in the streets, in the black community. Isn't it obvious this neglect of their people by the black elite and this display of black savagery in the streets can only cause additional contempt in whites who see us as too stupid and too socially lazy to help each other meet our very minimal needs of food, clothes and shelter, while providing a safe, clean and wholesome environment for family living? Whites know and we know too that if people other than blacks do not come into Detroit and open stores to sell us food and clothes and make available to us housing our scene here would be the same as it is in Haiti and Africa.

What is wrong with black folk! That is the question before us in Detroit, in the State of Michigan, the nation and the world. Why black politicians, ministers, entrepreneurs, civic leaders, blacks in media (that is blacks working for white media outlets), and black media (Michigan Chronicle, Michigan citizen, Ebony Magazine, etc.) do not cohere and build a public policy in Detroit that transforms the city from a crime scene to a place preferred? One of the principles of psychology is, you teach others how to treat you. Don't we know if we treat each other badly, others will see that and class us as socially deficient though we have our degrees from Harvard and other prestigious colleges and universities?

We most know that it is okay to talk about us, to critique us, to point to our deficiencies, and seek, trying hard, to improve ourselves.

Again, your focus was timely for a time past, when Jim Crow ruled the land. Paul W. opened telling about a white shop owner trailing and watching a black male in the store. When asked by Paul W., why was he following and watching the black male, the owner said that black male was a thief. The black panelists let that pass, and went on to talk about driving while black and white privilege. The owner was acting wisely, keeping an eye on the thief, thus protecting the merchandise. Under Jim Crow, the owner could/would have called in a pact of goons who would have taken the thief outside of town, beaten the hell out of him, busted a kneecap, broken two toes, and made him promise never to steal again, and let him know that if he did, they would kill him. Thus marked and crippled for life without due process, he committed never to steal again and kept the promise, because he knew the goons would keep theirs. Now the white man respects the humanity and the life of the black thief. Sure racism is a problem, thus driving while black is some danger; but we must learn to priorities. I think anyone with good sense would readily realize that having a white man watch you to keep you from stealing his property or having a white cop pull you over on the road is a lower priority than having a black male murder you or a member of your family.

Finally, your focus of bridging the racial divide is a recipe for getting a lot of black folk murdered by our own black sons in the black community, because that kind of focus today only enrages blacks and, getting no proper leadership from black leaders, they roam the streets of the community murdering, slaughtering and killing their own people of all ages, many times in cold blood. So Emery, if your hatred for your people is not so overwhelmingly fixed that in your view the only option you have is to continue, even if a huge spike in the murder of blacks, mostly by black males is certain, please change your focus. And Paul W., if your desire is not to see blacks present themselves as an innately deficient people, persuade Emery to change the focus.

There is a way to bridge the racial divide that could and would improve immensely conditions in the black community and, thereby, improve race relations. If you have even a modicum of respect for the lives of black people, please change your focus, and address the need black folk have to build a public policy that gets the best out of all of us, especially our black sons in our community. If you do, our sons will be so busy developing themselves, they will by omission quell their impulse to murder and steal and commit mayhem in the city and thereby gain a zest for life and living that will cause them to act civilized.

Let's say for argument, you are interested in reducing the threat of driving while black. Your focus is not the way to do that; it will instead increase the danger, because a spike in the black murder rate will cause whites assigned to contain and restrict black savagery to keep a keen eye on blacks stirring about.

By the way, murder in the city has spiked to date 17 percent this year.

Let's say the Whiteman does enjoy white privileges of walking about in his community in relative safety, running businesses there that meet his basic needs, plus those that make for the good life in entertainment, athletics, festivals, carnivals, etc. ad infinitum. One of the most inane statements blacks make is that black youth don't have anything constructive to do, when black youth being idle have for more to do than any other youth. The question is, why don't Emery and other blacks see the need for black privileges, and raise the conscience of our people to enjoy black privileges of safety, cleanliness and prosperity in the black community? Both of you, Emery and you, Paul W. are in the media, and polling now is an intricate part of the fabric of society. Above I questioned whether your motivation was out of some misguided notion to actually, with intent, do harm to black people. I based that assessment on more than twenty five years of research on how the black elite brutalize the mass of black people in America, Haiti and Africa. But let's just say you are, though misguided, sincere. If you truly are sincere in improving the condition of black folk, while at the same time improving race relations, in addition to suggestions made above, use your clout now to have a survey taken asking these questions: would you like relations improved between white and black people? Do you believe if blacks reduced homicides in Detroit from well over 300 per year (this level of slaughter has been maintained annually now for nearly 40 years) to well under 50, that would improve or hurt race relations? Do you believe that, if blacks cleaned up the city and made it a really safe, clean and prosperous place in which to live, raise a family and do business, race relations would be helped or setback? You get the thought.

Sincerely,
Shelton Vaughn

August 22, 2006
Dear Mr. Cabell:

This is a personal note just for you. I knew a lady named Terry and, therefore, was not certain your gender; so your picture in the paper cleared that mystery. I know you probably think I am the biggest advocate for advancing excellence in black media, when I say the black press today is fit mainly to carp and bark rather than being a sophisticated human resource fully capable of knowing right from wrong and demanding right from us toward us as well as right from others toward us. To share with you the kind of focus the black press once had, I am enclosing an article written by a church reporter once for the Michigan Chronicle. What happen to the black press is during the civil rights movement one of the things Dr. King did with SCLC was to demand that companies advertise in black publications; once black publications got that revenue stream, they turned their back on black people by not demanding our excellence, and set on the course of carp, whine and bark like a feist. I recommended in a letter, March 26, 2006, that MC assign one city beat reporter at least, and if resources allow assign a reporter for each the mayor, council and the schools. There should also be a reliable stream of information on black business development in the city, because without an economic base for wealth building in the black community, we will never be seen as anything other than subhuman animals, wearing the human form. I see Sam Logan wrote a responsible, factual and detailed article (MC August 16-22, 2006) on DPS rejection of the Compuware contract for 4 mini-companies with no credible track record; but he is all over the place with articles; black folk need a solid base of facts built up over time and retrievable for review and analysis when desired. Sam's main talent, however is not writing; it is selling newspaper, but a paper needs to do more than be sold; it needs to inform and educate the reader in a consistent and comprehensible manner. This idea is for from the publishers and editors of the black press today.

It did so in the latter part of the 1800s and, as the enclosed article indicates, during a good portion of the 1900s; but the current crop has not adjusted to the new reality of blacks in power. Even Ebony *is still stuck where it began. When it started, the main fair for blacks in white media depicted blacks as lazy surly idiots possessing little to no initiative, fit only to be told what to do by whites and then made to do it under the constant threat of lynching. And John Johnson saw that blacks were raising families, going to school, getting degrees and landing jobs here to fore closed to them. So* Ebony *found success in reporting the success of individual blacks. Black under the lynching threat perked up and tried to prove to the white he was human and that he could act with sense. Once Dr. King with SCLC successfully ended Jim Crow, most of the best educated, the most gifted, and the most wealthiest ceased all pretense of claiming to be human and sped headlong into the arena of the pathological lapdog.* Ebony's *list of the top 100 most influential blacks is an anachronism. We need now to know who is failing or succeeding in these positions of influence, prestige and authority. We need to know what black mayor formulated and carried out, or failed to, a public policy that made his jurisdiction a first-class, first-world, world-class jurisdiction in which to live, raise a family and do business. Where crime is as low as it is in the white's; where students are leading the state or region in academic excellence; where the family is stabilized at 80 to 90 percent of households headed by a mother and father in the home (which is the percentage sustain during Jim Crow when we were trying to prove to whites that we are human); where the overall economic well being of the people is second to none; where the black male develop businesses that meet the daily needs of the people for food, clothes and shelter and, yes indeed, where he is respectful, respectable and respected.*

Sincerely,
Shelton Vaughn

P.S. The enclosed article should prove that I am not off key, and that I am justified in believing that the black press can do its duty. As evidence shows, the lady in the picture is black. The power and authority which that lady writes seems unthinkable in the shallow headed, mostly feel good in blissful ignorant gibberish filling the whining and carping black press today.

Dear Mayor Kilpatrick:

This letter is about how to save upwards of 90 to 95 per cent of lives lost in Detroit on average per year during the past 37 years starting in 1968 through 2004. In this time we have had no year as low as 365 and we have averaged about 540 per year. Multiply 540 X 37 = 19980 (less than five thousand were lynched during the 70 year lynching season from 1882 thru 1951 in the whole United States, and over a thousand of them were white). Save 90 percent of 540, that is 486 lives saved, bringing homicides down to 54 per year. The plan I can present to you can bring homicides down below 50 per year, and keep them there. That is what this letter is about. Now let me tell you how this letter came to be written with the confidence and assurance I give that we can do it.

Mr. Mayor, I had a 3.42 GPA (but I chose not to pursue the masters and the PhD programs) upon graduating with a Bachelors of Arts Degree in General Studies from Wayne State University in 1981. I had learned in my course of study the scientific method of research, the method of raising questions and systematically searching and hopefully finding the answers.

Detroit had a very bloody decade of the 1970s, when over six thousand people were killed. These killings disturbed me with an impact that can only be guessed at. But there was contrast that made the horror of the killings even worse. During that decade we black people got everything in the city that we had been asking for since the first boatload of us was bought by the colonies in 1619 in Jamestown, Virginia. Since that day we had been asking for freedom from bondage, the right to vote—not just to cast a ballot but to run for office with a chance to win, and not just to be considered for a high level appointed position but also to be affirmed. In other words, all the rights, privileges and obligations of a full born, natural born citizen.

During the 1970s, we got the first black mayor in 1974, first majority city council and first police chief. In the school system, we got the first superintendent of schools and first majority school board. We went from mom and pop businesses to multimillion dollar auto dealerships and big general supermarkets. Regarding our clergy, we went from being Rev. this and that to being Dr. so and so. According to the U.S. census, the average household income in Detroit was greater for blacks than in any other of America's ten largest cities. Now here are some chilling facts, the year 1974 remains even to this hour the bloodiest year in the city's history; the decade of the 1970 still hold the record as being tops in killings. The images of the city for the decade, therefore, were not black achievements but black on black crime and murder capital of the nation. It was in 1968 that homicides went over one a day; the last year homicides were below one a day was that God awful year of 1967 when the city writhed and twisted, killed and slaughtered, in a messy riot.

We have shown that we can kill, murder and slaughter each other at high numbers in our homes, streets and neighborhoods; and that we can grieve; we all have seen the grieving mother following in the trail of the hearse carrying her murdered child's body to the grave; but now, because of research, we can save ever so many lives of our sons and daughters, especially our children.

Based on the research, I would like to present the plan to you and 25 people of your choosing. You are the central person in the city. I would be irresponsible not to bring it to your attention. The 25 people would have the responsibility of hearing the plan and deciding that we should work the plan and plan to work till the goal is reached, or to say not yet. The goal of bringing homicides down below 50 per year and keeping them there can be achieved in five years from the kickoff date.

Beginning an independent research project in 1981, I had to find the cause and the best possible solution to the city's homicidal problem. Having found the answer to the two questions ten years later, I wrote the article enclosed. But as the case would have it, there were five questions to be considered, not two. The other three were: can we solve this problem? Will we solve it? And if "Yes" to those two, then when? Through systematic study, I found the answers, to can and will we, to be "Yes." Now of the five, the only one left yet to be answered is, when. We can do it now; but, whether we do it now or wait a thousand years; when we do it, we will still look back and wonder why did it take us so long.

You should be remembered not merely as one who was mayor but as a man of history who responded to the call to hear the plan to check the death rider in the city and to let our sons and daughters live. And generations yet unborn in centuries yet to be, when they look back down through the corridors of history

SHELTON VAUGHN

and come to this moment in time and look in on us, they will be able to say these are they who cared enough to save the lives of our sons and daughters.

Your neighbor,
Shelton Vaughn

Enclosure
P. S. To present the plan will take at least 90 minutes.

Dear Councilman Cockrel:

Since black folk have been trying to run Detroit city governance, starting in 1974, it has been continuously spiraling farther and farther downward into the bottomless pit. Not only Detroit's residents but the whole world is watching and waiting and wondering when will Detroit's black politicians stop hatching excuses to explain their failures and boldly develop a public policy that makes their city reflect the level of their intelligence. Cynics say you already have given it your best shot. They say if black politicians had honed, intelligent, political skills, they would have shown them somewhere on the planet by now either in America, in Haiti or in Africa.

It seems the black politician lacks the mental ability to understand the fact that it is not about speech making and promises but actual results on the ground in the hearts and minds of the constituents. In the 2000 census, the black population in Detroit went down. Using the scientific method of inquiry, I began my dedicated research of black people in 1981. As word spread about it, people would ask me what did I think of Mayor Young when he was mayor, and ever since I have been asked upfront would mayor Archer or Kilpatrick do a good job as mayor, I have been able to predict and state unequivocally that neither of these three men would succeed as mayor, because neither had a clue what is the duty of the mayor. There is an absolute law of nature; which is, if the dot is not thrown in the direction of the board, you are certainly not going to hit the bulls eye. In that case you will not even hit the board. I have found only two blacks in American history to make effective public policy in the black community in the three main areas of safety, cleanliness and prosperity; they are Booker T. Washington: he lifted the veil of ignorance from his people; and Martin Luther King Jr., he lifted from the nation the scourge of Jim Crow, a system that forced upon blacks extreme measures of insult, open rebuke and contempt.

It is said in the paper that you, the council, voted not to raise the water rate because you wanted to keep it cheap enough for the poor to be able to afford it. That is not an intelligent reason not to raise the rate. That logic says if the poorest among us cannot afford the increase, then nobody should have water. Which is what will happen if keeping it at the current rate makes it impossible to generate the revenue necessary to tend repairs and overall upkeep of the system to the highest quality. Your action opens a path that denies top quality water to all. A more sensible approach would be to raise the rate for upkeep; and, if need be, seek charity benevolence to assist the poor in paying their bill as is done in the THAW program in home heating. You should keep before you always the story of Josephine Baker, who according to the movie of her life, by insisting that she save all unfortunate children ended up saving none and being kicked, yelling and screaming out of her own house.

Let me close by repeating these two views: 1. If your problem is not due to deliberate choice but is truly a lack of intelligence, you are doomed by nature to stew forever in the mess you are in. 2. The duty of the politician in office is to develop a public policy that ensures that the confines of his jurisdiction are safe, clean and prosperous. If this is not achieved, he is a failure. If he does not know and understand this to be true—well then, in that case, he is a pathetic fool.

Sincerely,
Shelton Vaughn
cc: to each council member

Dear Councilmember Reaves:

I knew you had for more in you than that cursory, inapt, nonsensical response you made to my first letter. Since you came from a background of song, I knew you knew you do not just run out and blab a song before any rehearsals. That is the reason I said gain fame on council as you did in song by becoming a real pro there. Recognize the honored situation you are in, the great opportunity you have which is to make this city sing again.

Fix in your head first just how Grand Boulevard renamed can become a magnet for nudging Detroit from her current state of lethargy into a sassy mode that will cause her to lift her voice again with song and invite the world to come. Make her the city where her sons will think and act like self respecting men and boys, and her women and girls will light up the world with discipline and supreme elegance.

Your idea is good. It obviously is not the quality of the idea that is the problem. Who is going to pay for it is. The old folk used to say the biggest fool on earth can ask a question the wisest and most learned man cannot answer. You say Berry Gordy wants GB named in his honor. Taking your points at face value: you want the city to rename GB after BG, because in your view that will help Detroit move forward by bringing in tourists. Now once you have those two points as a premise, you do not emblazon yourself before the world as an unskilled, lazy neophyte. Having conceived the ideas, the first thing you do is go to BG and get his support in the form of at least $10 million; then go throughout the city holding town meetings, at least 25 or more building support among the people by making clear your vision. With that kind of thought and leg work performed, when you present the resolution to council for a vote it would be greatly appreciated by the people, and your name would live in history as not only a great singer but a great leader.

Do not go to Berry with some muddleheaded claptrap. Layout your plan, your vision, with such clarity and precision that he grasp the idea. Justify every penny. Remember he was so good, he renamed a city. He made a sound world renown. When you say the motor city, people know you are talking about Detroit; and likewise when you say the Motown Sound. He did not half step when he put you all before the world. Do not half step this. If you are going to do it, do it right. You are talking here about one of the foremost innovators of all time. He now is like Max Fisher, a man of wealth and privilege. Do not demean his greatness with sloppy, half baked fuzzy thinking. Remember your idea is to honor the city by honoring him. That is by no means a small feat. So don't treated it like one. People from all over the world will come to Detroit to ride on the Berry Gordy Boulevard. Yes some of them may sing some of your songs, or play them as they ride along enjoying, perhaps, a romantic interlude, remembering what they once had or looking forward to pleasures yet to come.

If you and Berry really want this, it will truly be one of the most astounding miracles ever to occur in all the annals of human history. When one is at his level of wealth and prestige says one wants means one is willing to use one's resources and influence to make it happen. That is what Max Fisher did for the Max Fisher Orchestral Center, Henry Ford for the Henry Ford Hospital, and Andrew Carnegie for the Andrew Carnegie Library at Tuskegee University. Each of these men coughed up millions of dollars to enshrine their names forever in the hearts and minds of their countrymen. So it is not a matter of Berry saying he wants this. Any punk thug on the street can say he wants a street named after him. But can he make it happen? The answer clearly is, no. And the question you must ask is, is this something Berry wants? Or is this something he merely says he wants? It will take too much space here to explain why if you two get it done right it would be an astounding miracle. So let me close by saying you are nibbling at the edge of something grand, and that if it is done right generations yet unborn will call you the miracle lady and Berry Gordy a black man who did not let his people down.

Sincerely,
Shelton Vaughn

P. S. You may have serendipity. I hope you do. But as the old folk used to say: time will tell for sure.

Dear Ms. Martin:

It is likely you know that the most demeaning thing whites have ever said of blacks is that we lack ability for abstract thinking. So I hope you can understand how severely grieved my heart was, as I watched you ask Bill Cosby questions about his sex life, I saw you fumble for words and your lips quiver and you squirm as if your resistance were not there and that every stereotype ever uttered about the steam and heat of the loose sexual nature of the "colored gal" were flooding you to a degree that you had to segue from, the poor public policy issue in the black community he was their to discuss, to his sex life. But that program was not to discuss the over gorged sexual nature of the colored gal, nor the piped virility of the black male. The purpose of having Cosby on was not to talk about spousal infidelity.

Your performance said of you, I am just an old lazy, ignorant colored gal, lacking the industrious spunk necessary to rouse myself to get up and stir about in and among blacks so I'll be able to address a public policy issue, an abstract reality, without displaying and substituting my horniness in a lascivious, aggressive and degrading manor. If you are so unintelligent, you are incapable of understanding your problem, then may God have mercy on us all.

The black community today all over the world is a state of savagery because of our poor public policy, and this is so because we have not formulated the abstract idea coherently in our heads and then executed it effectively on the ground for the good of the total community. The white man gave you 30 minutes of precious air time to discuss poor black public policy, but you could not constrain yourself to sustain a discussion on policy for 30 minutes without a drift into sex. This naughtiness says you have more going on between your legs than in your head; and that is so sad, because that says there just may be no hope for us animalistic coloreds, as the white man says, to ever perform the abstract idea.

Here are eight questions every black so call journalist should ask of black policy makers to form the basis for discussion of the issue of black public policy in the black community:

1   What would you say is the public policy of black policy makers in the black community today?
2   Do you want the black community to be the best it can be? Explain.
3   Do you believe the black community today reflects the best of black intelligence? Explain.
4   Do you believe black pastors, politicians, business tycoons, and civic leaders are intelligent enough to build a coherent public policy in the black community that will make it safe, clean and prosperous on a first-class, first-world, world-class basis? Please explain your answer?
5   Of the four areas of leadership listed above, on which of the them would you put the greater portion of neglect for the problem of poor public policy in the black community?
6   Why specifically do you think black leaders are so slow about leading the black community to greatness?
7   Do you believe black leaders understand their responsibility to black people?
8   If they do not, is that a sign of their inferiority?

We need a public policy that speaks to and develops our better natures. Dogs and other animals have sex. Only humans develop public policy, an abstract notion, to meet their communal needs. How well they do this determines whether they are an inferior or a superior people. As you can see, sustaining the abstract idea is not about whether some blacks have college degrees and money. God bless you.

Sincerely,
Shelton Vaughn

Dear Mayor Kilpatrick:

As you know, October has become a period of dread, when flocks of human angels are called upon to come out to help keep the devil at bay during the Halloween season. But we have not yet quelled the impulse that makes Detroiters and, perhaps, others want to torch our city in a deliberate effort to burn it to the ground.

While what I am going to propose may not quell that evil and destructive impulse, it will certainly give the city a truly proper and positive focus for that month.

I am an officer in my optimist club, and I would like to meet with you or your representative and discuss a plan I have to work with you and one of the stadium heads for a grand event for mid October 2003. This will give plenty of time to meet with everybody and to adequately pull it all together.

This could be one of the truly grand events of the city. There are so many wonderful and capable people in the city and in the area who are wishing you and the city well, there is no reason why this event would not put a rise in the step of pride in the city for everybody. Detroit I believe shall shine again.

Yours sincerely,
Shelton Vaughn

Ebony Magazine Editor:

*In Nikitta A. Foston's article (*Ebony *September 2002), Why Women Cheat, the quote identifying the essential difference between men and women is of a white female doctor. Foston presents the female of her race as an animal in heat, "I cheat because I want variety," not as a human being with morals. The discouraging statistics in the article are so lopsided, they seem to make it accurate to conclude that the black woman—not just a particular one—lacks moral stamina; and that it is proper to conclude that she sees herself not as a human being who can find variety and joyous satisfaction in moral choices. When I consider, as I must, it is about the woman of whom I am a direct descendant, my heart becomes heavy and laden with grief.*

It was not always this way. In the 1940s and 1950s, the words in the black man's song were honey, baby and sugar. It was only after she dropped her morals did he change his words to whore, bitch and slut. I think that in the transition is a message somewhere that goes something like this: black woman pull up your morals by finding variety in moral choices; and the black man will change the words in his song to honey pie, sugar pudding and baby sweet so fast, it will make your heart flutter and your head swivel, causing you to light up with a brightness, a joy and a peace of which you had no idea was in you.

Sincerely,
Shelton Vaughn

Dear Mr. Leavy: Ebony Magazine

The historical paradigm is that whites discriminate against blacks because blacks are black. My more than forty years of research on my race shows that not to be the case. I have found just the opposite to be true: that no white person nor white system has ever enslaved, segregated or discriminated against a black person or black people because of their race or color. I would like to present this paradigm to *Ebony* for publication in a series of twelve essays over a period of one year. This will make history for *Ebony* and for black people. This as you can imagine will have a greater liberating effect than the switch from Negro to black which many thought would never occur. That switch, however, shows that blacks can change for their betterment. The relaxed swagger seen in black models in fashion shows and elsewhere on the world stage today would be utterly impossible without that switch having been made. Their supreme confidence reflects a high measure of assurance emitting as a source of pride from black people in the color of their race, now convinced black is made by God; black is beautiful; and are willing to say it loud, I'm black and I'm proud.

I began my research of blacks December 20, 1956, pretty much like Ebony *began, by looking at black achievement. There were things happening then I'm sure that spurred my interest causing me to focus on this topic. In the last half of the 1940s, Jackie Robinson had integrated Major League Baseball and Harry Truman, U. S. president, had integrated the U. S. Armed Forces; and in the 1950s the U. S. Supreme Court had struck down the separate but equal laws in education and the rise of Montgomery had occurred under the leadership of Dr. Martin Luther King Jr.*

Again, my focus like Ebony *was on black achievement, looking at our achievers in science, medicine, agriculture, education, entertainment, athletics, writing, publishing, preaching, business and of course reviewing the horrors of lynching and other forms of abuse at the hands of whites throughout the years. This pattern of study engaged me till 1981. In that year, I graduated from Wayne State University with honors with a liberal arts degree. At that point I had a choice, go on and get my masters and PhD or to investigate a most disconcerting phenomenon, blacks slaughtering blacks in high numbers in the black community with almost complete contempt for human life. This at a time when we were making unprecedented gains in achievement, especially in Detroit. In 1974 we got our first black mayor; during that decade we got the first black superintendent of schools, first black police chief, a majority on city council, a majority on the school board, the clergy raised themselves from Rev. to Dr. Yet it was during that decade blacks went nuts murdering blacks. The year 1974 was the bloodiest in the city's history and likewise was the decade; and for that, the city gained infamy in the title murder capital of the nation and noticed for the phrase black on black crime.*

This pattern shows that, though we are now proud of our color and individual achievements, we are not yet proud of ourselves as manifested in the way we treat each other and our surroundings. Our pride to date, therefore, is surface; this series will deal with us inside ourselves. Color is not glue. The bond of men is internal; they connect to each other from something inside of themselves.

Being a researcher I had to find the cause for and the solution to this pattern of slaughter. It was during this course of research that I made the amazing and astounding breakthrough to the fact that no discrimination we had ever suffered was due to our race or color. And *Ebony* being a historical black magazine, I thought it proper to give it an up-front opportunity to share with our people this beautiful relief from a burden we have borne for too long. Again this switch will be for more historic than from Negro to black. It will help assure as Dr. King foretold that we as a people will get to the promised land of safety, cleanliness and prosperity.

I must admit that from day one I was never quite convinced that the race problem was due to the color of either race, since neither had any say in his own creation. But who was I to question views handed down by some of the best minds of the race. The series will shine light in a dark place where truth has been hidden, and our people will realize in our time that a lie shall not live forever. In that realization we will be aided greatly in our march forward up and out of the dungeon pit, and see the day light of humanity and raise our voice in song in unison and sing coherently together the words: "Free at last, free at last, thank God almighty, we are free at last."

If you are any thing like I was, you may have thought about the matter but the old paradigm was so firmly set that you never thought to question it seriously. It was so completely convincing that we blacks were enslaved, segregated and continues to be discriminated against because of our race and color; that though skeptical, skepticism alone was not enough to convince me that my early hunch was right. Thus you will be able to benefit from my findings and to share them with our people. I can feed it to you, and thus the people, in bite size morsels of 15 to 25 hundred words per month. I am enclosing excerpts from three essays of my work. We can go forward from here together, if the match is made. Hoping to hear from you real soon.

Sincerely,
Shelton Vaughn

Dear Council Member Cleveland:

You pointed out two errors in my letter: the fact that the Michigan Chronicle got it wrong. (See copy enclosed). You should know by the way that black media is less (repeat less) responsible than the black politician. And you said not Detroit *but Atlanta on a per capita basis became the real murder capital during the 20 years Mayor Young was in office. If you can prove that, I'll give $25.00 (twenty-five dollars) to your favorite charity; and if you can't, you give the same amount to mine.*

On this we can agree, it was our behavior that gave those who first labeled Detroit the murder capital of the nation the ammunition to do so; it was our behavior that made the charge, if not technically accurate, creditable. Detroit was notorious in its murders; it first went over one murder per day in 1968; it has not been under 4 hundred any year since. That year it reached 426. It has averaged over 5 hundred homicides per year now for 33 years. That's well over 16 thousand. If Atlanta has murders above us per capita in this time frame, it is not by much. I doubt seriously if you can certify that it has.

I feel silly trying to argue this point, because it seems like the council is trying to explain these murders. These murders in Detroit in these high numbers are inexplicable. Our energy should be used in stopping, not explaining and comparing, them.

You ask what can the council and the people do to reduce homicides in Detroit. The council can take action that can reduce homicides in the city to about the same per capita ratio it was during the 1950s when whites was running the politics of the city. The ratio then was about one homicide per 18 thousand. To get to that ratio today we would have to reduce homicides in the city 90 percent. That is we would have to reduce them from the 500 average per year sustained during the past 33 years to 50.

You know, when whites were lynching us in high numbers, whites formed the NAACP to formerly and to structurally lobby their fellow white citizens not to lynch black folk. They took a two prong approach. They sort to get legislation passed in congress outlawing lynching, but that proved to be impossible due to the Southern filibuster, and they sort to change the white public opinion that tolerated it. When they began to take those actions, lynching began to decline. The sentiment today in white society not only does not support lynching blacks but to the contrary, it supports prosecuting the perpetrator(s). A la the case of James Bird in Texas.

The first thing the council can and should do is pass an ordinance in which the goal is set to reduce homicides in the city to the level outlined above. At this point in time, I may be the only person in this town who happen to think that black life is just as important as white and that if whites could prevail with whites to stop lynching us that we can prevail with us to stop murdering us in such high numbers, and that we can be effective in fact in reducing homicides in Detroit over 90 percent in 5 years. And do it in a way that would be sustained forever. And the spur could and should be to honor the late mayor who loved this city so much.

I would like to testify before council on this matter. Can you help me with that?

Respectfully yours,
Shelton Vaughn

Enclosure
P.S. Based on the record, to grant a holiday in his name would be an invitation to murder, would be in common parlance like throwing raw meat to dogs.

Dear Council Member Tinsley-Talabi:

I read in the paper that "Detroit City Council recently voted to have the city's Law Department draft an ordinance authorizing a paid /holiday commemorating the birthday of the late Coleman A. Young, Detroit's first Black mayor." That smacks of crass and impudent phoniness. The year he took office, 1974, we murdered more people in the city ever, before or since. We not only made the 1970s decade the bloodiest in the city's history, we made it the murder capital of the nation, and the coinage of the phrase "black on black crime." And also during his reign in the 1980s, we instituted a pathology called "Devil's Night," when we tried to burn his beloved city to the ground, and people came here from around the world to record us in the very throes of making complete fools of ourselves. Now do not compound this pattern of savagery in a pretense of honoring him by establishing a holiday for the date of his birth.

In memory of Coleman A. Young, the first black mayor of Detroit, for his life time of honored service to the city, his race, the nation and all mankind, we the members of the black race with the goodwill of others should reduce all crime committed by us in the city in the seven major crime categories (murder, rape, assault and battery, auto theft, larceny, burglary, and vandalism) reported by the FBI to over 90 percent per annum. If we do that, and sustain it forever as a legacy to his greatness, he will smile in his grave, and be glad.

This will please him for more than a holiday in his name, for he loved life. And it grieved him beyond measure while he lived that blacks murdered blacks in such high numbers in his beloved city. We certainly did not show that we gave a tinker's damn about him when he was mayor.

I would like to see, and hereby recommend that, City Council commission a scientific poll on these two choices in the city as a way of honoring the memory of this truly heroic and legendary mayor who at times in his life stood against the riptide of bigotry when it was a raging and violent storm unchecked hardly by law nor reason.

As some council members know, Mayor Young was a strong opponent of lynching. It may surprise some of you to know, however, that from 1882 when Tuskegee Institute began tracking lynching to 1952, there were just over 4 thousand seven hundred lynchings nationwide, peeking in the 1890s when a lynching on average occurred every other day. It may shock some of you also to know that during any ten year period during Mayor Young's reign, we murdered in this one city alone around 6 thousand.

After Rosa Parks was viciously beaten and robbed in her home, an old black man watched from his window as black males roamed the parking lot of his apartment building vandalizing and stealing the cars of black senior citizens, that same night a few hours later as a pack of dogs roamed through the lot sniffing and smelling, he turned aside and wept when he recognized through a discernment that dogs had more respect for old black folk and their property than those young black males.

To pass an ordinance in recognition of his birth, in a pretense of honoring him would be reflective not of honor of him but of a lazy and indolent council too stupid to provide the kind of courageous leadership needed to make his beloved city a safe, clean and prosperous place in which to live, raise a family, and do business. If this ordinance passes, the people of the earth will look again with pity on this city; and history itself will weep at the waste of so much blood for nothing.

Yours sincerely,
Shelton Vaughn
cc: to each council member

The Detroit News
August 2, 2001
To the Editor:

In memory of Coleman A. Young, the first black mayor of Detroit, for his life time of honored service to the city, his race, the nation and all mankind, we the members of the black race with the goodwill of others should reduce all crime committed by us in the city in the seven major crime categories (murder, rape, assault and battery, auto theft, larceny, burglary, and vandalism) reported by the FBI to over 90 percent per annum. If we do that, and sustain it forever as a legacy to his greatness, he will smile in his grave, and be glad.

This will please him for more than a holiday in his name, for he loved life. And it grieved him beyond measure while he lived that blacks murdered blacks in such high numbers in his beloved city.

I would like to see a scientific poll on these two choices in the city as a way of honoring the memory of this truly heroic and legendary mayor who at times in his life stood against the riptide of bigotry when it was a raging and violent storm unchecked hardly by law nor reason.

Sincerely,
Shelton Vaughn

Dear Councilmember Cockrel:

Upon attending "Where Do We Go From Here: A Town Meeting on Police-Community Relations," at Akwaba Community Center, Wednesday, April 17, 2002 at 6 p.m., I found something to compliment, and have a suggestion for your next one that might improve it. First, it was well attended; the speakers stayed pretty much to schedule; questions from the audience were good. The thing missing was, there was no community voice on the panel to speak to the relevance of the persona of the community. If there is to be formed a productive partnership with the people and the police department, there should be such a voice on the panel. The police state their position. The groups state their complaints.

The audience ask good questions. The persona would state what the community can and should do to make the partnership effective. Without this input on the panel, we are left with the stated position of the police and a catalog of complaints of the groups, and a list of questions effectively unanswered for the most part from the audience but no catalyst to transform these stated positions, complaints and questions into the desired result out where it really counts in the community.

When I was a youth, the old folk had this saying: charging somebody with stinking, when you don't bathe, don't make you smell good. Thus the breath of the wind of the charge bends and blows back on the accuser more than on the intended target. Challenging the police to be a good partner does not make us be good partners. I believe, and I sensed from the audience, the people want to be a good partner too. I would like to volunteer to be that voice on the panel.

Yours for a better city,
Shelton Vaughn

SELECTED BIBLIOGRAPHY

Abernathy, Ralph D. And the Walls Came Tumbling Down. Harper & Row, 1989.

Bacharach, Peter and Baratz, Morton S. Power & Poverty: Theory & Practice, Oxford University Press, Inc., 1970.

Ball, Edward. Slaves in the Family, Ballantine Books, 1999.

Baldwin, James. Notes of a Native Son, Harper's Magazine, 1955.

Baldwin, James. The Fire Next Time, New Laurel Edition, 1985.

Brodie, Fawn M. Thomas Jefferson: An Intimate History. W. W. Nortón & Company, 1974.

Bundles, A'Lelia. On Her Own Ground: The Life and Times of Madam C. J. Walker Washington Square Press, 2002. Carmichael, Stokely & Charles V. Hamilton. Black Power: The Politics of Liberation in America, Vintage Books, 1967

Current, Richard N., and Williams, T. Harry and Freidel, Frank., and Brownlee, W. Elliot. The Essentials of American History, Second Edition, Alfred A. Knopf, Inc. 1976.

Davis, Sampson and Hunt, Rameck and Jenkins, George. The Pact: Three Young Men Make a Promise and Fulfill a Dream, Riverhead Books, 2002

Du Bois, W. E. B. A Soliloquy on Viewing My Life from the Last Decade of Its First Century: The Autobiography of W. E. B. Du Bois. International Publishers, 1997.

Du Bois, W. E. B. The Souls of Black Folk. W.W. Norton, 1999.

Ellison, Ralph Waldo. Invisible Man, Random House, 1952.

Franklin, John Hope. From Slavery to Freedom: A History of Negro Americans, Third Edition, Vintage Books Edition, 1969.

Graham, Lawrence Otis. Our Kind of People: Inside America's Black upper Class, Harper Perennial Edition, 2000.

Graham, Lawrence Otis. The Senator and the Socialite: The True Story of America's First Black Dynasty, HarperCollins, 2006.

Harlan, Louis R. Booker T. Washington: The Wizard of Tuskegee, 1901-1915 Oxford University Press, 1983.

Hurston, Zora Neale. Their Eyes Were Watching God. First Harper Perennial Modern Classics Edition, 2006.

Johnson, Charles and Smith, Patricia. Africans in America: America's Journey Through Slavery, Harcourt Brace & Company, 1998.

King, Martin Luther Jr. Stride Toward Freedom: The Montgomery Story, Harper & Brothers 1958.

Lee, Harper. To Kill a Mockingbird, Warner Books, 1982.

Lewis, David Levering. W. E. B. Du Bois: Biography of a Race, 1868-1919 Henry Holt and Company, LLC., 1993.

Lewis, David Levering. W. E. B. Du Bois: The Fight for Equality and the American Century, 1919-1963, Henry Holt and Company, LLC., 2000.

Lewis, David Levering. King: A Biography. University of Illinois Press, 2nd Edition, 1978.

Lewis, Reginald F. and Blair S. Walker. Why Should White Guys Have All the Fun? John Wiley & Sons, Inc. 1997.

Lincoln, C. Eric. The Black Muslims in America. S. J. Reginald Saunders and Co., Ltd., 1961.

Madigan, Tim. The Burning: Massacre, Destruction, and the Tulsa Race Riot of 1921 Thomas Dunne Books, St. Martin's Press, 2001.

SHELTON VAUGHN

McMurry, Linda O. To Keep the Waters Troubled: The Life of Ida B. Wells Oxford University Press, 1998.

Niebuhr, Reinhold. Leaves from the Notebook of a Tamed Cynic, the World Publishing Company, 1966.

Redding, Saunders. On being Negro in America, Bantam Edition, 1964.

Oates, Stephen B. The Fires of Jubilee: Nat Turner's Fierce Rebellion, Harper & Row, 1990.

The Declaration of Independence and The Constitution of the United States.

Washington, Booker T. Up from Slavery. New American Library, 2000.

Williams, Juan. Thurgood Marshall: American Revolutionary, Times Books, 1998.

Young, Andrew. An Easy Burden: The civil rights movement and the Transformation of America, HarperCollins, 1996.

INDEX

K

Kennedy, John F., 181–83
Kilpatrick, Kwame Malik, 190, 219, 221
King, Martin Luther, Jr., 10, 12, 50,
   67, 80, 126–27, 175
   assassination of, 65, 68, 80–81, 83,
      97, 112, 125, 133, 213
   Booker T. Washington, compared
      to, 41, 82, 99, 103, 109, 131–32,
      134, 173, 196, 221
   leadership of, 40, 45, 47, 79, 87,
      90, 102, 105, 110, 127, 134, 151,
      168–69, 171, 215, 227
   during civil rights movement, 57,
      82, 106, 125, 157, 172, 180, 196,
      213, 217–18
   speeches, 124, 127
   views on
      human progress, 169
      integration, 33, 170

L

leadership, 102, 168–69
*Leaves from the Notebook of a Tamed
   Cynic* (Niebuhr), 180
Lee, Harper
   To Kill a Mockingbird, 29, 155
letters to
   Mr. Cabell, 218–19
   Mr. Cleveland (councilmember), 229
   Mr. Cockrel (councilmember),
      221–22
   the editor of *Detroit News*, 231
   the editor of *Ebony*, 226
   Emery King and Paul W. Smith,
      214–17
   Kwame Malik Kilpatrick, 219–20

Mr. Leavy (of *Ebony*), 227–28
Ms. Martin (TV host), 224–25
Ms. Reaves (councilmember), 223,
   232
Ms. Riley (columnist), 211–12, 214
Ms. Tinsley-Talabi
   (councilmember), 231
Lewis, Reginald, 165
Lincoln, Abraham, 87, 136–38
Locke, John, 89
lost generation, 43, 81, 97, 213
love, 49, 87, 169, 181
Lowell, James Russell, 167
lynching, 30, 55, 87, 104, 162, 199,
   218–19, 227, 229, 231
Lyons, Henry J., 41

M

Madison (grandfather of Willie
   Vaughn), 142–43
Mattie (mother of Willie Vaughn),
   142
McDaniels, Bootjack, 30, 162
me-ism, 80–81
middle class, 110–11
Montgomery, 79, 105–7, 156–57,
   171–72, 186, 188, 195, 227
Morgan, Clement, 52
mysterium transmondum, 124, 126

N

National Association for the
   Advancement of Colored People,
   56–57, 59–60, 67, 98, 104, 106,
   117, 229
National Baptist Convention, USA,
   Inc., 41, 132

National Urban League, 98
Nat Turner rebellion, 150, 195
New World, 40, 88
Niagara Movement, 51–53, 56–61, 83, 104
Niebuhr, Reinhold
  Leaves from the Notebook of a Tamed Cynic, 180
niggerism, 56, 132, 149, 157
Nixon, Richard M., 182
NM. *See* Niagara Movement
North, 136–37
Notes of a Native Son (Baldwin), 146

O

Oates, Stephen B.
  Fires of Jubilee, The, 195
Obama, Barack, 10–12
Old World, 88
On Being Negro in America (Redding), 151
Oprah Winfrey Show, 116, 164
organization, 61, 82–83, 213–14
Otto, Rudolf
  Idea of the Holy, The, 124
Our Kind of People (Graham), 66
Ovington, Mary White, 59–60

P

Parks, Rosa, 40, 79, 156, 172, 188, 231
Pavlov, Ivan, 32
phenotype, 111
Plessy v. Ferguson, 197
policy, 16–17, 46, 97, 100, 102–3, 111–12, 122, 138, 152, 154, 186
  definition, 106

formulation of, 46, 187
public. *See* public policy
samples of, 108–9, 164
social, 122
policy speech, 124–25
prosperity, 16–17, 29–30, 35, 38, 148
  in black communities, 32, 217, 228
    as duty of black leaders, 105, 108, 118, 129, 186, 200, 221–22, 231
    lack of, 47, 49, 76, 178–79
  as pathway to progress, 75, 179, 184, 201
  as reflection of superior intelligence, 37, 45, 67, 74, 90, 148, 166, 181–82, 225
  role of citizen in building, 92, 167
  key to progress, 187
  public policy needed to create, 39, 76, 98, 197
  in white communities, 32–33, 37, 166
public policy, 16–17, 46, 64, 197, 225
  black leaders
    as duty of, 47, 64, 69, 98, 101–3, 129, 186, 200, 215–16, 218, 222
    who made effective, 221
  black society, as key to transformation of, 9–10, 25–26, 38–41, 45, 58, 64, 101, 107, 146, 148, 151, 197, 199, 221
  children, for the safety of, 46
  difficulties in creation of, 45–46, 58, 148, 150
  failure of black leaders to create, 68, 76, 103, 105–6, 148, 151, 159, 178, 180
  as real cause of race problem, 28, 46, 113, 149, 151, 161, 177
  for poor blacks, 64, 224

SHELTON VAUGHN

leadership of, 54, 87, 99, 102–3,
109, 134, 151, 221
Talented Tenth, meets criticism from,
65–66, 68, 92, 131–32, 183, 195
Tuskegee Institute, founder of, 40,
57, 66, 82, 101, 104
Up from Slavery, 119
W. E. B. Du Bois
compared with, 54, 62, 100, 104,
118, 121–23
enmity with, 54–56, 131, 195
interview with, 52–53
leadership compared with, 10
Wells-Barnett, Ida B., 55, 199
White, Walter, 162
white contempt, 34, 83–85, 101. *See
also* racism
Whiteman, 78–79, 100–101, 123,
173, 185, 216
white media, 98, 128–29, 214–15, 218
white people, 27, 31, 61, 64, 66, 72,
92, 97, 102, 120, 138, 151, 171,
184–85, 188, 212
black people
abuse of, 106, 122, 227, 229
compared with, 108, 115,
149–50, 157, 159, 164–66, 186
enslavement of, 101, 148–49, 153,
156, 160, 170, 174, 192, 218

relationship with, 31, 57, 59, 75,
84, 108, 117, 149, 157, 159–60,
172, 175, 188, 229
view of, 37, 39, 49, 58, 101,
149–50, 154, 158, 160, 172–73,
212, 215, 224
educational opportunities, 116
intelligence, 48, 161
definition of, 160–61
public policy of, 109, 111, 150
as a race, 152, 158, 165–66, 178,
187
racism of, 32, 34–36, 56, 79, 98,
101, 106, 109, 129, 132, 156–58,
193, 226
types of, 115
Willie Vaughn Post Office, 144
Winona, Mississippi, blowtorch
lynching, 30, 162
Wright, Richard
Black Boy, 147

Y

Young, Andrew, 80–81, 83, 97–98,
125–27, 168–69, 213
Call to Conscience, A, 124
Young, Coleman Alexander, 38, 41,
221, 229–31